D1871872

FERTILITY TRANSITION IN RURAL SOUTH INDIA

FERTILITY TRANSITION IN RURAL SOUTH INDIA

ABUSALEH SHARIFF

GIAN PUBLISHING HOUSE
NEW DELHI - 110002

GIAN PUBLISHING HOUSE
4348, Madan Mohan Street
4-C Ansari Road, Daryaganj,
New Delhi-110002

©1989, Abusaleh Shariff

ISBN 81—212—0268—X

PRINTED IN INDIA

Published by Mrs. Gayatri Garg for Gian Publishing House, New Delhi and Printed at Godwall Printers, Delhi.

Preface

During 1960 and 1970 there were numerous surveys and research studies to assess the Knowledge, Attitudes and Practices (KAP) of family planning methods in India. These surveys and studies have been subjected to severe criticisms for the limited scope and stereotypic findings. Almost during the same period a Sample Registration Scheme (SRS) was designed and implemented by the Registrar General to estimate the demographic indicators such as the birth, death and infant mortality rates. Although this system is the best available source to get impressions about the demographic trends ; both the KAP surveys and the SRS remained silent about the need to explore the causes and mechanisms of declining fertility. There, however, have been many speculations and powerful after-thoughts about the determinants and consequences of fertility decline. 1980, nevertheless, witnessed a revival of concern in investigating the underlying causes of the demographic transition which is in progress in India.

One important contribution in this direction has been from a team of investigators from the Australian National University (ANU), Canberra and the Population Centre, Bangalore. Professor J.C. Caldwell of the ANU showed that the demographic change and its composition can be better explored and understood by conducting first hand research using a combination of survey and anthropological research methodologies. The present work is one of realizations of such a concern. The field work and research on which this book is based was undertaken in a cluster of four villages during 1980-84.

In the process of conducting a research project one becomes indebted to many people. My deep gratitudes cannot be adeqately conveyed in a brief acknowledgement. Nevertheless, this work would not have been possible without the co-operation and involvement of the village people of the research area. I not only developed a memorable association with them but was also inspired by each one of them to conduct my field work successfully. My sincere gratitudes are due to all of them.

It is my bounden duty to express my deepest gratitudes to Professor J.C. Cadlwell and Mrs Pat Caldwell, who since the time I met them in 1979 have been my best tecahers, both in India during my field work and while I was at the Australian National University. The time I have spent with them has been a period of learning and the discussions with Bruce Caldwell were stimulating and fruitful.

I have greatly benefited from discussions with my friends and colleagues especially Dr. S. Krishnamoorthy, Dr. Mrs. Goon Tan, Dr. Lado T. Ruzicka, Dr. Gavin Jones, Mr. M. Guruswamy and Mr. Ramesh Kanbargi ; my many thanks are due for them. I wish to express my thanks and appreciation to my wife Shahnaz Begum who not only helped me in field work, data collection and coding of data but also proof read the final draft of this work.

Finally, it is my pleasure to express my indebtedness to the Australian National University, Canberra, Australia for facilitating me with adequate funds to undertake field work in India and to complete this work while I was in Australia during 1981-84.

ABUSALEH SHARIFF

Contents

List of Tables

List of Figures

List of Maps

Maps Showing the Geographical Distribution of Families by Caste and Location of the Family Planning Acceptors

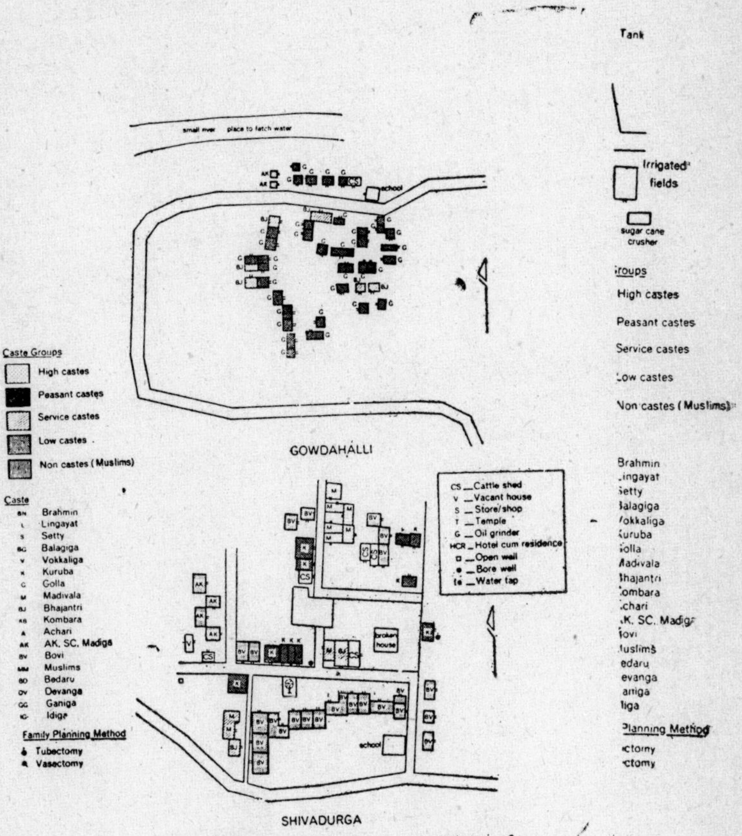

Map Showing the Geographical Distribution of Families by Caste and Location of the Family Planning Acceptors

MAP 3

1

Introduction

Hitherto demography in India has largely been studied in its quantitative dimension, and a qualitative evaluation of the demographic process is rare and fairly recent. Demography has remained a study of population, of its size, structure distribution and growth, but the understanding of demographic transition is incomplete without a clear understanding of social change and the interrelationships between them. The interrelationships are two-sided. Social change may occur in response to changes in demographic or ecological conditions, and demographic transition may occur as a result of social change. The Pre-British period in India is regarded as an indicator of the former and the post-Independence period is an example of the latter. A more recent example of the former kind is the sociopolitical unrest in the state of Assam originating from massive immigration. The subject of this research is focussed on the latter relationship.

A common notion that village society in India has remained unchanged and does not show a positive desire for change can be regarded wrong, as social change in India has undergone an evolutionary process. Under the British rule and during the two World Wars there were changes in social mobility, the economic system and in general style of life. Since Independence, the rate of change has enormously increased and change is multidimensional.

Village society has emerged as an important element in social, political and economic changes in the recent times. This change is often attributed to the exogenous influence (national and even global oriented) of modernization which includes industrialization, urbanization, increase in socio-political awareness, change in economic relationships, monetization, and a move towards secularism. Nevertheless, social change requires internal adjustments and the intrinsic causes of change represent the levels of social adaptability leading to appropriate changes in social behaviour. The process of change is complex and a macro-perspective fails to give a clear account of the causes and nature of change. The micro-anthropological perspective and intensive village studies not only contribute to a systematic social enquiry in their own right but also provide the correlates for a macro-understanding.

There are a few accounts in India which have demonstrated the importance of this approach in social research. Beals (1955, 1962), Epstein (1962, 1973), Hobson (1978), Ishwaran (1970) and Srinivas (1976), are the notable examples in south India. Slater's edited work in 1918 was a good lead and, in 1961, the Census of India also undertook village studies presenting detailed statistics and data which are part of this approach. The use and benefits of this approach to the study of demographic change was neglected until recently when the Caldwell and Reddy started their Karnataka Fertility Project in 1979. The only exception was a study by Poffenberger (1969, 1978) in a north Indian village which was initially intended to investigate socialization practices and social change, but latter also investigated certain aspects of the dynamics of fertility behaviour and family planning. Nevertheless, Caldwell's foundation for a systematic study of the relationship between society and demographic process has bridged the gap between facts and knowledge and at the same time has prompted many to evaluate the methodological merits and demerits of the macro and micro approach. Demography may start with numbers in its effort to summarize social behaviour but has to end in social interpretation. I have, therefore, chosen the micro-approach to investigate the cause of fertility decline and fertility decision-making, which also provides support for understanding the macro-perspective.

India for long has been regarded as a high fertility country yet, fertility as measured by the crude birth rate was never as high as in some of the contemporary Middle Eastern and African countries. This was due to the effect of cultural taboos regarding marriage, remarriage, sexual abstinence, coital frequency and breast feeding. It is also possible that low health and nutritional status of women restricted births from occurring at the biological maximum. Nevertheless, even in India, fertility levels are considered high and have elicited the increasing concern of policy-makers in the course of economic and social planning. The policy objectives are to reduce the current levels of both fertility and mortality. The current levels of fertility and the consequent rate of growth of population is considered an impediment to development and national well-being. It has been argued that evidence for this is provided by the consistent increase in the Net National Product, while per-capita income remains almost constant. For the south Indian region the birth rate worked out to be 30 per thousand in the early 1980s, close to 40 per thousand in early 1970s and as high as 45 per thousand in the early 1960s.[1] There is ample evidence in demographic literature to support the view that fertility in India has indeed been consistently falling at least since early 1950s.[2]

What are the explanations that might be offered for the decline in fertility ? The simplest answer is that married couples are beginning to have fewer births during the course of their marriage.[3] Because of declining infant and child mortality and a substantial increase in child survival, it is expected that the number of births per couple will be lower now than a generation ago. The notion that the demand for children is for ones who survive to particular ages (Davis, 1963) is an important one, because families are interested in a certain number and in a specific sex combination of children who would survive until adulthood or death of the parents. To achieve this goal, under the conditions of falling mortality, parents may choose to have fewer births by resorting to voluntary fertility regulation using either traditional or modern family limitation methods.

1.1. Fertility Decline and Demographic Transition

It is widely recognized that India is undergoing a demographic transition where both mortality and fertility have been consistently falling in the recent past (see Appendix I). However, if one is broadly investigating the casual factors responsible for the decline in fertility, there is a controversy whether to give credit to the development effect or to the family planning effect as it can hardly be a coincidence that family planning was popularised in India in almost the same period that fertility declined. Is it then development that brings change in fertility, as held by Kuznets (1964), Notestein (1956), Raulet (1970) ? Or is it acceptance of family planning *per se* which reduces fertility (Mauldin and Berelson 1978), or is it something else ? Any answer to such a question which ignores, particularly in the Indian context, the nature of the ongoing changes in the culturally accepted value system, orientations and norms would not be a satisfactory explanation. Value system change in response to new or alien forces which intrude into a traditional static structure. The socioeconomic development and the modernizing process seem to have this capacity[4] enabling the inert values to change.

A few, for instance Clifford (1971) and Fawcett (1970 : 114) have subscribed to the existence and importance of value orientations, where traditional value orientations, support high fertility and modern value orientations support low fertility. However, value systems or value orientations themselves seem to have less demonstrable capacities for influencing fertility change (Spengler, 1966 : 129). The push has to originate from elsewhere. Poston and Singelmann (1975) have examined this hypothesis among Indian males only to conclude that, without the effects of socioeconomic status, value orientations would not be related to fertility behaviour, and the mediation between socioeconomic status and fertility behaviour is only partial. More recent work on the relationship between value orientations and family planning indicators, arbitrarily assuming that family planning helps in bringing down fertility, have subscribed to a similar hypothesis. Mukherjee (1981 : 40) worked on data from four Indian states and concluded that value orientations can be of some use in predicting different aspects of family planning, but at the same time cautions that his analysis cannot be construed to imply that modernity variables indicate a person's family planning status.

There are critiques of both these approaches. In the first place there has been an attack on demographic transition theory, which holds that broad developmental changes and fertility decline go together, or that it was socioeconomic development which depressed fertility (Teitelbaum, 1975). The second argument emerges from Davis's criticism (1963 : 345) that one way of oversimplifying the complexities of the theory[5] is to regard demographic behaviour as a function of a traditional culture or value systems. Thus, any researcher, who attempts to establish the casual factors for fertility decline as emerging from modern economic development or social transformation, is attempting a difficult and perhaps impossible task. In spite of this risk, an attempt follows to identify the factors involved in falling fertility rates during the socioeconomic transformation. The fact is that there is no second approach yet discovered which can give an alternative explanation of such a change which would be more appealing. This calls for an explanation of two interrelated concepts, *development* and *social transformation*, which in fact are not mutually exclusive.

Development is frequently used to mean economic development, which is characterised as change in the technology in use, production methods, infrastructural extension, level of commercialization and the like. Inevitably, as a result of development, there must also be a change in social structure in the society through the changes in occupation patterns, education, social and geographic mobility, inter-personal commercial relations and intra-family relationships. These are the social developments which in India appear to be barely elastic enough to accommodate further economic development and cultural change. However, there exists a circular but casual interrelationships among these factors. Progressive changes in educational standards and literacy, occupational shifts from a more agricultural or traditional to a less agricultural base, urbanization, commercialization and modernization, communication and transport and income levels are labelled as the indicators of the development process. Contradictions arise if the per capita income or per capita gross national product is considered as the chief development index, because, although income has increased considerably in monetary terms, it has recorded little increase in real terms and there still exists a wide disparity in the level of incomes within the population, the majority falling into the low income group among whom in fact real income has probably fallen during the 1970s (Dandeker and Rath, 1971; Sethuraman, 1974; Bardhan, 1970). This has arisen from two counteracting forces : decreasing labour productivity and almost constant agricultural wages in real terms in the presence of consistent inflation (Maddison, 1971 : 90; Sethuraman, 1974 : 687).

In the context of rural south India, the concept of development can be stated as follows. Many in India believe the government's effort to be the principal reason causing and facilitating economic and social change through its policies (Mandelbaum, 1970 : 636). The governmental extension of the infrastructure and organization (bureaucracy) at the rural end facilitated the measure of development. A village with a secondary school, health unit, electricity, good road connection, tap water facility and similar other facilities is always regarded as more developed than the one which has fewer such facilities. However, this alone will misrepresent reality, for such facilities may in fact be used only by the few relatively wealthy, the high castes and the land owners. Therefore, the proportion of the population who actually may have benefited from such facilities or who have the potential to utilize them, and the subsequent progressive changes in their life-style, are the real measures of development.[6] Therefore, one would expect that if the proportion of population utilizing these facilities is higher, it is certain that the rate of change has been substantial, and a lower proportion suggests that the rate of change is slow or even non-existent.

Social change is reflected in different spheres like education, health, agricultural output and occupational diversity. With change, the proportion of children attending school increases and the school drop-out rates fall. An increase in hospital attendance, not due to rise in morbidity but due to increased awareness of the value of hospital treatment and a greater willingness to utilize existing facilities, is likely to improve general health conditions, Better nutrition and child health care would cause a decline in mortality, especially infant mortality. People will prefer the use of modern technology in agriculture to increase yields. More and more people will resort to non-traditional occupations based on education and newly acquired skills. They also appear to exhibit a willingness to accept increasingly modern family planning technology.

There may be parallel changes in the social structure in relation to inter-family and intra-family behavioural and production relationships. During the process of transformation the family relationships, especially between young and old and between males and females, move towards more egalitarian ones (Caldwell 1976a). Simultaneously the division of labour, work responsibilities and the priorities of work within families also change. The whole question here is one of priorities and decision-making. Children will be viewed as expensive to maintain and the contribution from children to the family income will decline. In the process, both the concept and extent of dependency changes. A large number of children become less desirable because of the increased emphasis on modern education and skill formation which is expensive. Children also appear to depress the current income of the family because working mothers develop the concept of opportunity cost which is readily converted into monetary terms based on the local wage rates. The situational gains or the benefits from the exploitation of the children and women by the patriarch fall and a situation emerges where the cost of maintaining children is higher than the immediate as well as latent benefits from them. This mechanism leads to a reversal of intergenerational wealth flows where the older generation has to forego their current consumption in order to improve the quality of children and meet the demands of the younger generation while the anticipated tangible rewards from child bearing are not equally assured. Eventually the situation leads to the first anti-natal decisions emerging from the younger generation, and, if associated with more egalitarian status, the family may allow these new ideas to flow faster leading to conclusive decisions with less antagonism.

Caldwell brings together these issues and argues that it is the social transformation of the family through the acquisition of new values which determines fertility decline. Accordingly the essential forces are the social ones, as he emphasizes:

> ...the forces sustaining economically unrestricted fertility are frequently strengthened by economic modernization unaccompanied by specific types of social change and that this is the explanation for sustained high fertility in a situation in which "modernization"—urbanization, increase in the proportion of non-agricultural production, and so on—is demonstrably occurring. The social revolution—one of familial relationships and particularly of the direction of intra-familial flows of wealth dictated by familial obligations—need not by its nature accompany economic modernization (1976a : 322).

and stresses :

> Obviously the fundamental choices are social ones and economic behaviour is rational only in so far as it is rational within the framework established by social ends (p. 326).

Again in 1978 Caldwell wrote:

> ...the conditions of stable high fertility, and of subsequent destabilization, lie largely in the nature of economic relations within the family. The family that determines economic advantage and demographic decisions...encompasses those groups of close relatives who share economic activities and obligations. Within this larger and demographically more significant entity, the locus of economic and fertility decision-making is of prime importance, but has not as yet been adequately investigated (pp. 553-554).

He, however, leaves a note of caution:

> The implications for demographic transition theory are that transition is made possible only by profound changes in the social structures of such societies, and the analyses of the economic rationality of high fertility reach different conclusions in different social structures (1976a : 336).

Caldwell's explanation goes much further than this social and economic debate. Accordingly, it is the new western way of life, produced by the penetration of imported values which brings the decline in fertility, and hence urbanization, high incomes and shifts in occupations are not the major forces in causing a decline in fertility. Such a way of life may precede development or even modernization (1977 : 100).

> Fertility in the developing world will decline as the decision-makers no longer secure decisive material advantage from high fertility—which means changes both in the identity and authority of those gaining material advantage. These changes will be a product of economic change—of capitalist production outpacing even industrialization—and of largely imported social change (broadly speaking, Westernization) (1978 : 571).

Caldwell also emphasises that in transitional societies the pronounced change which occurs simultaneously is a shift in primary emphasis and obligation from the extended (larger) kin to the immediate family. Such a shift usually involves a major change in husband-wife relationship to one of emotional involvement and egalitarian relationship. He notes:

> As the conjugal bond become closer, or more sentimental, and as the mother's maternal feelings play a greater role in family decision-making, the sex and age differentials in material advantage are likely to be increasingly eroded (1978 : 572).

There are those who argue, that the effect of the development process or modernization may be to increase fertility

(Nag, 1980 ; Krause, 1963 ; Das Gupta *et al.* 1956) through the general improvement in health, hygiene and nutrition (Frisch, 1975 : 20; Mosley 1977 : 4-7; Srinivasan *et al.*, 1978 : 262) and change in norms relating to breast feeding, abstinence, widow remarriage and proportions married (See for instance Caldwell and Caldwell, 1981 ; Caldwell, 1982 ; Nag, 1980 ; Wyon and Gordon, 1971 : 142 ; Hull, 1983). It is believed that this usually increases the fecundity of the population in general, and, unless checked proportionately, there may be an increase in the growth rate which may be further accentuated by a decrease in death rate. However, this would be a temporary phenomenon, since the traditional values subsequently change accommodating the shifts in individual priorities which would be anti-natal in nature. Nevertheless, Caldwell argues that:

> The major implication of this (decline in fertility) analysis is that fertility decline in the Third World is not dependent on the spread of industrialization or even on the rate of economic development. It will of course be affected by such development in that modernization produce more money for schools, for newspapers, and so on: . . . But fertility decline is more likely to precede industrialization and to help bring it about than to follow it (1976a:358).

This contention is explained on the similar lines for the Indian situation where he argues that the decline in fertility is the result of changes in social values and a process of secularization which has emerged from westernization. Nevertheless, to explain the determinants of fertility decline in India the study of fundamental changes in the society, both social and economic are seen as essential.

The failure of the fertility transition theory to provide a satisfactory explanation of fertility decline in terms of the socioeconomic macro changes is also given by Teitelbaum (1975) who states that a modified transition theory could provide only a high level of generality. He gives the Latin American example that it is more likely that the experience of initial fertility decline would be first among those countries with relatively high levels of development. He, however, emphasize the incapacity of this approach to predict the timing of the onset of the fertility decline. The relevance of the demographic transition theory in explaining the cause and timing of fertility decline is under attack, due partly to its unsatisfactory demonstration of the mechanisms of the European demographic transition. However, it may still retain its predictive utility in the case of less developed countries, where fertility decline is evident among the countries with faster development, like Singapore, Taiwan, and Korea, and the regions or countries claiming to be successful in the equitable distribution of development benefits like Sri Lanka and Kerala state in India.[7] What is evident here is that without push or pull factors of developmental benefits which would operate at micro or family level, society may not respond with declining fertility (Namboodiri, 1980). Westernization, a concept distinct from modernization and development, would, however, be an element in the incipient development process.

Once westernization is accepted by the society as a way of life and utilizes the gains of development process, such as education, monetization, transportation and media, then the impact of future development and modernization may become less effective. Nevertheless, in the absence of westernization, modernization may continue to exert its strong influence to bring change in the society. Thus what seem probable here is that, given a certain level of modernization or development, changing values may gather velocity, especially through a series of changes in the form of subsets of the whole system. Consequently, many of the norms and traditions regulating fertility may change faster to outpace the process of development. Since development is a function of capital, technology, political will and social acceptance in a country like India at some stage it may lag behind the process of social change. Once the issue is outside the limits and control of development, change depends entirely on the capacity of the society to sustain and accentuate the issues of change in terms of values, orientations, norms and way of life.

1.2 Family Planning and Fertility Decline

A different issue but one parallel to the above is whether to consider contraception or family planning as an independent factor responsible for fertility decline. Family planning, appears to be a segment of the modernization process itself (Demerath, 1967:181) which provides couples with a more convenient means of regulating their fertility. Mauldin and Berelson (1978) have established that the social setting and programme efforts go together most effectively, and suggest that a certain level of development is essential apart from its continuing influence for a successful programme. Cutright and Kelly (1981:145) demonstrate a most important effect of the family planning programme on fertility change in developing countries. They distinguish a strong as well as rapid programme effect on declining fertility. The qualifying explanation given by them, however, suggests that the family planning programme represents only a cost-effective strategy to decrease fertility. What is arguable in their presentation is their implied emphasis on programme effort rather than development. Blake (1965) and Davis (1967) did not rely much on family planning programmes because high infant and child mortality[8] keep fertility high even if the programme suggests an increase in acceptance. They believed in the effectiveness of the promotion of the small family norm as well as motivation to help people to reduce desired family size. Davis believed that the usual family planning programme is not an effective fertility control programme at all, but only a first step in the desired direction and advocated the next and subsequent policy steps to follow to reach intended results (1967 : 737). Demeny (1979) and Weeks (1977) also suggested that socioeconomic improvement should precede the programme effort for the best results. While evaluating the programme impact in Costa Rica, Reynolds (1972) concluded that 35 to 45 per cent of the decline in fertility was due to factors other than organized family planning. An alternative strategy linking both efforts seems to be practical as well as acceptable for developing societies. Freedman (1979) summarizes that the motivation for low fertility may come from a relatively small subset of developmental changes without western-type modernization and industrialization.[9]

Caldwell (1975), while establishing the relationship between the fertility decline and the family planning programme, states that, for some developing countries with a governmental family planning programme, some consider the programme to be a failure and few others assert its inevitable task of fertility reduction. But he rejects both these views on the ground that the family planning services are often inaccessible for varied reasons, and further that such services are often unequally distributed so enabling only a privileged few of its use. However, for India he argues that:

> Although the existence of the family planning programme and its very considerable degree of efficiency has been a major force in accelerating the fertility decline, there is little doubt in the community that there have been underlying forces reducing the value of unrestricted fertility (p. 432).

These underlying forces in India are said to be found in the changing social structure since the post-war period, and the change has occurred faster after Independence.

It is now evident that a scrutiny of the underlying forces is a precondition to understand any social phenomenon. Fertility decline is a demographic resultant of a social phenomenon. One can also argue that fertility decline is a demographic means to a social goal. As already pointed out, in this study emphasis will be given to the former proposition. Therefore, the research has concentrated on the scrutiny of the social and economic structure. Special emphasis is given to understanding the nature of the family as a primary social institution, followed by the current and past fertility levels, and understanding its specific behaviours in regulating fertility and the choice of family planning methods.

Understanding fertility behaviour of a particular culture is essential to understand the demographic process Demographic change is found to be the consequence of the interplay of the *intermediate variables* (Davis and Blake, 1958). Nevertheless, the concern of this research is to investigate what is happening before the intermediate variables come into picture or what determines the intermediate variables. This study, therefore, is concerned with the changing social structure of which family is an institution where changes occur. The unique feature of the Indian family is its nature within the extended family system which for long was regarded as the essential characteristic of the Indian society. This thesis is an attempt to reveal the village society, and its specific behaviour and responses. This task is attempted by using a micro-framework to study a cluster of four south Indian villages.

1.3 Scheme of This Thesis

The following section of this chapter presents the scheme of this thesis. Chapter 2 discusses the methodological debate concerning the micro and macro approach, and describes the methodology used to collect and analyse data for this thesis. Chapter 3 is devoted to introducing the research area and its people with special emphasis on the aspects of social structure and change. Chapter 4 presents in detail the fertility and mortality indices followed by a discussion of differential fertility in the research area. The last section of this chapter presents a multivariate analysis undertaken to bring out the variables which have significant effects on fertility. Chapter 5 describes the isues regarding the type of family of current residence of the pepole and reproductive couples and its relationship to fertility. Chapter 6 explores the aspects of the family planning programme in this area and brings out the norms regulating the choice of modern family planning methods. Chapter 7 reviews the theoretical debate about fertility decision-making and provides a scheme for the fertility decision-making analysis in the Indian family. Chapter 8 presents the facts and figures regarding the fertility and family planning decision-making process where case histories are used to substantiate the findings. In Chapter 9 aspects of the status of woman and value of children are discussed which together appear to be responsible for the growing acceptance of family planning and the emergence of a voluntary desire to control fertility. Chapter 10 brings together some of the major hypotheses and arguments developed and tested in the preceding chapters.

NOTES AND REFERENCES

1. A detailed discussion on fertility and mortality trends for India and Karnataka is presented in Appendix I.
2. The only exception to this is the results from 1981 Census of India which counted more than projected population for the country as a whole. But speculation that the birth rates during the preceding decade has remained unchanged or has only slightly declined is yet to be conclusively proved. Nevertheless, there are wide regional disparities between the States and Karnataka is supposed to have failed to bring down birth rates from its early 1970 level of around 30 per thousand population. For more on levels and differentials in birth and death rates for India and Karnataka during 1971-81 see National Academy of Sciences (1981).
3. The socio-cultural norms in India do not recognize births outside wedlock. Although such births are found they are rare and such statistics are not available in India.
4. This relationship gives credibility to the demographic transition theory in explaining fertility decline.
5. This refers to the application of the theory of change and response in modern demographic history.
6. Chapter 3 highlights certain issues concerning this argument with reference to the four south Indian villages selected for the study.
7. Even at lower levels of development the equitable distribution of health nutrition and education in Sri Lanka and Kerala State in India is indicated as chief reason for surprisingly low levels of fertility and mortality in recent times. For further reading in this direction refer to Radcliffe (1978) and Nag (1982).
8. This still is the case in the south Asian countries where the infant mortality rate is in the vicinity of 100 per thousand live births. Some new thoughts in the case of India suggest that mortality has increased lately due to improper expenditure policies of the funds allocated for health, nutrition and welfare. However, these findings are based on thin set of data and are excessively speculative.
9. Note that Freedman refers only to modernization and not to westernization or western way of life.

2

Methodology

Early demographic literature was found in works on philosophy and theories with demographic implications in disciplines like political economy and sociology. The basis was generally intuition and largely theoretical. In the late nineteenth and much of the twentieth century, social scientists and governments depended on periodic census and large-scale nation-wide surveys for the demographic data base and evidence to support theories. Now there is a tendency and a growing measure of agreement among demographers, as well as other social scientists interested in demography, about the need and usefulness of a semi-anthropological or micro-approach for a better understanding and explanation of contemporary demographic change.

2.1. Demographic Data Base

The mechanisms and explanations of demographic change and phenomenon, such as the change in population size, structure and distribution, has its origin in various disciplines and schools of thought. Thomas Malthus (1798) and the early classical economists considered population as an imporant factor of production.[1] Malthus in his theory of population explained the interrelationships between population growth, food production and wage rates. He also explained the mechanism of increase and decrease in the size of population in a country using the laws of nature. This served the early social scientists, theoreticians and governments as an impetus to investigate the issues concerning the growth, structure and distribution of the population. This curiosity encouraged the advent of periodic censuses and large-scale national sample surveys. Subsequently, newly emerging nations and states heavily depended on these kinds of information and statistics for planning purposes. These needs laid the foundation of the systematic enumeration and estimation of populations, including population projections.

After the World War II, many nations came to believe that their respective populations were either too large or small for the requirements of economic growth and the nation's well-being. This seemed to be an awakening after the realization and vision of peace in the post-turbulent days after war and devastation. Reconstruction and development were the immediate objectives of many nations and the pressure of huge populations on limited land areas and resources was strongly felt. This led to the outburst of large-scale surveys apart from periodic censuses to get frequent and exhaustive information on various issues such as population, income, land utilization, family planning and education.

The censuses and periodic surveys provided an excellent set of data in terms of size and scale, covering areas like the states or a region. Statistical techniques were developed to help secure more reliable figures on birth, death and migration rates. More recently in the 1960s the knowledge, attitude and practice (KAP) surveys provided useful statistics and helped the extension of the newly instituted family planning programmes in many countries. However, the emphasis was on the totality of the issues, considering often the state or a country or even a region encompassing many countries as a unit. This approach is often referred to as a *macro-approach.* A specific approach is distinguished more from its goals and scope rather than its contents. This concept was introduced to demographic literature by economists who were interested in population, and it served as a basis for the proponents of many eco-demographic theories like the economic theories of fertility and theories concerning population and development. The issues studied varied in nature concerning social, economic, demographic and attitudinal aspects of population. Data were collected on a sample basis using standard pretested questionnaires.

Such investigations provide essential first steps in seeking explanations, but do not go far enough in this direction. The conduct, size, division of labour and organizational expertise presents a feeling of great efficiency, but it is this high level of professionalization that obscures the realities existing in a society (Caldwell, *et al.*, 1982b). By and large such surveys undertaken in a country enabled the comparisons of data for two different time periods or two different regions at the same time. Although macro-analytical approach can discern the understanding of the dynamic aspects of a social phenomenon, such analyses are rarely found in survey results. They appear to reflect situations of a static nature. Large scale surveys did not go deep enough to investigate the causal relationships of a given phenomenon. Assuming the existence of certain relationships *a priori*, macro data enabled comparisons, and helped to measure the effect of different variables. For example, on the assumption that increased education may cause a decline in fertility, the data gathered on education and fertility through surveys presented a direct or inverse relationship between the two. What is difficult to explain by such analyses is the mechanism through which education affects fertility.

Hitherto, demographic research depended heavily on statistics and its macro-application ignoring largely the multi-disciplinary nature of the subject. It has been only in the recent times that we have observed a shift in emphasis from a quantitative analysis for establishing fertility, mortality and migration levels and trends to a scrutiny of these levels and trends. An investigation detailed and largely interdisciplinary in its nature and scope can be termed as the *micro-approach.* Recently there has been a shift in some quarters toward the micro-approach as a method of demographic investigation (Burch, 1980 : 2) which owes more to anthropology than to other disciplines (Caldwell, *et al.* 1982b; Nag, 1982). The advantage of this approach is that it enables investigation into those issues and questions which ordinarily escape the survey, due either to the limitation imposed by the questions framed for interviewing or due to the time factor.

The dimensions of micro-approach are at least two sided. The first and foremost is the structure of investigation. A detailed structural understanding of a specific phenomenon is the central issue. This cannot be done on a large scale to reach a high degree of precision and concentration of the subject. The desirable approach is to study an issue within a social context deeply enough to relate any social process to social change. It is ordinarily less feasible to undertake such a study on a large scale. Thus the second dimension is the limitation on geographic or physical coverage to smaller areas like a group of villages. These are local studies which facilitate not only concentration on the issues of research but also help in fitting this into a social perspective. This in other words is also identified as a *holistic-approach* (Epstein, 1977). Such are the requirements and desirability of social research which lead to the development of a micro-approach which is being now used in demographic investigation as well.

Caldwell (1976, 1982b), Cassen (1975), Epstein and Jackson (1977), Leibenstein (1981), Nag (1977, 1978), Namboodiri (1980), Poffenberger (1973) and Srinivas and Ramaswamy (1977) have advocated the usefulness of a micro-approach for explaining demographic transition which has gained much from anthropological techniques. Although micro-economic theories of fertility have been in existence since the late 1950s, their approach has relied mostly on the level and type of analysis rather than the pattern and method of data collection and analysis. In other words the micro-theory is put to a macro-test to find out how a population behaves on average, although such tests seem to be unsatisfactory to explain the maximization process (Leibenstein, 1981 : 385). Becker (1960), Easterlin (1969), Leibenstein (1957), Namboodiri (1972) and Schultz (1974) proposed different dimensions of the micro-economic theory of fertility based on the household decision-making model under the umbrella of the theory of choice and the consumer theory. There were a few other attempts, of an independent nature by sociologists, anthropologists and psychologists.

The study of family interactions, intergenerational role changes, family mode of production and wealth flows has come into vogue in recent years. The relationship of family interaction and fertility were studied by Blake (1960); Hill, Stycos and Back (1959) and Stycos and Back (1964). The last study was carried out in Jamaica and Puerto Rico, using a three stage research methodology: the first stage consisted of intensive, unstructured interviews with a small sample of women and their spouses. Hypotheses developed from these pilot type studies helped in developing semi-structured questionnaires used in large scale surveys in the second stage, and the action research programme used the survey findings, for field experiments and evaluation purposes was the third stage of research (Fawcett, 1973 : 41). But it is not clear, whether the authors ever participated in the interviewing, participative observation and field work. This methodology remained short of presenting a model viable for future experimentation. Rainwater (1960, 1965), used interviewing techniques to study conjugal role relationships and the pattern of sexual behaviour and related these variables to family size preferences and contraceptive practice. He emphasised the role of the individual's perceptions, motivations and constraints in fertility behaviour. His analysis was more quantitative in the first study but the second study was presented more as a qualitative analysis. Rainwater's work although very close to a micro-approach, restricted itself to a narrow scope.

The micro-approach as a method of research and investigation used in this study refers to a methodology involving semi-anthropological research tools along with some of the survey methods. The emphasis on this kind of approach is more recent and the active initiation and application have been found in the works of Caldwell since 1974 with African, Bangladeshi and Indian data. The problem and need of micro type research in India has been discussed only by a few others in recent times. Nag (1977 : 273-276) identifies the need for micro level studies[2] and such data requirements for policy planning and proposes collection of data relating to human fertility. Srinivas and Ramaswamy (1977 : 28-29) emphasize the areas where KAP studies have failed to explain the fundamentals of fertility behaviour, and suggest a socio-anthropological approach in understanding fertility along with aspects of culture in its wider social context. Caldwell and Caldwell particularly used this approach[3] during 1974-75 in Nigeria. Later in his theoretical essays of 1976a and 1978 Caldwell very strongly emphasized the need for a micro-approach. This methodology was later used in the South Indian Fertility Study (SIFS), an Australian National University—Bangalore Population Centre joint project.[4] Caldwell in 1976a stated that,

> There has also been a research failure: failure to investigate in detail the ways of life and circumstances of individual acceptors parallel (family planning acceptors) to similar studies of the population as a whole (p. 335).

and Caldwell, *et al*, in 1982b wrote that,

> The statistical techniques are ever more impressive and are both needed and valuable in that they measure the true demographic position and the direction and speed of change. But in themselves they do not tell us anything about the nature of the change.

Such observations, led to the onset of micro-demographic surveys. Although few others have come fairly strongly in support of the use of micro approach in demography, most have failed to put it into practice. For instance Cassen states that:

> The emphasis on the village studies is there not for their statistical significance but for their depiction of a process that may be characteristic; they illustrate some of the features of rural life . . . (1975 : 51).

He added,

> The studies of ordinary villages cannot be said to constitute a random sample, although further investigation may show them to be on the whole 'better' than average in certain respects and therefore indicative of what may be going to

> happen elsewhere; and it should be possible to establish common characteristics of villages where given classes of events occur (p. 52).

Freedman records the usefulness of demographic data collected by anthropologists. He explains that, due to the importance of the kinship structure for fertility and the difficulty of studying this phenomenon in the quick cross-section surveys, co-operation with the anthropologist seems essential (1961-62 : 42).

While writing on "Economic Decision Theory and Fertility Behaviour", Leibenstein advocated the desirability of intensive village studies (1981 : 397). However, the most important reason given by him for such studies is that most of the population in low-income developing countries lives in villages. Nevertheless, such an intensive project could also be planned to study a sect, community or a smaller area in the modern day urban areas. In this regard, Ryder (1963) is of the opinion that it is the relative importance of micro-analytic and macro-analytic levels of inquiry which is important for the explanation of fertility. Vance (1959) has explicitly called macro-analytic explanations inadequate because they fail to specify the ways in which macro-variables are translated into individual motivation.

The usefulness of the micro-approach can be well understood only if one has a fair knowledge of its application in other disciplines like developmental economics and sociology in the developing world. The works by Srinivas (1976), Hobson (1978), Epstein (1962, 1977), and Ishwaran (1970) would not escape such a review. Srinivas has very well demonstrated the usefulness of studying the social structure at the village level, where the interrelationship and effect of caste, kinship, family can be well understood. Epstein has used this approach[5] to explain the problems of economic development and social changes in two south Indian villages. Later (1975, 1977) she extended this methodology to development studies and demography. However, her later work depends heavily on the second hand reports of her students.

2.2 Survey Versus Village Studies

The fundamental goal of inquiry in social science research lies in explaining the nature of social change; that is, the why? How? When and where? of change. The demographer's interest is also in this sphere of explaining the nature of demographic change in a given socioeconomic and political environment. Demographic patterns are the reflections of the specific nature of change in the respective sociocultural, economic and political conditions of the society. In this context the study of the details of the social system becomes essential while attempting to present the mainstreams of demographic change. Revers as far back as in 1913, defined the nature of field work and distinguished between 'intensive' and 'survey' work. Radcliffe-Brown latter reaffirmed this distinction. Nevertheless the methodological debates are polemic (Reinherz, 1979 : 9) and the discussions of experiences are largely personal (Caldwell, *et al.* 1982b : 1). Both the qualities of this debate are inherent in the following discussion.

The major merit of the survey approach is its ability to provide quick data on varied aspects of inquiry covering huge areas and large populations. The analytical results which by nature are quantitative, attempt to present an understanding of the overall situation and produce patterns and correlations to suggest where relationships might be established. But they do not provide insight into the cause and sequence of demographic change nor can they help in interpreting the reported behaviour differing accross different cultures. Such an inquiry is possible through an in-depth, anthropological type investigation. An advantage in micro-village level study is that it allows the investigator to follow and keep a track of those households and individuals who may move away to different residential quarters in the same village. This happens either by a change in residential quarters or by a division of a joint family. In a survey design it is normally less feasible or difficult to keep track of people for such movements. Thus for a longitudinal study the micro-approach is the best suited methodology. Short of explaining the process of change in a particular social system the survey undoubtedly presents a static situation at a given point of time or at the most a comparison of several points in time. This gap is filled only through an investigation which is historical in perspective and anthropological in nature which provides an opportunity for both retrospective and prospective investigation.

The sampling procedure is a unique aspect of the survey which is assumed to provide representation of a population at large, but it often gives a notion of selectivity by its nature, and certain apparently trivial, but important sections of the society are usually omitted, for instance, households having no currently married women, or the ones with a single person in them. For a substantive research topic, one has to take into account the fact that there is no specific guideline to support the selection of a specific type of persons, families and even interviewers. Survey methods essentially rely on interviewing the selected respondents, which not only presents the views of a selected few like the husband or wife or the head of the household, but also runs the risk of superficiality due to instant replies from them. The answers are less likely to be counter-checked and the views of others in the family are not included. The problem of selectivity, superficiality and spontaneity leads to vague answers and general bias. This bias arises from the uncontrolled behaviour of the respondent, such as, excitement, fear, anger or even intentional misreporting for want of basic information about the research which the respondent would expect to be told which can easily be done during intensive field work. Under such circumstance, the respondent's reply to the investigation cannot be relied upon without his choice of words, tone of voice, gestures, and expressions (Cicurel, 1967). Therefore, the survey may deal with an atypical section of the given community.

It has been widely recognized that the social relationship between the interviewer and the respondent during the course of the study is the most important factor which reflects the quality of data. Interviews are the conversations with purpose, and the kind of relationship required to elicit information, often personal in nature, demands a high degree of cordiality, acquaintance, faith and trust between the interviewer and the interviewee. Such an environment of cordial rapport is likely to be achieved when the researcher stays with the community for a fairly long period, participates in day-to-day living, and has had at least some kind of non-formal social interaction before the interviewing. This helps in motivating and in keeping the community's interest high before the actual interviewing. For the specific purposes of interviewing, different visits for different issues lead to fruitful data during the field work, about family routines and problems. The intensive field work also provided an opportunity to the researcher to record those observations which were not regarded important for the research at the start of the work. Better relations with the respondents were frequently established by making appointments convenient to them for interviewing. During interviewing one normally feels each interaction will have problems of a different kind which are to be negotiated at each step with a variety of solutions (Cicurel, 1967). Such an elaborate and tactful conduct of data gathering is one of the characteristics of micro-approach. Surveys by their nature induce quick conduct on the part of both the interviewer and interviewee, and do not grant importance to a specific person or family which is often highly desirable in social research. An advantage of the micro-approach is that all members of a community are given equal attention during the interviewing. Nevertheless, the major strength of the micro-approach is its capacity to absorb and accommodate additional investigations on different dimensions, which can be included at any stage of the field work. Unlike survey research where hypotheses and choice of questions are often based on prior research, and are chosen because they have worked elsewhere before, in the micro-approach they are also generated during the course of field work which provided a great flexibility in the conduct of field work. It is possible during the course of field work to develop, modify or even reject hypotheses according to the requirements and feasibility of the field work.

Surveys are ordinarily the source for quantitative data which are used for statistical manipulations. But qualitative material, *even if gathered*, in the course of a survey, may be seen as too problematic for analytical purposes due to difficulties involved in coding and standardizing of the responses. The usual presentation of results, based on the subsuming and standardization of varied responses into a few sets of categories, may not lead to an adequate representation of the findings. This problem is overcome by qualitative analysis and the presentation of facts and figures gathered by the micro-approach. The additional strength of the data gathered from the micro-approach is that the application of advanced statistical tests and analyses becomes ever more desirable. It is possible that a large set of data may provide meaningful results by the application of a simple analysis like cross-tabulation and it is not ordinarily required to resort to sophisticated techniques. But because of the usually small set of data, the application of advanced techniques like the analysis of variance and regression becomes more desirable and essential. This, however, emphasizes the fact that micro-approach and statistical analysis are not mutually exclusive, rather the quantification and its qualitative interpretation increases the desirability and authenticity of the micro-approach.

Surveys are efficient for collecting data on variables which are scientifically important rather than those seen as practically important. For example, the interrelationship between age and parity as presented by estimating mean parity for the women from different cohorts or the mean number of children according to different lengths of marital duration in itself cannot sufficiently explain but just add to the pile of indices and statistics. What is more relevant is the explanation of why a certain proportion of women have fewer children than the mean parity while others have more. Practically, more important considerations for explaining fertility differentials emerge from the family power and economic structure. The normative behaviour of an individual is controlled in any society by the interplay of family and community interactions. This practicality is quite conveniently truncated into a matter of family size differentials or at the most a differential expressed in terms of simple and complex household structure. The apparently scientifically important variables emerge largely from the status of a couple like the educational attainment of the husband or the wife, whereas in the real situation emphasis should instead be given to educational levels and patterns of the whole family. It is known, however, that the very size of large-scale surveys make it almost impossible to collect such a detailed information. On the other hand, a detailed, informal and in depth investigation, in spite of the sample and geographic coverage being limited to a smaller set of population or a few villages, enables a better understanding of demographic behaviour.

The skills and standards required to undertake a micro-study are enormous, and this limits the frequency of such research. This approach is attached, involved, personal and both objective and subjective. Thus there appears to be a high degree of bias inherent in this approach, but the extent and nature of bias can be explained by the researcher himself and can be reviewed and evaluated by others, whereas the multiplicity of biases in the survey cannot be easily explained, nor can it be evaluated.

Macro-analysis has been identified as a valid procedure perhaps more suited to developed than developing countries by Epstein (1973 : 3). Her argument is that the institutions, attitudes and behaviour in the developed countries are more in harmony with the fast pace of development and show an extraordinary adaptability. Whereas in the developing countries like India, the social institutions, individual attitudes and behaviour are not turned to such an extent as to withstand the forces of development and change. In such situations the quantitative analysis suited to market conditions alone become unreliable and misleading.

Present-day requirements for data on huge areas and greater populations, however, make it inevitable to have surveys as the source of data, and often the objectives of such surveys are simple to be investigated within a short time. Yet micro-studies should be carried out to strengthen results and interpretations. However, the micro-method not only can supplement the surveys but also can exist in its own right as an independent method of investigation (Caldwell, *et. al.* 1982b).

2.3 Methodology of the Present Study

The following section deals with the methodology and data used in this study. This section also deals with the technical aspects of data collection and the analytical procedure used for this thesis. The problem for investigation at the start of the study was to explain the beginning of fertility transition in a south Indian region. A close analysis of the figures on various demographic indices so far available gave a general answer that fertility in this area indeed was falling. The South Indian Fertility Survey research had also made possible the timing of fertility decline in a neighbouring area of south India. A wide range of investigative findings gave an insight into the issues of socioeconomic change in general and demographic change in particular. The researcher was keen to find out if a similar change was occurring in other areas of the region, namely a decline in fertility. The prime objective of the current research was to know the responses of the villagers to the family planning programme and to investigate different aspects of fertility decision-making among rural families of the research area. For a better understanding of these issues the research had also to be supplemented by a study of the community, nature of family and social change, economic role of children, and women both in economic and sociocultural context. The best way to find out this reality is to live with them for a sufficient period of time, win their confidence, and observe and ask them about their way of life.

A cluster of four villages was selected for the purpose of this study. The requirement was that the villages had to be as far as possible typical of the plain region or *maidan* of south India, which is mostly a dry area, with subsistence agriculture, cultivating cereals and millet suited to local climatic conditions. However, the unique feature of the settlement patterns of the Indian villages is that a few villages settle around water tanks of different size.[6] These tanks enable the cultivation of small quantities of wet crops especially paddy and sugar cane. An apparent uniformity among the villages of this area is that these villages almost have a common tradition but the impact of social change is felt differently in spite of exposure to similar levels and patterns of socioeconomic transformation as a result of government programme implementation.

The selected villages are found in a circular area within a radius of seven kilometres. They are located sixty kilometres north of Bangalore city the capital of the State of Karnataka and fifteen kilometres off the state highway, from which a moderately good road connects the larger of the villages to the *taluka* headquarters.[7] These villages are also a part of the village *panchayat*,[8] which has its headquarters in the larger of the villages.

The taluka centre, namely Doddaballapur is the nearest town which caters to many special requirements of the population of all these villages. The largest of the four villages selected for the study is connected to the taluka headquarters by a bus service of sufficient frequency to allow an emergency trip to the town and back within a day. Ten kilometres north-east of this village are the famous Nandi Hills which are the start of a seventy kilometre mountain range stretching north-west. This area has a long history and a feeling for the past, the people tracing their ancestors at least to the late eighteenth century. It is over this period that the largest of these villages has grown into a multi-caste village.

The other three villages are in the hinterland, being connected by pathways and non-motorable roads. They stand out as single caste village units close to self-sufficiency in their daily needs.[9] The total population of these four villages was 2,747 living in 525 households according to the 1971 census. The greater proportion of this population was engaged in agriculture and agriculture-based occupations. A few households also draw their supplementary income from a seasonal household industry namely *leaf-plate* making.[10] Thus the villages are typical of the Indian peasant economy undertaking near subsistence agriculture while only a small share of produce is sold or exchanged to meet the cost of miscellaneous purchases.

Both the survey and micro methods were employed for data collection. Data collection was done at different stages using different techniques and the field work for a period of twelve months was planned. For this purpose, the investigator stayed in the larger village for nine months and the area was frequently visited for next four months. The strength of this approach was that the researcher became a part of the village society and after some time the people thought that he was in fact going to settle in that village for a long period. This obviously was the case, as the day-to-day contacts with the local population as a customer of the local vegetable grower, milk suppliers, manager of the fair price depot, electrician, plumber, bicycle mechanic, flour mill owner and so on served as good contact points. The relations with some of the neighbours were close enough to become involved in emergency exchanges of items essential for village life such as salt, match sticks, betel leaves and kerosene. A few people developed monetary contacts in the form of frequent borrowing of small amounts of cash for their requirements which they opted to repay in kind like milk, eggs and fruits. These contacts were possible since the investigator stayed in the village with his wife and presented a feeling of settled village life to the people around. The investigator and his wife being members of the same culture and language group were advantaged and it helped to establish a good rapport among the target populations.

Recurrent visits over many years will provide sufficient opportunity to understand fully the local conditions but for reasons beyond the control of this study it had to be a single but continuous period of field work for one year. This approach has its own advantage over the other, to the extent that it made it possible to observe the behaviour of the population round the year through an understanding of the effect of seasonality on occupations and family events in these village community.

During the course of field work and interviewing, offerings in the form of tea, coffee, a glass of milk and invitation to share their regular meal were frequent and were accepted without hesitation. Many families belonging to the lower sections sought advice on issues like the health and education of their children despite having a health dispensary and schools in the larger village. However, one incidence left a lasting impression on the investigator's mind. One evening a research team was involved in a detailed conversation with a fifty-five-year-old villager at his door-step where the cattle were tethered. During the course of the talk one of the cows started urinating. The respondent spontaneously collected the urine using both his hands and drank it. Then he collected some more and sprinkled it on the interviewers as a gesture of blessing. He had already learnt that the interviewers were newly weds and also that they were Muslims. Muslims are known for their disapproval of this Hindu practice, and yet the respondent considered them a part of the same culture and belief. This reflects the fact that familiarity, and recurrent interactions with the local population helps in eliminating suspicion and fear from the interviewers and intensifies rapport with the local population.

The preliminary data or the base line data was collected through a hundred-per-cent household survey using standard pretested proformae. The following proformae were used during different stages of data collection.

1. Household Information Card (Form I) : The general identity of village and the household [11] and listing of all the persons ordinarily living and sharing food cooked from a common kitchen was done in Form I. The socio-demographic information collected was name, age, sex, relationship to head, marital status, education attained, expected highest level of education, primary and secondary source of income, occupation of the individual and the annual individual income. This proforma was designed also to identify the currently married women between ages 15-49 years and information about the occurrence of any birth and death in the household during the previous twelve months. The information thus collected was expected to help in the analysis of the family structure, age and sex distribution, marital status, occupational classification and annual gross family income. A detailed analysis of educational levels and patterns according to sex and age was possible using this data.

2. Supplementary Household Information Card (Form II): This card was included to record information about those persons who ordinarily resided in this household, but were not

doing so now for various reasons. Such reasons were marriage, employment, education, health and others. The intensity and type of contacts retained by these people with the original household as well as any monetary and or contributions in kind to the family were collected. The extent of each person's involvement in family decision-making was also investigated through this proforma. This form was designed to investigate the extent and scale of wealth flow or remittance and involvement in major decisions relating to family management.

3. Pregnancy History Card (Form III): This card was used to collect detailed pregnancy histories of all the identified currently married women of ages between 15-44 years. Details included age at marriage of both of the spouses, list of all pregnancies irrespective of the nature of pregnancy outcome. This provided information on live births, still births and other kinds of foetal losses. For all live births, the age, date of birth, sex, living status, duration of breast feeding, and for dead children, the age at death were collected in detail. The nature of labour activity of the grownup children was recorded in great detail. For all women interviewed with Form III, information about the practice of any family planning method was noted, and from acceptors, the date of acceptance, and place and method of family planning were collected. This information helped in estimating demographic indices and rates for the research area.

4. General information on the households, livestock, and agricultural possessions, land onwership and yields and type of house. A detailed record of common possessions of a village household and other information relevant to assess the economic standards of the household was gathered using standard proformae. Two additional questions on the perception of the change in economic condition, living style and change in the family structure since the last five years were put to all the households.

Those data which were collected using survey approach served as the base-line data for the intensive investigation of special topics. The household in which at least one couple had adopted any of the family planning methods were singled out for in-depth interviewing (eighty-eight in number). Informal in-depth interviewing was done in eighty of the *acceptor families* covering various predetermined topics. This involved repeated contacts over the whole year. The idea was to know the reality about why couples from these households decided to limit their family size and how exactly the decisions were taken. The topics covered in these informal interviews were as varied as a brief family history, information on the couple's parents, relationships between marriage, the spouses before marriage, the couple's own kin and their affinity in terms of residential arrangement contacts and bondage, source of emergency and mutual supports during crisis and a brief marriage history. Some of these issues have been regarded by other researchers as trivial for the explanation of fertility behaviour, but they were found to bear an important influence upon family planning decision-making in this study. Thereafter, the interview proceeded with the detailed questioning about the sequence of marriage, births, and deaths, and their effect on the socio-economic status of the family at each stage. Questions covering socialization, education, work and labour distribution were asked to all the family members which also provided data for the investigation of sex differentials as well. Views felt about the costs and benefits of having children particularly the last child before acceptance, and future births which could have occurred in the absence of acceptance, were also recorded. The issues concerning the arrangements of the marriage of daughters and sons in the household drew the special attention of the interviewers. A separate set of unstructured question were brought in to investigate the decision-making patterns, day-to-day family affairs and family planning in the context of respective household structure and economic conditions.

An equal number of in-depth interviews was undertaken to cover those families where *there were no acceptors* but had currently married couples having at least three or more living children with the last child being less than three years of age. Almost the same set of question were asked of these non-acceptors, with an emphasis on the non-decisions on family size to be treated as a form of fertility decisions. Reasons for such non-decisions were investigated in detail. Each in-depth interview when completed became an essay on the whole family, while the information was usually collected from not only the husbands and wives but also from other adult members of the household. This enabled the cross and counter cross-checking of the information reported from different people of the household. However, care was taken to retain the independent views about family planning acceptance and decision-making. Two more areas were added for further investigation : health expenditure and labour market family data. This information is available from selected households.

Three investigators were employed to undertake the survey work in the initial period of the field work. These investigators had sufficient experience in data collection, for they had been involved in the South Indian Fertility Project since its inception in 1979. All the in-depth interviews and observations were done first-hand by the researcher and there was neither scope nor need to employ informants from the local population. Personal notes based on the day-to-day observations and various essays written on general topics provided a valuable source of support data for a qualitative analysis of this study. The information on pregnancy histories was gathered in a series of repeated visits to the households. The respondents this time were the couples and frequently the wives. In-depth interviews with the selected couples were conducted during separate, often repeated, visits contacting the husband, wife and other elder members of the family. On a few occasions children were questioned for information about themselves and their younger brothers and sisters, about their age (using school certificates where possible), education and work. Very old persons often provided valuable information about the past and an attempt was made to obtain as much information as possible from them.

NOTES AND REFERENCES

1. Labour (meaning the population) was identified as one of the factors of production and its relationship with wages, was the essence of many classical economic theories.
2. Nag calls them as the community level studies.
3. Caldwell tried this approach as a supplement to a large scale

longitudinal type survey in Africa. Few issues which required a detailed investigation were researched through the in-depth and informal interviewing technique in 1974-75 in Nigeria and Ghana.

4. The South Indian Fertility Survey was initiated in 1979 and field work continued until 1983. For more details about this project see Caldwell *et al* (1982a, 1982b).
5. She considers this approach as a joint application of economics and anthropological techniques for her study of two villages in South India.
6. Numerous tanks and small lakes are the characteristics of maidan of the Deccan Plateau. Almost all large villages are found beside a water tank.
7. Taluka is the lowest administrative unit of the government bureaucracy where an official namely *tahsildar* is stationed as the administra tive head. A taluka normally covers a population of a hundred thousand residing in 150 to 200 villages.
8. Panchayat is the village headquarters of the local self-government, which is based on the design of the traditional village councils. In the modern days the members of the panchayat are elected through a popular vote from among ten to fifteen villages to cover the population residing in as many villages. There are certain regulations which are meant to guarantee the representation of women and as many communities as possible.
9. Single-caste villages are characteristic of this region ; often they are smaller in size and population ; but they may also contain a few persons of other castes especially the Scheduled Castes and Tribes and a few persons belonging to other service castes like the Madivala and Nayanda.
10. *Leaf-Plate* is a traditional disposable plate used for serving food. They are professionaly knitting using a specific variety of wild leaves and sharp bits of sticks. The knitting requires a special skill of arranging many leaves to give circular shape which do not allow liquid to spill around.
11. Each household was identified and was given a separate household number which was used to identify the household in the later part of the Study.

3

The Study Area and Its People

3.1. Location and Description

As discussed in Chapter 2 it was decided that a rural population would be selected for the study. This population had to be from a different area but similar cultural group to that of the population covered by the South Indian Fertility Survey (SIFS). Apart from the original nine SIFS villages which were about one hundred kilometres west of Bangalore, two other villages were being studied in the south and south-eastern parts of the region. In contrast, the four villages selected for this study are sixty kilometres north of Bangalore. The area selected for research constituted four villages in Doddaballapur *taluk* of the Bangalore district. *Ramagere*[1] is the largest of all, situated beside a small pond locally called *kere*[2] which apparently had a very small population a century ago.[3] This village now is approachable by a secondary motor-ble road connecting two state highways stretching about 40 kilometres and linking two major towns of the area. It is this communication network which has enabled Ramagere to grow into a larger multi-caste village with diverse occupational opportunities. The second village which is relatively smaller in terms of population is towards the south of Ramagere in the hinterland. It is about three kilometres away from Ramagere by a pathway and about four kilometres by a rough road mainly used by bullock carts. This village named *Laxmipura* is also situated on the banks of a pond slightly larger both in depth and in capacity thus enabling at least some wet cultivation. This settlement is a dominant caste village engaged in agriculture.[4] Its proximity to Ramagere has precluded the establishment of modern institutional infrastructure except for a primary school and a milk producers' co-operative.

The other two villages, named *Shivadurga* and *Gowdahalli*,[5] are situated to the north of Ramagere. They are about three and six kilometres respectively in distance from Ramagere and are located about half a kilometre away from a non-motorable road which starts from Ramagere and leads into the hills fifteen kilometres further in the north-east. They are smaller, predominantly single caste villages, where people are engaged mainly in stone-quarrying, animal husbandry and wood cutting besides agriculture. These villages are characterised by specialized economies due to their natural environments. Thus, Ramagere presents itself as a multi-caste, heterogeneous, active and central village, whereas Laxmipura, Shivadurga and Gowdahalli are dominated by single castes, and relatively homogeneous in character.[6]

These villages are found within a diameter of about nine kilometres. Ramagere and Laxmipura are in the plain areas of the region and the other two are located in a hilly terrain, closer to the dry forests. The location and settlement patterns of the smaller villages suggests their long history, which dates back at least three hundred years. This is demonstrated by the fact that they are found on the elevated tableland adjacent to the remains of early stone walls which surrounded these villages in the past. This was the feature of villages in this hilly area during the reigns of early chieftains and *pallegars*.[7] Usually a large village and sometimes a group of villages were ruled by a chieftain and the rivalry between such rulers resulted in wars and killings. There were also instances of large-scale looting and robbery in the olden days. For these reasons the villages were protected by circular stone wall around them and often the settlements were on hills and mountains. Though the two smaller villages are not quite on the hills, they depict the characteristics of the settlements of the past. This makes us think that Ramagere is of comparatively recent origin and grew faster due to better organization and infrastructural facilities. Laxmipura, however, is a much older village than Ramagere and it is on the plains which is the feature of the land mass south of a shallow valley originating in the hills. Though Laxmipura is older than Ramagere, what is not found there is the stone wall which is the feature of other two villages. This is due to three factors. The first is that Laxmipura has always been a comparatively large agricultural village. Secondly, the major caste (*Vokkaliga*) of this village is the dominant caste of the region thereby having an advantage of greater security due to large numbers.[8] Lastly, this village has no near access to rock and stone, rendering it difficult to construct stone walls around the village. However, the security aspect of this village in the olden days is worth investigating further from a historical perspective.

The above mentioned topographical features have moulded the subsistence pattern of the villages under study. Laxmipura, however. has remained a purely agricultural village, only difference is that the cultivators use modern agricultural methods such as tractors, fertilizers and pesticides electric driven irrigation wells, sugar cane crushers and modern marketing of the produce. The people of Shivadurga and Gowdahalli, who were earlier sheep and cattle graziers, milk and firewood sellers, have adopted subsistence agriculture more recently. The original population of Ramagere was agricultural but in recent years this has given way to other occupations such as animal-husbandry, trade and other non-agricultural occupations. The selection of Ramagere as a centre for village level planning activities has created a number of government jobs since 1952. In 1981 almost 14 per cent of the households reported government salaries as the primary source of income and another 2 per cent reported this as the secondary source of income. Practically all these people work in Ramagere.

This area falls within the dry zone of the south Indian

peninsula, where even the average of 72 centimetres of rainfall is only marginal for the dry crops.[9] The rainfall is spread unevenly between the months of May and October each year and allows only for a single annual crop, *Ragi*, a local variety of finger millet is the chief crop, while sorghum, horse gram, field beans, peanuts and rice are grown in small quantities. Sugarcane and grapes are the commercial crops cultivated only by a few large agriculturists. Vegetables and greens are grown close to the villages both for local needs and exports to nearby towns and to Bangalore city. Water from the irrigation wells is used to cultivate these produce. However, agriculture still is a gamble with the rainfall. In four of the last seven years the rainfall has been below average. In 1980 the area received an annual average rainfall of only 51.6 centimetres, which caused a severe drought-like situation in the area. The soil around the villages, except some near Laxmipura, is rocky and brown which has a poor absorptive capacity and is not really suitable for good cultivation. The land surrounding Laxmipura is of relatively good quality and due to better water resource from a tank adjacent to the land it enables at least a comparatively good yield of dry crops and also some wet crops like sugarcane and rice. Thus the population depending entirely on agriculture in Ramagere, Shivadurga and Gowdahalli are worst affected by bad rains. This is the main reason for the diversity of occupations in these villages. Agriculture and dairying are the main occupations in Laxmipura and incomes are relatively better when compared with other three villages.

For the last twelve years a few people in Ramagere and a comparatively larger proportion of the population of Laxmipura have been engaged in dairy-farming as a secondary occupation. Danish breeds of cows were introduced in this area by the Indo-Danish project on an experimental basis at the beginning of the last decade, and many people of these villages are utilising this expertise. Even in this field, however, Laxmipura has shown remarkable success in terms of daily milk production which is marketed through the milk Producers' Co-operative Society units, one each in these two villages. Such developments did not take place in the two smaller villages where sheep and cattle grazing have remained predominant. This is both due to the limitations of the project and the reluctance of the people to invest in expensive breeds of cows which normally have a high risk of catching disease, and in the absence of proper insurance farmers have a high risk of loss.

Being the *Panchayat* headquarters, Ramagere has a panchayat office, a farmer's bank, a producers' co-operative society (distributor of food grains, cloth and fertilizer), a private commercial bank, a milk co-operative, a high school and a *Kannada* and a *Urdu*-medium primary schools.[10] A revenue official called the village secretary is stationed here who collects the local land taxes from this and other surrounding villages. A veterinary and a health dispensary cater to the requirements of this and various surrounding villages. The village was electrified in 1936, the flour mill was established twenty years later, the health dispensary in 1968, the veterinary dispensary in 1977, while tap water and the telephone services were provided only in 1979. Laxmipura, which is three-and-a-half kilometres away by the pathway, depends greatly on Ramagere for daily requirements. The village is also electrified and has primary school. It has a separate milk co-operative. Other smaller villages are connected with an unmetalled non-motorable road. They have a single-teacher lower primary school each, which are rarely open for want of students, at least during the peak agricultural seasons. Nevertheless, Ramagere caters to the normal commercial and other requirements of the people in various surrounding villages including the three included in this study. The taluka headquarters is the nearest town which caters to many of the special requirements of the population of all these villages. This town is about twenty kilometres away from the largest village and is connected to it by a bus service of sufficient frequency to allow an emergency trip to the town and back within a day. Each day the bus service, managed by different private enterprises, stops six times going in each direction.

3.2 Social Structure of the Population

(*i*) *Castes in the Research Area*

The indigenous castes of the area are the *Vokkaligas*, *Gollas*, *Kurubas*. There are also a few *Scheduled Castes*,[11] and

Tribes, some *Brahmins* in this area. In Ramagere, the *Balagiga* caste people are dominant not only in power[12] but also in numbers. Next in importance are the six households of the *Edigas* who by virtue of their ability to recruit agricultural labourers on their large farms have come to wield substantial political power. *Settys* (*Vaishyas*)[13] although traceable back for at least three generations, they are the most recent addition to this village. They control the grain and other large businesses of the area. However, this rich caste does not claim political power, but has the respect of all other residents of the area through its money lending and business contacts. Ultimately, the Settys' group strength is sufficient to protect its economic interests, as shown by the fact that they managed to shift the village *shandy*[14] to a neighbouring village about forty years ago. Settys and Balagigas are the migrant population from neighbouring areas of present day Andhra Pradesh which lies on the other side of the mountain range. The remaining Hindu population belong to different Service Castes some of whom are still engaged in respective traditional occupations. They are *Ganigas* (oil crushers), *Madivalas* (washermen), *Bhajantris* (barbers) and *Acharis* (gold or black smiths). Vokkaligas, the indigenous peasant caste of the region, are mainly found in Laxmipura, and the *Bovis* (stone cutters) live in Shivadurga, the village situated next to a large rock which is being cut and sold by the Bovis. Table 3.1 and 3.2 gives an idea of the different castes, and their size and distribution in this area. The segregated pattern of village settlement based on caste can also be found from Maps 1 to 3.

The *Muslims* migrated to the larger village in the late eighteenth century from the northern parts of the then Mysore (now Karnataka) and Hyderabad (now Andhra Pradesh) provinces. They migrated in connection with the flourishing trade in horses and donkeys, and as members of the armies of Hyder Ali and Tippu Sultan.[15] Now, there are twenty-nine Muslim households in Ramagere, mostly occupied in small trade, agriculture and simple mechanical jobs.

The area is as yet a traditional entity. Old inter-caste relationships exist, though altered or disordered by commercialization. *Jajmani* or *adade*[16] systems of service payments still

TABLE 3.1

List of Castes, their Traditional and Present Occupations

Caste	Traditional Occupation/s	Present Occupations
Brahmin	priests, landlords	priests, agriculturists, teachers, bureaucrates.
Lingayat	agriculture	agriculturists, teachers, hotel owners.
Balagiga	bangle sellers, peasants	politicians, panchayat members, agriculturists, lower professionals, small business, tailors, agricultural labourers, bangle sellers.
Ediga	toddy tappers	politicians, landlords, agriculturists, toddy sellers, liquor shop owners. mill-owners.
Kuruba	Shepherds	agriculturists, shepherds, agricultural labourers.
Golla	shepherds	agriculturists, shepherds, agricultural labourers, firewood sellers.
Ganiga	oil crushers	peasants, oil crushers.
Madivala	washer men	washermen, peasants, agricultural labourers, tailors.
Achari	Smiths	gold smiths, peasants, musicians.
Nayanda	barbers	barbers, peasants, musicians.
Vokkaliga	peasants	agriculturists, politicians, panchayat members, teachers, tractor owners, cane crusher owners.
Setty/ Vaishya	traders, money lenders	traders, money-lenders, agriculturists.
Bovi	stone cutters	stone cutters, peasants, agricultural labourers.
Scheduled Castes	menial jobs, labourers	agricultural labourers, peasants, bonded labourers, servants, leather workers, lesser professionals, other menial jobs.
Muslims	small traders	small traders, shop cwners, bicycle mechanics, black smith, tailors, agriculturists, labourers, teachers.

TABLE 3.2

Households and population distribution of important castes by village

Caste	Ramagere			Laxmipura			Shivadurga			Gowdahalli			All villages		
	N	P	%	N	P	%	N	P	%	N	P	%	N	P	%
Brahmin	23	77	3.9	3	10	1.4	—	—	—	—	—	—	26	87	2.8
Lingayat	20	88	4.5	1	5	0.7	—	—	—	—	—	—	21	93	2.9
Balajiga	104	602	30.7	12	60	8.2	—	—	—	—	—	—	116	662	21.0
Idiga	6	39	2.0	—	—	—	—	—	—	—	—	—	6	39	1.2
Kuruba	41	230	11.7	—	—	—	10	54	22.1	—	—	—	51	284	9.0
Golla	12	78	4.0	—	—	—	—	—	—	31	181	81.2	43	259	8.2
Ganiga	17	86	4.4	—	—	—	—	—	—	—	—	—	17	86	2.7
Madival	4	15	0.8	6	19	2.6	11	48	19.7	—	—	—	21	82	2.6
Achari	10	58	3.0	1	6	0.8	—	—	—	—	—	—	11	64	2.0
Vokkaliga	7	20	1.0	62	378	51.8	—	—	—	—	—	—	69	398	12.6
Setty/ Vaishya	17	92	4.7	—	—	—	—	—	—	—	—	—	17	92	2.9
Bovi	1	6	0.3	—	—	—	24	121	49.6	—	—	—	25	127	4.0
Scheduled Castes	57	286	14.6	43	201	27.5	6	15	6.1	1	5	2.5	107	507	16.0
Muslims	29	200	10.2	—	—	—	—	—	—	—	—	—	29	200	6.3

exist in a weak form. Because of the fact that the labour inputs are not usually estimated in monetary terms, these systems of service payments are continuing in a weak form. However, payment in kind is preferred less both by the employee and the employer. One finds the system of traditional exchange of service obligations still in practice in this area at least among the members of the same kinship group. The traditional washerman now prefers to obtain cash for his services, and the barbers have established their own permanent place of service inside the village limits. The latest addition to the list of the local occupations is *hotel* trade,[17] most of the caste groups having a hotel of their own. The customers originally had to be from the specific castes who are traditionally allowed to enter a house or eat with the caste person who owns the hotel. However, the competition among hotel owners has made them relax this rule to allow all caste people to enter and be served although Scheduled Castes and Scheduled Tribe persons are not yet encouraged to enter a hotel. The government has also made it illegal to refuse entrance to such common places on the basis of caste, religion and region of origin.

Brahmins still have their traditional feeling of caste supremacy, the Gollas and Kurubas retain their old rivalry, they were originally hill-based caste people with similar occupations, and seem to be at odds with each other ; while the Ganigas and Acharis reside very close to the inner village circles where the Brahmins and other, non-vegetarian castes normally reside. People belonging to Scheduled Castes and Tribes still feel obliged to do their traditional jobs for no monetary payment either from the community or the panchayat and expect that one day they will be regularized in those jobs for a salary. Traditionally they in Ramagere and Laxmipura used to sweep the village streets, clear the dead animals, carry dead bodies in case of death by drowning and suicide, lift night soil from the landlords' back yards, work as servants and announcers to the landlords and the village panchayat. They, however, make situational gains, like occasional small payments made to undertake such tasks. The Scheduled Caste and Tribe people live in a separate colony and have a separate source of water in the largest village. The public tap distribution system was introduced about three years ago, and these communities have access to a tap connection which does not provide water. However, this caste group has mixed feelings toward the other communities. They continue to respect the High Castes as a traditional practice, which becomes binding for those low caste persons who work as labourers. In recent times they have begun to feel and know that they are exploited.

The area has no great history of its own to leave remarkable traces behind. However, two temples are prominent in Ramagere which are unusually old and beyond the capacity of the natives to trace their origins. The largest of the two temples is the one which has Sri Venkateshwara as the deity. This deity is found only in a few place in Karnataka. Staunch believers in this deity are the Balagigas and the Settys. Therefore, the presence of this temple suggests the presence of these communities for a long time. There used to be a few *Devanga* caste[18] households earlier this century and in 1930 there were at least six handlooms producing cotton and silk cloth in Ramagere. Though electricity was available in Ramagere in 1936, these families migrated to Doddaballapur, a town twenty kilometers away and with them went the looms and industrial activity. This movement occurred due to the establishment of organized silk manufacture at Doddaballapur using powered looms. There is no other evidence of any factory type or industrial enterprise in this area excepting a cart making factory (non-electric) owned and managed by a Muslim joint family. However, there are three additions to this village which operate on electricity on a commercial basis. They are the flour mill which was opened in 1968, a rice mill owned by the richest of the landlords which rarely operated during our stay due to crop failure, and lastly one of the Brahmin families operates a wetgrinder[19] on a commercial basis since 1977. In Laxmipura, since the introduction of electricity, three sugar cane crushers and one flour mill have begun operating.

(*ii*) *The Village Scene*

While entering the village area during the months of May to October one cannot fail to smell the green ragi fields around the village, but closer to the settlement a pungent odour emerging from the cow dung pits greets a visitor into the village. One finds innumerable numbers of small pits half filled with cow dung and stagnant water in the close vicinity of the rural dwellings. These are left for fermentation through the year to get good quality loam soil or organic manure for the next cropping season. Vegetables, like pumpkins and bitter gourd, are grown around these pits as they require no manuring and watering. Unfortunately these pits are mosquito breeding places. When a visitor arrives, he is met by the dogs whose barking announces the presence of the stranger to the people, especially the children. The children of a village, who are comparatively exposed to communication and schooling, are less suspicious of strangers visiting the villages and their excitement in speaking with strangers often helps provide directions to the health centre, or the school or even a specific household. Children of interior villages are comparatively more suspicious and always keep their distance. The entrance to Ramagere is by a metalled road. As one enters the first settlements to the right of the road there is a row of eight small shops which come alive in the evening where *toddy* and *arack* are sold to the local population. A permanent smell of this locally brewed liquor greets one at any time of the day or night. Next to them is a prominent concrete structure with a brick compound which was originally constructed as the 'Sub-centre' headquarters of a female health worker. This is used as a health dispensary by a government appointed medical practitioner and also as the residential quarters of the female health worker. The medical practitioner, who is locally referred to as *doctor*, comes to this dispensary every day from Doddaballapur as part of his official duty. Next, the residential dwellings are found which are locally called *mane*. On the left of the road is the new extension to the village under the Janatha Housing scheme of the state government, and behind this extension is the Harijan colony where the castes belonging to the classified caste groups, the Scheduled Castes and Scheduled Tribe population live in their huts. This colony is called *madigara keri* by the local population. By now one has reached the front of the village and the landmark is a bus stop. Two huge *pipal*[20] trees surrounded by a square shaped stone platform around their trunks provide a shady place to the waiting travellers. This place was originally used by the panchayat as a court-room to hear and settle village disputes. There are a few small shops selling *beedi*, *betel* leaves, and other items. More recently a few roadside restaurants have appeared where sometimes travellers spend hours together waiting for the bus. Once at this bus stop people identify a stranger to the village and a few will even ask questions about the visitor's where-abouts. One of the most frequent enquiries the villagers make is about the rains in the area from which the visitor comes. Beside this bus stop there is a bicycle repair shop and a flour mill, and there is a huge sign board hung outside the wall of the adjacent building which reads in English, 'Milk Producers' Co-operative Society Ltd'. This society is kept open in the early mornings and also in the late evenings each day to collect milk from the villagers which is sent to a chilling plant at Doddaballapur. A few metres further on the left side of the road is another large concrete building with wide steel shutters ; it is a godown or a grain silo, of the Farmers' Co-operative Society, which is meant to store and distribute fertilizers and seeds to the local agriculturists. This building is also used as a place to store and to distribute scarce food grains, as well as sugar and kerosene at the government controlled prices to the people of this village and various other villages in the periphery.

From here narrow streets lead us to the densely packed houses of Ramagere. In the centre of the village is the main shopping area, which is a straight but narrow street mostly occupied by the business community of this village. All the Setty households are found in this street, each one of them having an annexe to the house used as the grain shop. People of this caste are traditionally known to be business-oriented and have retained their occupational identity intact unlike many other castes. This street is close to the inner circle of the village where the Brahmins generally used to live. Now most of the Brahmin households have disintegrated and many Brahmins have migrated leaving behind only a few. The old mansion-like houses of the Brahmins are now rented in parts to the officials of this village.

A distinguishing feature of the multi-caste villages of this region is that the residential prtterns are closely related to the caste hierarchy in the village. In Ramagere, the Brahmin households are found around the bigger temple, and their immediate neighbours are the Settys and the Lingayats (see Maps 1 to 3). Acharis, not near in the caste hierarchy, but being a vegetarian caste, live in the immediate vicinity of Brahmins. Politically powerful and numerically large is the Balagiga caste who occupy a part of the village facing on to the main road and the streets which connects the main road with the shopping area. The Golla and Kuruba caste people have found a place towards the back side of the village, and the Scheduled Castes and Tribes live in a separate colony. The Muslims occupy an area in between the 'madigara keri' and the dwellings of the Balagigas.

The village schools are located in an area opposite to the big temple which are separated by an unusually wide street starting from the temple. The High School building is impressive yet it is not large enough to accommodate the ever increasing number of students. Students to this school, it is claimed by the Head Mistress, come from as far as fifteen kilometres. During the course of the conversation she expressed her appreciation of a girl student belonging to a distant village for her distinction in the 1980 Secondary School Leaving Certificate examination and asked us to find out the possibilities of an admission for the girl into a college in Bangalore with some financial assistance. Two other school buildings in the vicinity are the Middle and Primary level schools. They are old buildings and the local panchayats are not able to mobilize local resources to renovate them. Just in front of these schools is a small house-like structure which is used as the veterinary dispensary. The veterinary practitioner, the medical practitioner, travels on his motorcycle daily to and from his native village twelve kilometres away.

Behind the schools is the cemetery and crematorium of this village. Since the construction of residential quarters for the village officials by the Department of Public Works just in front, the burial ground has been rarely used. However, there is a practice among certain castes to bury or cremate the dead in their own lands provided the land is not under cultivation, or in a corner of the land set aside for this purpose.

The majority of the house units in these villager are made of either mud or unburnt bricks with thatched roofs. There are a few two-storey tiled roofed buildings belonging to locally rich persons. All the Scheduled Castes and Scheduled Tribes population live in huts roofs made of coconut leaves. The doors of these village dwellings open directly to the street and often children play on the streets. These are contiguous buildings and many are demarcated with a wall rising only half way to the roof. Such houses are the result of recently split joint families where a single house structure has been divided among many sons. However, the dwellings can be divided into five kinds based on their use : (i) residential, (ii) cattle shed, (iii) residential-cum-cattle shed, (iv) shop and (v) residential-cum-shop. Many average farmers impound their cattle within the residential dwellings, while the ownership of a separate cattle shed is a sign of relative wealth and prestige.

Though a few village lanes are paved with stone slabs which drain aside the rain water, many other streets lack drainage and sanitation. Recently introduced public taps in Ramagere add to this problem even in summer. The taps provide water thrice a day at specified times. It requires an enormous amount of time waiting in the queue with buckets and vessels lined up in front of the tap before the water starts flowing. This task is entrusted to children, especially girls, in almost all the families. Thus children are more exposed to contamination in the streets and near the taps. In the summer of 1981 children in Ramagere were seen to be engaged in varied activities other than household duties. Nearly in all the households, with the exception of the very rich and the Scheduled Castes the women and girls knit *leaf plates*. Leaf plate making is a cottage industry in this village. During the same season of the year children belonging to the trading community especially Muslims, work on sorting, cleaning and storing *Tamarind* and *Pongamia* seeds.[21]

The adult males of the village do varied activities depending upon their respective occupations and season. However, these villagers spend a substantial amount of time gossiping at their favourite spot like a village restaurant, the platform around the pipal tree or on the stone bench usually fixed in front of shops. Such places have a great significance in the villagers' life. It not only helps them to relax and forget momentarily the miseries and problems of the family or business, but also, more importantly serves as an dissemination centre for valuable information such as availability of paid work. Due to the absence of newspapers, public radios and other kinds of formal communication systems, the villagers are exposed to information only from a variety of people, local as well as visitors, at these places. Such are the places for gossip and entertainment. This phenomenon is found only in Ramagere, while the other three villages are too small for such daily social occasions, and also that there are no restaurants and shops in these villages.

Women are the busiest in the village. They work for longer hours, mostly within their homes and sometimes outside in the fields as agricultural labourers. Usually the public wells in rural India are the places of conversation and gossip for women ; while this is largely true in Laxmipura and Shivadurga, in Ramagere it is not so. This is because the village panchayat has provided the facility of public tap water distribution as a result now mostly children obtain water from the taps using vessels and buckets made of plastic which are lighter than the conventional vessels and buckets made of brass or iron. Well water is rarely used by the families in Ramagere.[22] On the other hand, there is no public well in Gowdahalli, and residents have to walk more than a kilometre and half to fetch any kind of water which is often done by men.

These villages, like all others in this region, are peaceful, serene and seemingly motionless. By the late morning many leave for work, mostly to the fields, children go to school and the few left in the village are kept away from the streets by the tropical sun. In the evening the streets become lively because of people returning home, and the sound of cattle arriving home from fields provides a unique pleasure. This is the time when the activities within the home speed up. In the dusk the village smells of smoke and a dark cloud of it encircles the village. Wood and cow dung cakes are the chief sources of energy used for cooking purposes. Though Ramagere has good access to electricity, no one in this village uses electricity for cooking. There are 113 kerosene stoves among the households of these villages, but very few of them use these stoves regularly due to a shortage in the supply of kerosene. The daily routine in these villages stretches from dawn to dusk and beyond. Adults, especially women, get up early and work till they go to bed in the night. Generally, women are the last to go to bed in a rural family and the first to rise. Only 164 (32 per cent) households in Ramagere and Laxmipura have electricity for domestic lighting and even among this privileged group the fear of heavy electricity bills make them go to bed earlier in order to minimize electricity consumption.

Generally, the life style of the local people appear to be easy going and lazy. Though village society is closely knit by the family, kinship, caste and inter-caste ties, each individual lives in a world of his own. There are only a few occasions when a villager becomes involved in village-wide or extra-village social activity. One such occasion is the cattle fair in the nearby temple village called *Ghati*. The annual fair usually falls in the month of January each year, and the farmers who wish either to sell or exchange their pair of bullocks plan almost a week-long stay at the fair. Farmers generally do not keep the same set of bullocks for more than a year. On this occasion farmers as well have to demonstrate their business and professional skill. To such fairs a farmer goes with his family to attend the annual *puja* at the temple. Other people visit such fairs either on business or on a pilgrimage. Politics is of no great interest to most people in the village areas. Political activity is a rarity at the village level. The only political happening in which some of the local population participated during 1981 was the 'state level *kisan* (farmer's) rally' organized by the oppositon political parties of the state. Incidentally, the chief organizer of the rally was the local leader who was also a Member of the Legislative Council. The Ediga and Balagiga caste people were particularly obliged to attend the rally at Doddaballapur, the Taluka headquarters. However, an interesting point in the village was that the families who used to sell daily labour particularly those of the Scheduled Castes and Tribes were without work that day and did not approve of the kisan rally.

South Indian villages are relatively peaceful and free from communal tensions compared to north Indian villages. There is no report of any incidence in the recent past of any tension or fight between communities. Though there is a strong feeling among the Scheduled Castes and Tribes, Gollas and Kurubas against the higher castes, it is more due to class differences than due to traditional caste differences. Many of the voluntary complaints made to the researcher by these communities are related to the discriminative distribution of certain essential commodities like rices, sugar, kerosene and controlled cloth through the public distribution system in Ramagere. The public distribution is done through the local village panchayat and the Farmers' Co-operative Society which is in practice controlled by the dominant caste of the village. A few other instances indicate a certain rivalry between groups but they are more in the nature of personal rifts between two individual families. One such clash was due to the impact of recent land reforms which made a tenant claim ownership rights denying the original owner any income from the land. There are a few other examples of trouble originating from the event of marriage. Yet Ramagere has a peaceful environment. In spite of the single caste in Laxmipura there are two rival groups among themselves. Some of the very close relatives belong to two different factions. These factions in Laxmipura are based more on the state level political rivalry, yet there is near perfect harmony in work relations. Differences sometimes arise during the village panchayat elections and the arrangement of marriages.

(*iii*) *Caste Groupings for the Study Purpose*

For convenience of analysis of the basic data, various Hindu castes have been grouped into four categories. The grouping has been done with great care and a careful observation of the socio-economic situation and inter-caste relationships in the villages. However, the ritual aspect of the caste system has not been exhaustively considered. Thus, the grouping and the ranking do not attempt either to suggest or to present the hierarchical caste ranking of the area. On the other hand, they present the status of caste in the local social and power structure. To a large extent the Hindu caste groups do represent the economic status in that order in the research area. A list of castes and respective traditional and modern occupations are presented in Table 3.1, and the size and distribution of castes is presented in Table 3.2.

The *High Castes* are the *Brahmins*, *Lingayats* and *Settys* (*Vaishyas*). Members of this group are vegetarians (although two youngsters reported that they had eaten meat on a few occasions when they visited Bangalore), live in the inner circles of the village and tolerate the presence of each other in the neighbourhood. They are relatively better educated, many work in non-agricultural jobs, and some landed persons undertake cultivation either by recruiting labour on a daily wage basis or by tenancy arrangements. Economically, this group is the richest in the area.

The second caste group is categorised as *Peasant Castes*. These are the intermediary castes, and most traditionally are agriculturists. However, all members of this category are either agriculturists or peasants with only a negligible proportion working in non-agricultural occupation. *Vokkaligas*, *Balagigas*, *Edigas*, *Kurubas* and *Gollas* are the main castes which constitute this group. Excepting all Edigas who are all rich and a few rich Vokkaligas and Balagigas, the economic level of the group is uniform. Vokkaliga and Balagiga being numerous in numbers, control the panchayat administration in the respective villages where they have dominance. Balagigas are dominant in Ramagere and Vokkaligas in Laxmipura. These villages are the headquarters of two different panchayats comprising different villages from around them.

Service Castes is the third category which includes *Acharis*, *Ganigas*, *Madivalas*, *Nayandas* and *Kumbars*. Though occupationally and culturally each caste is distinct the common feature is that they are traditionally engaged in caste specific service occupations. People of all these castes except those who were

Ganigas used to work under the Jajmani system. In recent times they have been undergoing an occupational transformation as a result of technological and related changes and a few have shifted to agriculture as the primary occupation. A few others are seeking non-agricultural pursuits, whereas many continue in their traditional occupations but with the modern touch of commercialization and the cash economy.

The last of the Hindu caste groups is *Low Castes* consisting of *Bovis, Scheduled Castes and Scheduled Tribes*. All but one Bovi family live at Shivadurga along with some Madivals and Gollas. Though occupationally Bovis are different from the Scheduled Castes and Tribes, they all are the major source of manual labour for both agricultural and non-agricultural work. The system of sending young male children to work, for a specific period, as permanent or bonded labourers is still found among all these low caste families.[23] Low caste women work on paid work as well in fields and other places. Economically they are the poorest and the landless.

The only other segment of the population of the area is the *Muslims*. In spite of their difference in religious affiliation, they are very much an assimilated part of the overall culture of the area. There is a Muslim who even practises the Hindu way of chanting mantras and prescribes *yantras* to the suffering Hindu children. He uses the Kannada language to chant and write *mantras* for Hindus and uses Urdu if dealing with Muslims. Muslims, however, live only in Ramagere and their major occupation is small trade. Some undertake cultivation and a few others work in the nearby town as weavers. Economically they are better off than the low caste Hindus and fall between the economic status of Peasant Castes and Service Castes.

3.3 Economic Structure of The Population

(i) *Landholding*

The economy of the research area is essentially based on agriculture. Agriculture is not only a source of subsistence but peasantry continues to be a way of life. People have both an emotional and economic value attached to land, cattle and agriculture. It is frequently found that many families are tied to a small land area which also encourages them to stay in the village. A Bovi caste family which migrated to Bangalore returned to the village after eight months to seek refuge in their disintegrating house and a small piece of land. Land, thus, is the ultimate security to a rural dweller. It is true not only of the traditional peasant and newly emerging agriculturists but also of the population engaged in non-agricultural pursuits like trade, commerce and government jobs. There is a growing effort among the latter to buy land not only for returns from agriculture but also as a sure investment and greater security for their money. Although, the returns from land are generally lower than from investments in non-agricultural pursuits, it is considered a safe and trouble-free investment. This also happens due to the local credit system, where a farmer who requires money to repay his debts or to arrange the marriage of daughters and so on, mortgage out land to get cash.[24] Over the years, due to the borrower's incapacity to repay the loan and high interest he is usually forced to sell the pledged land either to the creditor or to another wealthy person. Even the presence of a Farmer's Co-operative Credit Society and agricultural credit programmes in the village have not yet affected the existence of these older monetary practices. Similar finding has been reported by Mishra (1982) from a study of five villages which are only fifteen kilometres away from our research area.

Issues concerning the land ownership, income, education, occupations and landlessness are discussed below. The household survey data are analysed to bring out the differences between villages and caste groups. Tables 3.3 and 3.4 present the distribution of households by landholding categories for each village and caste group.

It is clear from Table 3.3 that the grouped villages Gowdahalli and Shivadurga, and Laxmipura are relatively more agriculturally oriented than Ramagere. Practically all the landless in grouped villages work as agricultural labourers with a strong commitment to land as the source of living. In contrast, more than half the landless in Ramagere are the families engaged in bureaucratic jobs or trade as the source of income. However, some of these have their share of land in their original place of residence or birth place. They live in a non-agricultural life style which propagates an urban way of life. The remaining landless are the Low-caste Hindus and the bulk of the Muslim families. Little over one-quarter of the households in Laxmipura and one-third of the households in the grouped villages have more than three acres of land although not at the same place. Clearly the intensity of agriculture and related activities are greater in these villages.

TABLE 3.3

Distribution of Households according to Size of Landholding by Villages

Land Holding (in Acres)	Ramagere		Laxmipura		Gowdahalli Shivadurga		All Villages	
	%	N	%	N	%	N	%	N
Landless or <0 5 acres	32.7	119	21.6	30	9.9	9	26.6	158
0.5–3.5 acres	49.2	179	51.8	72	50.5	46	50.0	297
Above 3.5 acres	18.1	66	26.6	37	39.6	36	23.4	139
All	100.0	364	100.0	139	100.0	91	100.0	594

Table 3.4 presents the proportion of households from different castes who belong to the different landholding categories. The Muslims and the High castes are least agriculturally oriented. The households belonging to other caste categories depend entirely on either their own family agriculture or on agricultural labour for a living. The only exception is the case of a small number of Service caste landless families who are engaged in their traditional occupations. A substantial proportion of peasant caste households own larger landholdings thus justifying their caste status.

Continuing the discussion on land, it is worth while to discuss a few related issues which reflect the pattern of agriculture in the area. It has been worked out from the reports of the families in the area that the villagers own a total of 1643

TABLE 3.4

Distribution of Households according to Size of Landholding by Caste Groups

Landholding (in acres)	Caste Group/Religion													
	Intermediate													
	High		Peasant		Service Castes		Low Castes		All Castes		Muslim Castes		All Hindus	
	N	%	N	%	N	%	N	%	N	N	N	%	N	%
Landless, <0.5	48.4	31	15.3	44	34.6	27	27.4	37	24.6	139	65.5	19	26.6	158
0.5—3.5	34.4	22	48.6	140	52.6	41	63.0	85	51.0	288	31.1	9	50.0	297
Above 3.5	17.2	11	36.1	104	12.8	10	9.6	13	24.4	138	3.4	1	23.4	139
All	100.0	64	100.0	288	100.0	78	100.0	135	100.0	565	100.0	29	100 0	594

acres of land, of which 77 per cent is dry, 16 per cent was and another 7 per cent is waste land. The total avreage is close to the amount of land given by the Census of India which is 1913 acres. The difference is due to the fact that our calculations refer to the land owned by the people from among these villages whereas the Census provides figures on the total land area of the villages.

The area is predominantly under dry cultivation, and only 16 per cent of the land was reported as having some irrigation facilities. Mishra *op. cit.* also provides almost the same proportion (17 per cent of the total land owned) which has access to irrigation in his villages. However, the wet land in the research area helps to grow only one crop a year because of the poor water supply from the tank. It is evident from Table 3.5 that Laxmipura has a little edge over Ramagere in wet land and the last two villages have it in negligible quantities. Since the failure of rains during the past three years and the meagre inflow of water into the pond adjacent to Ramagere there was no wet cultivation at all the during 1980-81. Only a few rich land owners, who have sunk wells and use electric driven motors to lift water, irrigated part of their land to grow commercial crops like grapes and vegetables. The people of Laxmipura, however, managed to cultivate one crop of either rice or sugarcane, though many had to cut sugarcane about 55 days earlier than the normal harvesting time. Thus the cultivation in the area depends on rain and it can be considered as the dry part of the state.

TABLE 3.5

Type of Land by Village

Type of Land	Ramagere		Laxmipura		G. Hali S. Durga		All Villages	
	Acres	%	Acres	%	Acres	%	Acres	%
Dry Land	589	77	348	70	323	87	1260	77
Wet Land	157	20	109	22	3	1	269	16
Waste Land	23	3	44	8	47	12	114	7
Total Land	769	100	501	100	373	100	1643	100

Another striking issue investigated in the area is the average yield per area (see Table 3.6). The average yield unit acre in the area increases as the size of landholdings increases. This is the opposite of what many others have found in the wet cultivated areas, where the yield per acre increases while the size of landholdings falls. The explanation for such a phenomenon is that, as the size of landholding falls, people undertake intensive cultivation with extra inputs of labour, and capital. But the fact is that the additional inputs of labour without accompanying inputs of capital will not increase the yields. It is, however, evident from the data that the per acre yield value increases phenomenally for the land size 7-10 acres and above. This is mainly due to the easy access and availability of agricultural loans to the farmers who own larger land areas. This credit provides for the increasing use of fertilizers, improved seeds and use of machinery. Generally, it is the large land owner who gets such loan from the government subsidized co-operatives and other institutions, because they are more likely to return the loan within a reasonable time. The larger farmer is also more likely to have an irrigation well sunk in his land area, and to use modern means and technology for cultivation. A large agriculturist who owns in total over fifty acres of land, grows on average Rupees 6,000 worth of yield annually per unit acre, mainly by undertaking cultivation using hired labour, water from three irrigation wells, improved seeds, adequate fertilizer, better technology and the guaranteed market for his produce.

TABLE 3.6

Average Value of Yield and Value of Yield Per Acre by Size of Landholding

Size of Land Holding	Number of owners	Average yield value in Rupees	Yield per acre value in Rupees
<1 acre	—	—	252
1—3 acres	279	638	301
4—6 acres	89	1765	345
7—10 acres	30	4362	514
11—50 acres	19	18289	1019
> 50 acres	1	482000	4300

(ii) *Income*

Table 3.7 presents differentials in income. Value of income for an agricultural family is the converted value in rupees of the total produce of a household less the wages paid to the hired labour, value of fertilizer used that year and expenditure if any on electricity and water charges. Wherever applicable incomes from secondary occupations and home industries are added to arrive at the annual income of a household. The average income per household for the area works out to be Rupees 5,357. The households in Ramagere fall very close to this average while those in Laxmipura enjoy a 20per cent higher and those in the last two villages a 27 per cent lower income than the average income. The per capita income for these villages works out to be Rupees 984, 1,227 and 262 respectively which average to Rupees 1,008 per person in the area. However, these figures on average household income and per capita income provide a misleading picture due to wide disparities between various groups. Thus an examination of the percentage of households falling into different income levels help in understanding reality. Almost 19 per cent of all households have annual income of less than Rupees 1500. Another 56 per cent belong to the Rupees 1,501 to 5,000 category and the rest or 26 per cent, have an annual income above Rupees 5,001. Ramagere records the highest percentage of the households (22.3%) falling in the first category followed by Laxmipura (18.7%) and the last two villages (11%). On the other hand, 33 per cent of the households reported annual incomes above Rupees 5000 in Laxmipura compared to 23 and 22 per cent respectively in Ramagere and the grouped villages. This suggests the relatively wide disparity of incomes and economic wellbeing in Laxmipura which incidentally has the highest per capita income of Rs. 1,227.[25] Sixty-five per cent of the households in the last two villages fall into the middle category, thereby suggesting relatively more economic equality at a relatively low level of income. It is evident from the percentages on main source of of income that Laxmipura and two grouped villages depend entirely (over 90%) on aggriculture-based occupations for their livelihood. It is because of the diversified occupational opportunities that the households in Ramagere have achieved a fair economic standard. Close to 30 per cent of the households engage in non-agricultural occupations in Ramagere.

Much of the income differentials between villages, and within villages, can be explained by the land owning pattern and the quantity of produce which depends on the quality of land, pattern of cultivation and use of fertilizer. Although the average landholding among the landed households in the grouped villages, the average annual yield value per household is the least at Rupees 1,172. It is in Laxmipura that average yield value is the highest which is twice as much as in Ramagere. Even the per capita value of yield for the persons living in the landed households is twice as much in Laxmipura than in Ramagere and little less than thrice when compared with the grouped villages. To summarize, relatively more economic, as a consequence social, homogeneity is found among the populations of the grouped villages. Whereas Laxmipura presents a wide economic disparity between the Vokkaligas and the Scheduled Castes (the only prominent castes), Ramagere in spite of the wide social diversifications, economically

TABLE 3.7

Average Annual Income Per Household, Per Capita Income and Proportion of Households in Different Income groups by Village*

Income (in Rupees)	Ramagere		Laxmipura		G. Halli S. Durga		All Villages	
Average Income	5304		6442		3910		5357	
Per capita	984		1227		762		1008	
Number of Households with	N	%	N	%	N	%	N	%
< Rs. 1500	74	20.3	26	18.7	10	11.0	110	18.5
Rs. 1501—5000	205	56.3	67	48.2	61	67.0	333	56.1
>Rs. 5000	85	23.4	46	33.1	20	22.0	151	25.4
All	364	100.0	139	100.0	91	100.0	594	100.0

*These figures are arrived at by accounting for incomes occurring from all sources based on information collected by a retrospective enquiry of earnings during the agriculture year 1980.

projects relatively more homogeneity than other villages, which is mainly due to the occupational diversities leading to fairly equal annual incomes.

With regard to the differentials in income according to caste there are some useful findings (see Table 3.8). The average annual family income varies widely between castes. The lowest annual income is among the Low castes at Rs. 2,583 followed by the Service Castes (Rs. 2,927), Muslims (Rs. 6,051) Peasants (Rs. 6,502) and the High Castes (Rs. 8,711) in ascending order. The per capita incomes as well takes a similar order beginning from Rs. 537, followed by Rs. 875, Rs 1,129 and Rs. 2,050 respectively.

The proportion of households having an income less than Rs. 1,500 is 19 per cent in total which is highest for the Low Castes at 30 per cent followed by the service (24%). Both Peasants and High Castes have 14 per cent of their households, each falling in this income category. Among Muslims, however, the percentage of households falling in this category is only 4 per cent. Muslims, Low Castes and Service Castes record greater than 60 per cent of their households falling into the income category of Rupees 1,501 and Rupees 5,000 thus representing relatively greater economic homogeneity among the respective cultural groups but at a relatively low level when compared to other castes in the area. Whereas the 14 per cent having less than rupees 1,500 and 32 per cent having more than rupees 5,000 annual income from the Peasant households, and 14 per cent with less than rupees 1,500 and 41 per cent with more than rupees 5,000 annual income from the High Castes families present a wide disparity of income within the castes. Thus, the disparity of incomes within the Peasant and High Castes households is wide when compared to the relatively low level among the Muslims, while the Service Castes and the Low Castes are relatively more homogeneous at low levels of income. On the other hand the disparity of income between castes is also high, placing the Low Castes and Service Castes at the lower end of the list, the Muslims and Peasants in the intermediate level and the High Castes at the top of the list.

The high economic standards has been possible by the

TABLE 3.8

Average Annual Income Per Household, Per Capita Income and Proportion of Households in different Income brackets by Caste Groups*

Income (in Rupees)	High Castes		Intermediate Peasant Castes		Service Castes		Low Castes		Muslims		All Castes	
Average Income	8711		6502		2927		2583		6031		5357	
Per Capita Income	2050		1129		604		537		875		1008	
Households with	N	%	N	%	N	%	N	%	N	%	N	%
income :												
< Rs. 1500	9	14.1	41	14.2	19	24.4	40	29.6	1	3.5	110	18.5
Rs. 1501—5000	29	45.3	154	53.5	51	65.4	81	60.0	18	62.0	333	56.1
Above Rs. 5000	26	40.6	93	32.3	8	10.2	14	10.4	10	34.5	151	25.4
All	64	100.0	288	100.0	78	100.0	135	100.0	29	100.0	594	100.0

*See note in Table 3.7

High Castes due to their involvement in diversified occupations available both within and outside the village area. Thirty-one and twenty-seven per cent of the households draw income mainly from business activities and salaries respectively, and another 23 per cent from agriculture, whereas 62 per cent of Peasant Castes depend entirely on agriculture and another 15 per cent on Wage Labour. Only 10 per cent of the households draw income from salaries and another small proportion from trade or business. For the Service Castes the proportion of households engaged in agriculture is 32 per cent followed by another 32 per cent as labourers and only 22 per cent of the households earn their livelihood from the continuation of their traditional skills and occupations. The Low Castes are mainly the labourers who constitute almost 65 per cent of all Low Caste households and only 27 per cent depend on own farming as the chief source of income. On the contrary, 52 per cent of Muslims depend on small business while only 30 per cent of households are engaged in agriculture, service and labour-oriented occupations with almost equal proportions in each category. Thus, though agriculture accounts for close to 60 per cent of all income in the area, it only places families in the intermediary economic status as judged from the local economic conditions. While trade has helped the High Caste households to maximize their incomes which has also helped Muslims to maintain their intermediate economic levels without substantial support from agricultural sources.[26] Salary is another source which has helped the High Castes to increase the income levels to the top of the list in this area. Labour and near subsistence agriculture among Low Castes and the traditional occupations among the Service Castes have not helped to improve the economic standards of the population of these communities, while they lack alternative source of income due to lack of education, skills and expertise.

(*iii*) *Education*

From among the households with at least one child of primary school age (5.14 years) 74 per cent are found to have sent their children to primary school. This percentage varies greatly among the villages. It is 81 per cent in Ramagere, 73 per cent in Laxmipura and only 49 per cent in the last two villages. Similar percentages for the households with children of secondary school age (14-16 years) are 42, 29 and 22 respectively. But, the percentages on tertiary education give a different trend, only 25 per cent of the households who had children of tertiary school age (above 16 years) in the last two villages having ever obtained tertiary education, followed by 18 per cent in Laxmipura. In Ramagere this percentage is only 6 per cent. This variation is due to a small number of households who have children of tertiary education age, in different villages. Another feature is that the continuation of education for higher standards depend on two factors. Immediate opportunity to study and the inclination for continuation of education. In Ramagere the youth, especially the males have comparatively more job options outside agriculture. There is also a greater opportunity for them to move out of the village on various jobs. In Laxmipura, however, the people's attachment to land and agriculture restricts the youth from entering non-agricultural activities like business or trade. They, however, are more inclined towards better education and white collar jobs. Because of the caste homogeneity the competition among Vokkaligas to produce at least one educated son is great. An example was set about twenty-five years ago when one of the families produced a veterinary graduate who now works in the Bangalore Turf Club as the resident veterinarian and earns a relatively high salary. The effect is that during the research period two of the Vokkaliga youths were studying in the Agricultural University in Bangalore. Due to the strong family ties present in this community and also due to the commitment and relatively greater incentive for the youth to come back to the village, these students have been normally reported as family members currently staying in the household, while they have been staying at Bangalore for quite some time. They, however, visit their families at least once in a fortnight. In Ramagere, on the other hand, only the youths pursuing higher education in Doddaballapur were considered a part of the present family and current residents. A few others who were studying and living in towns were not included as family members currently residing in the family unlike the case in Laxmipura. This is because the perception of the parents that these children will not return or that parents do not expect educated children to return to the village after completion of their education. Rather, they expect that they will get an urban job and send monetary contributions to parents. This is understandable for there is no incentive for such youths to come back to the village unlike the case in Laxmipura. Thus the percentages worked out for the category 'above secondary' do not present an accurate picture of the situation when comparing villages.

The educational achievement of the middle-aged and those above forty-five years of age present some encouraging patterns. Twenty-nine per cent of all persons aged 45 and above reported having done some schooling while this percentage is close to 50 per cent for the middle-aged persons in the area suggesting roughly a 60 per cent increase in the literacy level over a period of two decades. The population of Ramagere, however, is more widely educated than other villages. The percentage of the families where at least one middle-aged person had some formal education was 59 in Ramagere, 40 in Laxmipura and only 26 in the grouped villages. The percentage of the families having persons aged forty-five and above with at least some schooling was found to be only 36, 26 and 6 respectively. Thus, there has been a 400 per cent increase in the literacy levels among families with adults of middle-age in the last two villages during the last two decades, whereas this increase was only 154 per cent in Laxmipura and 163 per cent in Ramagere. The improvement in the literacy rate in the grouped villages is due to the opening of the primary school in those villages in 1960s. However, people report themselves to be educated if they have attended some years of schooling and even currently have forgotten how to read and write. Thus the figures on the educational patterns discussed above have to take into account this aspect of reporting before establishing any kind of inferences.

The proportion of households having children of primary school age who sent them to school is highest for the High Castes (93%) followed by Muslims (91%), Peasants (81%), Service Castes (75%) and the Low Castes (41%). The

TABLE 3.9

Pattern of Education in the Households by Village

Educational Category	Ramagere		Laxmipura		G. halli S. Durga		All Villages	
	N	%	N	%	N	%	N	%
Households having children of Primary school age : 6-14 years								
* but no Schooling	46	19.5	24	27.0	23	50.8	103	26.4
* Primary Schooling	190	80.5	65	73.0	32	49.2	287	73.6
All	236		89		55		390	
Households having children of Secondary school age : 15-18 years								
* but no Schooling	73	57.9	35	71.4	21	77.8	129	63.9
* Secondary Schooling	53	42.1	14	28.6	6	22.2	73	36.1
All	126		49		27		202	
Households having children of Tertiary school age : 19-24 years								
* but no Schooling	46	93.9	18	81.8	6	75.0	70	88.6
* Tertiary Schooling	3	6.1	4	18.2	2	25.0	9	11.4
All	49		22		8		79	

Households with Middle aged persons who have : 25-44 years								
* no Schooling	123	40.6	68	60.2	60	76.9	251	50.8
* some Schooling	180	59.4	45	39.8	18	23.1	243	49.2
All	303		113		78		494	
Households with persons of above 45 years of age and :								
* no Schooling	131	64.5	62	73.8	49	94.2	242	71.2
* some Schooling	72	35.5	22	26.2	3	5.8	97	28.6
All	203		84		52		339	

TABLE 3.10

Pattern of Household Education by Caste Groups

	High Castes		Intermediate Peasant Castes		Intermediate Service Castes		Low Castes		Muslims		All	
	N	%	N	%	N	%	N	%	N	%	N	%
Households with children of primary school age and : 6-14 years												
* no schooling	2	6.7	38	18.6	13	25.0	48	59.3	2	8.7	103	26.4
* primary schooling	28	93.3	166	81.4	39	75.0	33	40.7	21	91.3	287	73.6
All	30		204		52		81		23		390	
Households with children of secondary school age and : 15-18 years												
* no schooling	4	17.4	73	64.6	18	75.0	23	82.1	11	78.6	129	63.9
* secondary schooling	19	82.6	40	35.4	6	25.0	5	17.9	3	21.4	73	36.1
All	23		113		24		28		14		202	
Households with children of tertiary school age and : 14-24 years												

* no schooling	12	92.3	40	87.0	7	77.8	9	100.0	2	100.0	70	88.6
* tertiary schooling	1	7.7	6	13.0	2	22.2	0	0.0	0	0.0	9	11.4
All	13		46		9		9		2		79	
Households with middle aged persons and : 25-44 years												
* no schooling	4	8.3	104	42.8	38	60.3	98	83.1	7	31.8	251	50.8
* some schooling	44	91.7	139	57.2	25	39.7	20	16.9	15	68.2	243	49.2
All	48		243		63		118		22		494	
Households with persons Above 45 years of age and												
* no schooling	9	23.7	124	69.7	26	74.3	69	98.4	14	77.4	242	71.4
* some schooling	29	76.3	54	30.3	9	25.7	1	1.6	4	22.6	97	28.6
All	38		178		35		70		18		339	

contrasting situation is that the similar percentage for the Secondary School category are 83, 35, 25, 18 and 21 per cent respectively. This suggests that the proportion of children continuing education beyond the primary levels is highest among the High Castes and for all other castes it is generally low. Similar percentages for the educational standards above secondary level give an entirely different picture as in the case of differentials by village discussed in earlier paragraphs : 7.7 per cent of the High Castes, 32 per cent of the Service Castes and 13 per cent of the Peasant Castes households, who had children of the secondary school age, sent their children to school. The figure concerning the High Castes needs a similar qualification as was the case for village differentials. Those who enter tertiary education proceed to an urban place like Bangalore city for better education. Such students are not included as family members by their original families among the High Castes. This decreased the number of the households in the category. On the other hand, the relatively high proportion of Service Castes pursuing this education may be largely due to the problem of small size of this group.

The educational attainment of the middle-aged and the ones above 45 years of age is interesting to study. Almost 92 per cent of the households having middle-aged persons and 76 per cent having persons of age above 45 years reported at least some schooling among the High Castes. Eventually, the proportion of High caste families with some schooling is even today far higher than all other caste groups including Muslims. The tendency to study has, however, increased substantially among the Scheduled Castes followed by Muslims, Peasants and the Service Castes in that order. Yet the level of educational attainment and the proportion educated are far less than those belonging to the High Castes of the area.

(*iv*) *Response to Landlessness in the area*

According to Table 3.4 over three-fifths of Muslim households and one half of the high-caste Hindus are landless. Traditionally, Muslims are the trading community and many of them continue to be small business people. They visit various villages to collect produces such as surplus grains, oil seeds, pulses and tamarind from the rural families. These goods are usually sold to the local trader. The local traders (thirteen Settys, two Lingayats and one Muslim) control the business activities of the small businessmen by advancing money and buying goods at pre-determined prices. The landed Muslim households in Ramagere do not possess the type of agricultural skills which are found among the Peasant-castes of the area. Muslims of Ramagere thus have a non-agricultural outlook but retain a strong desire to own sufficient land for family agriculture. The High-caste Hindu households who are landless belong to the richer class of the community. They are the bureaucrates in the villages, generally belonging to Brahmin or Lingayat castes, and they are the large traders.

However, landlessness among the communities discussed above has nothing to do with abject poverty which is to a large extent true of other three caste groups. A substantial percentage ; 15 per cent of Peasant Caste families, 35 per cent of Service Castes and 27 per cent of low-castes are landless in the area. Landlessness among the peasants is largely due to the subdivison and sale of landholdings. Certain families own such a small land area that it cannot be subdivided any more. The male descendants from such households remain landless after either selling or leasing out their share of land to one of the others for some monetary return or for a meager share in the produce each year.

Balagigas, Vokkaligas, Kurubas and Gollas are large in numbers in that order within the Peasant Caste group. Vokkaligas are predominant in Laxmipura which is an agricultural village in its true sense. All Vokkaliga families own land which at least can provide a subsistence living. The quality of land, land per capita, the proportion of wet land and the average yield per capita are all relatively high in Laxmipura. The incidence of landlessness among them is negligible. The Balagigas who dominate in Ramagere are all peasants. A few landless, however, continue their traditional occupation of selling bangles in the surrounding villages. They also supplement their income by knitting and selling *leaf-plates* and working as wage labourers. Leaf-plate making is undertaken only by women and female childern of Ramagere as an household industry. The panchayat chairman, who is a landlord, and other landed Balagigas employ a large number of labourers for cultivation. It was reported that during the 1940s through to the 1960s there was some sort of shame attached to work as a labourer for the same caste person. Apart from the exchange of labour, hiring of labour service among the Vokkaligas and Balagigas within the same caste was virtually non-existent. Due to the economic pressures and growing surplus of labour in the area, the labourers have now developed a new tradition of seeking wage employment from the landlords of the same caste as a matter of right. Although, there is only a negligible proportion of permanent labour contracts between the persons of the same caste, the landed households now prefer people from their own caste and kinship to work as labourers during the normal agricultural seasons, and as a result, the landless Balagigas have easy access to paid work and also receive supple mentary incomes from bangle selling. Thus, the impact of landlessness is not felt to a maximum by this community as well. Kurubas and Gollas rank last in the list of peasant castes. They are culturally as well as economically lower than the two castes discussed above. They predominate in Shivadurga and Gowdahalli respectively and have large landholdings. As discussed elsewhere, the quality of land on which they depend is poor, and consequently income is substantially lower when compared to other catses discussed above. Since, there is no demand for agricultural labour in these villages, most of the landless Kurubas and Gollas have settled in Ramagere. Many of these landless work as non-agricultural manual labour like house construction, brick laying, well digging, road repair and digging trenches in the nearby forest. Two other activities are worth mentioning with regard to these castes. Gollas who live in Shivadurga collect wood from the nearby forest and sell it in the town thirteen kilometres away. Even an eight year old child who is not in school earns around three rupees in two days. Secondly, certain families from these two castes who own livestock often sell a sheep or two in the weekly market and a few specialize as the middlemen in the sheep selling business. Nevertheless, the impact of landlessness is relatively high among these castes in spite of the existence of alternative sources of income because these sources are highly seasonal and sometimes illegal.[27]

Castes grouped under the category Service-castes were traditionally occupied in caste specific crafts (see Table 3.1). Those crafts or occupations which require considerable skill and training are usually restricted to members of the specific caste, and hence others would have little opportunity to learn the required skills. Such occupations involve ritual or ideological components as well and are drawn from the caste-specific culture. Ganigas, Madivalas, Nayandas, and Acharis are the Service Castes found in considerable numbers in this area. The women of these castes to some extent even today perform co-operative functions along with the males in their traditional services to other castes. There is one Kumbara (Potter) family as well in Ramagere. Traditionally all these but for Ganigas were involved in the *Jajmani* system in which services and goods are rendered at a fixed or customarily fixed price and wages which were paid in kind. The Jajmani system, however, is not merely a means of distributing goods and services in exchange for grain but has a ritual component as well. The amount of transactions and the number of families involved in the jajmani systems have declined in this area due to the onslaught of wider technological change and the increase in monetary transactions in the villages. As a result many families belonging to Service Castes are facing difficulties in continuing their traditional crafts. A few who had managed to keep land have shifted to full-time agriculture, and a few have established the modified version of old crafts like a barber shop or a washing and ironing shop. What remains of the old jajmani system is the ritualistic service to be provided by certain Service Castes during the life cycle rites of other Hindu castes. For this purpose one or two families from among each service caste work around the year and rotate this privilege among others of the same caste over the years. The persons belonging to the Service Castes are in a way highly specialized in their respective skills, and, therefore, they do not manage to enter into other kinds of skills including agriculture easily. This has, eventually reduced the economic well-being of the persons and generally they have turned towards manual labour.

The oil pressers in Ramagere, however, are the worst hit by this kind of change. They were never a party to the Jajmani relationships in its strict sense and they have no ritualistic component attached to their craft. Now the villagers prefer to buy their requirements of oils from a wide range of brands available in the local stores. The consumption of vanaspati (a brand of vegetable oil) and coconut oil has increased among certain communities. This has caused a great decrease in the demand for the services of the Ganigas. Only one of the five oil pressing yards was operating on a few occasions in Ramagere during our stay in these villages. Now oil is extracted only from Pongamia and castor oil seeds which are traditionally used as a supplement to kerosene to burn the little lamps in the homes. The Ganigas, however, claimed medical value in the use of the pongamia oil but this has not helped to increase the demand for this oil.

The Low Castes category includes Bovis and the Scheduled Castes. Traditionally many of them were considered outside the Hindu varna system. They generally were always dependent on some landlord for work and a living. Since Independence they have been protected by law against oppression and exploitation. However, as always the majority continue to be landless. In the last few years government programmes have allocated some land to these families. But, due to a shortage of cultivable and good quality land, more often they have been allotted land which cannot be profitably cultivated. This land is either dry and of poor quality or requires large investment to make it cultivable through initial cleaning and levelling which is beyond the reach of these people.[28] These lands are usually located at a distance from the village which has discouraged cultivation because of inconvenience in travelling and the wastes of time. It works out that the wage earnings have a better returns than cultivating these lands. There are instances where others buy these lands from the Scheduled Caste owners at a cheaper price and invest in sinking wells and raising cashew crops which are highly rewarding. Thus, in spite of having some land, these families are forced to resort to daily wage earnings. However, the labour from this community is clearly the marginal labour of the villages which is employed only in times of high demand for labour. Secondly, as this labour is cheap and easily available, many landed households persuade and invite them to retain their old master-servant relationships in exchange for what is argued to be security and total care. Thus, most of the SCs in Ramagere and Laxmipura work for only a few rich landlords. It appears that the wage labourers were never a party to agricultural contracts and tenancy agreements where they had to pay rents. Thus they could not as a matter of custom expect to obtain loans of money, food and other help in crisis.[29] On the other hand the labourers were involved in the hiring of bonded labour. In this system the labourers offer their own or their children's labour in exchange of an advance payment by the landlord. The labourers were expected to work for the landlord until the value of their labour services equalled the borrowed money and its interest. However, this system even today exists with a variation : the labourers, especially from the Scheduled and other Low Castes, sell the labour services of their sons aged seven to sixteen to a landed family for an advance payment of a sum which is agreed upon by the parties. The money and the duration of work is determined on the basis of the age of the child (labourer) and nature of the work. Such contracts can be made either for a full year or even a part of the year based on seasons. Normally such contracts are not prolonged for many years which was the case in the past in the bonded labour system. Although this system of selling labour is not efficient, for the majority of the families from among these castes this is a easy way to secure support and help during crisis.

The Bovis of Shivadurga also work as agricultural labourers for the landlords in times of high demand for labour, and, during the normal days, they work on stone quarrying on a rock which in fact is owned by the landlord. Bovis, who are by tradition stone cutters, have long since been under the threat of the increasing use of bricks and tiles in the area. Now practically every house constructed uses burnt brick and tiles and for huts they use coconut thatch. Thus, due to the decline in the demand for stone slabs, they are jobless for most of the year. They, however, know that it will cause displeasure to the landlord if they decide to move long distances in search for jobs and do not return in time when they are required to work on the landlord's estate.

The consequence of landlessness and the low demand for labour from the Scheduled Castes, Bovis and some Service Castes is a drastic fall from their already low economic standards. The agricultural wage rates in the area are extremely low when compared to the non-agricultural and the urban wage rates. The agricultural wages are also affected by the seasonality of agriculture. The average wage for a normal agricultural activity is barely seven rupees for an adult male, five rupees for an adult female and three rupees for a grown up child. In the recent years there has also emerged a system where one can work for the part of the day as a labourer. For example, the wage rate is two rupees and one-and-a-half rupees respectively for a male and a female if they work between 8 A.M. and 10 A.M. between 10 A.M. and 1 P.M., or between 3 P.M. and 5 P.M. This system especially helps women and children who can perfrom household duties and child care besides working as labourers. The agricultural wage rates appear to have remained unchanged for over four to five years while the cost of many local as well as imported goods for a village life have gone up manifold. This has forced practically all adults and many grown up children among the landless families to wage labourers.

NOTES AND REFERENCES

1. The names of the villages used in this thesis are pseudonyms.
2. Pond is an artificial reservoir formed by a dam or earth or earth and stones built across a small river or brook.
3. According to one of the reports of a local person there were about eighty families living in 1935.
4. Dominant castes are those within local areas that control much of the land, have fairly large numbers, and are sometimes relatively high in the local caste hierarchy. For more on the definition and categorization of castes as dominant refer to Srinivas (1959) and Cohn (1971).
5. These villages are grouped together while presenting the results as they are small and are also close in sociceconomic levels. They are,

however, discussed separately whenever necessary to bring out the differences which are purely local in nature.

6. This village classification is based on the criteria developed by Beals (1961). He classifies villages into three categories. (i) villages with a small population of a single caste (ii) small multi-caste villages with a single head caste and (iii) multi-caste villages with dominant caste residents.

7. Pallegar was the local word referring to a physically strong local leader. Often such persons were the rulers of a small community. Political power in those days was closely associated with the physical strength of the person in power and with numerical support.

8. Vokkaligas constitute about twenty per cent of Karnataka's population and almost all of them live in the southern part of the state.

9. Data on rainfall presented here was gathered from the records maintained by a part-time official in charge of noting the rain gauge reading at the village. He is appointed by the Department of Mines and Geology, Government of Karnataka.

10. *Kannada* is one of the four South Indian state languages which has a Dravidian origin. This is the state language in Karnataka and about 66 per cent of the state population speak this language. *Urdu* is an India language but with admixture of Persian, Arabic, Sanskrit and English. It is a language mainly spoken by the Muslims and about nine per cent of the state's population speak urdu.

11. The Scheduled Castes and Scheduled Tribes are those classified castes which are listed after Independence under the constitutional directive to extend special support and privilege to their members. This is an effort of the government to increase their social and economic standards. They were earlier known as Harijans or Adi-Dravida and Adi-Karantaka. Some of the castes included into these groups were traditionally Sudras, one of the Hindu Varnas.

12. Power in the local context refers to the influence and particular community or group exerts so as to be capable of making or altering a major community decision such as the placement of a street light or a water tap. Such power, however, leads to political power by controlling village level political positions through claiming a larger proportion of votes. The village rivalry is often found in a village where there are two castes or community groups of almost same population size and economic status. Such rivalry may also exist in a single caste village with equally strong sub-groups.

13. Traditionally the Hindu population was divided into four *varnas* based on occupations and social division of labour. They are the *Brahmin*, the *Kshatriyas*, the *Vaishyas* and the *Sudras* in that order of hierarchy. Brahmins were priests and learned men, Kshatriyas were warriors, Vaishyas were businessmen and Sudras were to do menial jobs and work as labourers and servants.

14. The shandy is the weekly market where people from among the surrounding villages gather on a specific day to sell and buy requirements for day-to-day use including food-grains, grocery, vegetables and meat.
15. Hyder Ali and Tippu Sultan were father and son respectively, who ruled the southern parts of Mysore state during the second half of the eighteenth century. Both were prolific warriors and Tippu Sultan died in a war while fighting with the British in 1799.
16. The *Jajmani* system (local Kannada word *adade*, in India is a system under which the labour services and other crafts and services are rewarded in kind at some fixed time such as during harvesting involving no proper measure of labour or service inputs.
17. A hotel is a restaurant, often a part within the residential dwelling meant for common access, in which tea, coffee and local snacks are served for a price.
18. Devanga is a caste who are traditionally weavers.
19. Wetgrinder in a modern appliance which is used to grind wet rice and wet pulses to get a thick liquid out of it which is used to make *idli* (a local dish for the breakfast), and, *pakoda* and *bajjee* which are the common snacks.
20. *Pipal* is a kind of fig tree which has a religious significance among the local population. There are five such trees in Ramagere, two in Laxmipura and one each in the remaining two villages.
21. *Tamarind and Pongamia* are varieties of commonly found nuts, there seeds are used in making colours and dyes.
22. The only exception is a public well in 'madigara keri'. There is no tap connection yet to this colony.
23. Bonded labour traditionally was a relationship which was akin to the master and servant relationship. Labourers used to work permanently for one landlord in an effort to repay the borrowed sum and its interest. The pre-fixed annual wages were so low that it used to take generations to repay the loan which was transferred on to sons. This system has slightly changed yet works in similar lines. Now often a father borrows a certain sum from the landlord and sends his son to work in the landlords home for a specific period which is agreed upon by both the parties. Before the completion of this contract the father may borrow again and may ask his son to continue to work for additional period of time. Such contracts can go on till the marriage of the son after which time he may decide to beeome a labourer hiring out labour on daily basis.
24. Immovable property is a recognized and preferred collateral by the local money lenders for advancing loans.
25. Thimmaiah (1983) in a recent work on Inequality and Poverty in Karnataka has discussed in detail drawing upon his empirical findings

the issues relating to absolute poverty and inequality. However, the pattern of poverty and inequality discussed in this thesis need not necessarily follow the one described by Thimmaiah.

26. Levels of income and economic standards among the Muslims of Karnataka are relatively low, and the poverty is very high among them and the Scheduled Castes and the Scheduled Tribes. See Thimmaiah *op. cit.*, p. 43.

27. The government has a policy to stop deforestation and the penalties for deforestation are high for the offenders.

28. Some families estimated an initial investment of around two thousand rupees to clean and level an acre of land. This amount is close to one full year's income of such families which is impossible to raise either by savings or by loans.

29. There is a considerable variation across the country in the custom of obtaining loans and support during crisis by the wage labourers. For more on this see Bardhan and Rudra (1980) and Greenough (1982 : 65).

4

Demographic Description and Fertility Differentials

4.1. Population and Growth

The demographic description of the study area starts with an analysis of the growth of population since 1941 which is followed by a discussion on the fertility rates and differentials. The figures on the village population are available since the 1941 census.[1] Shivadurga and Gowdahalli population have been combined together since the census does not provide separate data for each village. Sex-wise population data for every ten years since 1941 for the villages together with the percentage annual exponential growth rate are given in Table 4.1.

The population of these villages together was 1,903 in 1941 and it rose to 3,158 in 1981 which implies a 66 per cent increase over a period of forty years. The highest increase was recorded in Ramagere (73.7 per cent) and the lowest in Laxmipura (52.4 per cent). The other two villages together have experienced a 58.3 per cent increase during the same period. This growth has occurred in the absence of a substantial migration into or from Gowdahalli, Shivadurga and Laxmipura, other than that caused by marriage.[2] A 58.3 per

TABLE 4.1

Decadal Change and Annual Exponential Growth Rate of the Population of Villages Since 1941 by Village

Year	POPULATION											
	Ramagere			Laxmipura			Shivadurga Gowdahalli			All villages		
	T	M	F	T	M	F	T	M	F	T	M	F
1941	1129 (1.43)	—	—	479 (1.31)	—	—	295 (1.03)	—	—	1903 (1.34)	—	—
1951	1302 (0.45)	644	658	546 (1.14)	283	263	327 (1.21)	165	162	2175 (0.74)	1092	1083
1961	1362 (1.79)	667	695	612 (1.37)	303	309	369 (1.20)	197	172	2343 (1.59)	1167	1177
1971	1629 (1.86)	835	794	702 (0.39)	351	351	416 (1.12)	222	194	2747 (1.39)	1408	1339
1981	1961	996	965	730	368	362	467	237	230	3158	1601	1557

Source : Different Census volumes ; Census of India publications.

Figures in parentheses are the percentage annual growth rates for the total population of respective villages.

The official population census of 1981 gives a total population of 1916 for Ramagere, 753 for Laxmipura and 493 for Shivadurga and Gowdahalli. These population totals have been worked out from the village level population reforms of the 1981 census data.

1981 population is counted by the scholar in February 1981.

T=Total Population, M=Male population, F=Female population.

cent increase in the population of the last two villages is most likely the result of natural growth.

The increase in population of the last two villages is found to be consistently spread out over each decade presenting an initial increase of 10.8 per cent between 1941 and 1951 and then stabilizing around 12.5 per cent, whereas, in Laxmipura after a consistent increase of around 13 per cent till 1971, it fell steeply to only 4 per cent between 1971 and 1981. In the absence of the possibility of increased death rates and large-scale out-migration this fall seems to be due to a decline in fertility. Ramagere is found to be different from the other three villages. The 15.3 per cent growth rate between 1941 and 1951 was followed by only a 4.6 per cent growth in the period 1951-61. However, the growth rate was 19.6 per cent and 20.4 per cent during 1961-71 and 1971-81 respectively. The percent-tage annual exponential growth rates also present a similar trend in the population growth of the area. It has been reported that Ramagere was one of the worst hit villages during late forties and early fifties by a bubonic plague epidemic which appears to be the reason for a steep fall in the rate of population increase between 1951 and 1961. Ramagere, a village of open access which is located on a plain area, is more susceptible to epidemics, while the other villages are more in the hinterland and the last two are in fact located on elevated tableland so isolated that they are less susceptible to epidemics. Besides, even today, the last three villages are much cleaner due to greater sanitation in Laxmipura and there is no scope for the water to stagnate on the slopey rocks in the other two villages. The sudden increase in the population size after 1961 in Ramagere is explained partially by the in-migrants to the village due to the newly established governmental offices and the infrastructure, and consequent flow of official or bureaucratic population. During the same period there was a substantial growth in commerce and trade in this village which attracted traders from elsewhere. The evidence for in-migration in Ramagere after 1961 is found in an unusually greater increase in the number of households between 1961 and 1971, and also between 1971 and 1981 (See Table 4.2) which cannot ordinarily be explained by an increase in the division of joint families.[3] In fact, the total number of households fell between 1951 and

TABLE 4.2

Decadal Change in the Household Size since 1951 by Village

	Ramagere			Laxmipura			G. Halli and S. Durga			All Villages		
	HH	P	P/HH	HH	P	P/HH	HH	P	P/HH	HH	P	P/HH
1951	274	1302	4.8	118	546	4.6	64	327	5.1	451	2175	4.8
1961	256	1362	5.3	120	612	5.1	71	369	5.2	447	2343	5.2
1971	327	1629	5.0	123	702	5.7	75	416	5.6	525	2747	5.2
1981	364	1961	5.4	139	730	5.3	91	467	5.1	594	3148	5.3

HH=Households. P=Persons. P/HH=Persons per Household.

1961, while they consistently increased over the years in the other three villages. Nevertheless, this discussion is based on the assumption that the likelihood of errors at the village level in counting the number of households and population are minimal.

Table 4.2 also presents the change in average household size since 1951. For Ramagere there was a recurrence of increase and decrease in average household size over the years. In 1951 the average size of household was 4.8 persons, which increased to 5.3 in 1961 and then declined to 5.0 in 1971 before rising to 5.4 per household in 1981. In 1951 Laxmipura had 4.6 persons per household which increased to 5.7 in 1971 but by 1981 had fallen to 5.3. The average household size for the other two villages together was almost constant until 1961 and then it increased sharply to 5.6 in 1971, later falling to 5.1 by 1981.

4.2. Age Structure of the Study Population

From the age structure it can be inferred that the population of the area is relatively young. Forty-three per cent of the total population is less than 15 years of age, the highest proportion being 15.4 per cent for the age group 5-9 years [Figure 4.1]. For the total population there is a successive decline in the proportion of the population in the higher age group excepting the 25-29 years category. The proportion of population above 60 years of age is 6.5 per cent. The proportion of population belonging to the ages between 15 and 60 years is 51 per cent with only a slight differential by sex representing a dependency ratio of 96 per hundred active population defined in terms of age.

The age distribution presented separately by sex shows certain peculiarities. The proportion of males less than 15 years of age is 21.7 per cent and this proportion for females is 20.8 per cent. But for different age groups the percentage of males is uniform whereas among females those aged 5—9 years constitute a relatively high proportion compared with what could be anticipated. This is also reflected in the high sex ratio favouring females in this age group. In his work on the age distribution of the Indian population, Mukherjee (1977) notes that the proportion of females in age group 5—9 years for the then State of Mysore (now Karnataka) was a little

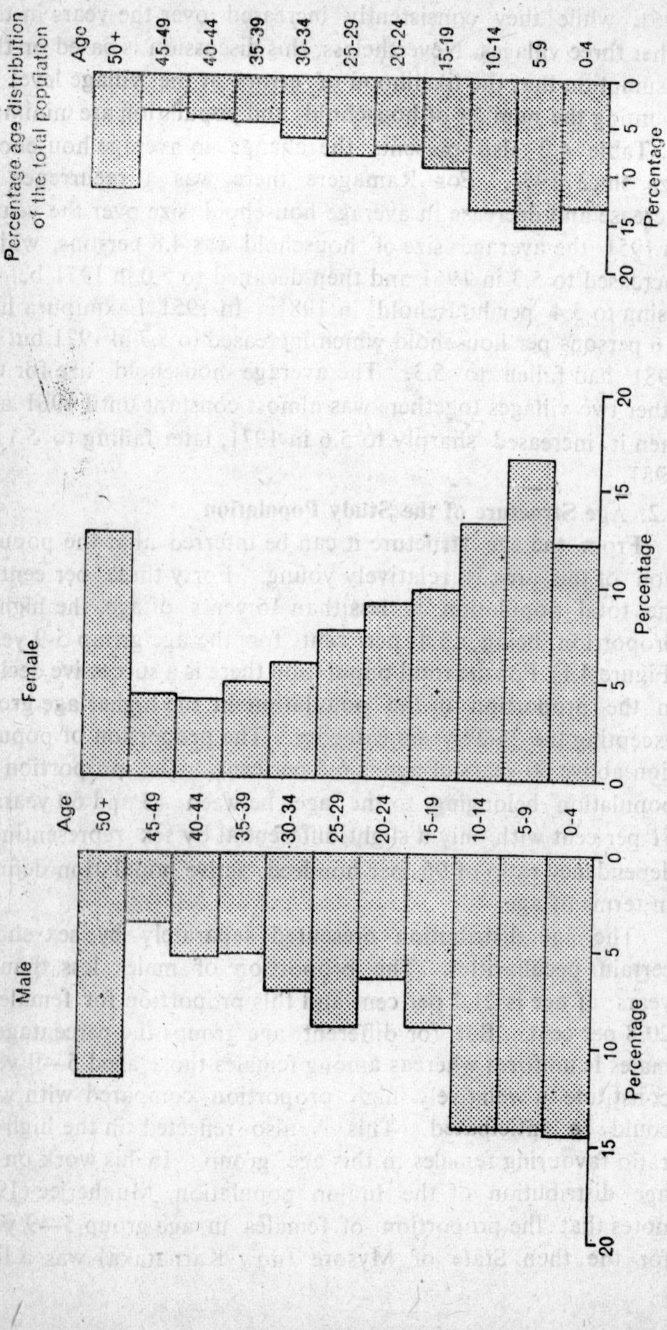

Percentage Age Distribution of Males and Females (All Villages)

FIGURE 4.1

higher in the censuses starting from 1921 to 1971 excluding 1951. This occurs because of two reasons. First, the age misreporting among females is believed to be higher than males in the area. In a society with strong son preference the event of a son's birth is distinctly remembered and many families record the date of birth of a son. On the other hand, the birth of a female child is taken as an ordinary event. It has been found that in the past when a son was born in a rural family, a public announcement was made so as to inform all the people of the village of the event, whereas in the case of the birth of a female child this was usually not done and the event often went unnoticed. In the research area grand ceremonies were arranged while naming male babies,[4] whereas no such arrangements were made for the naming of female children. These cultural practices help recall the age of sons better than that of daughters. While collecting age data, especially for the school-going population, school records containing the date of births as approximate proof of the age were used to assess correct age. Such records were more frequently available for the male children than for the female children, because boys constitute a relatively greater proportion of the school-going population.[5] On many occasions the horoscopes[6] were also provided as proof of age for male children whereas such records were provided only on a few occasions in the daughters. Secondly, the uniform proportions in the early age groups for males perhaps suggests a relatively lower incidence of deaths among males in these age groups than among females. This is to a large extent true of the village area. Though the practice of female infanticide does not exist, the incidence of female neglect and discriminative treatment can be observed. Boys are customarily better fed than girls and they are more likely to continue in school for a longer period. Sons also draw a greater attention from the elders for treatment during illness than the daughters. Practically everyone was of the opinion that sons should get more and better education than daughters. The investment in education of daughters is least rewarding to the parents because, after marriage they are expected to contribute their labour and services only to their husband's family. Nevertheless, a few persons suggested equal educational opportunities and only one was of the strong opinion that his daughter, after completing the matriculation that year, should continue to learn formal tailoring so that she could earn money to save for the dowry to be paid on her marriage. All these factors support the greater survival of male children than their sisters. The proportion of sons surviving in the area is 0.850 compared to 0.801 for daughters. The aspect of female neglect is however, evident from the figures on proportion of daughters surviving presented in Table 4.8 which are low in practically all socio-economic groups of the population. This does not, however, explain a relatively higher proportion of females in the age group 5—9 years, for which the only plausible explanation is the misreporting of age.

Beyond the age of 15 years, there is a consistent fall in the proportion of women in successive age groups as a result of attrition due to death. However, for males there is steep fall in the age group 20-24 and a steep rise in the following age group. This is mainly due to the differential migration patterns of the male population.

Among the villages there is a uniform pattern in the age distribution excepting the age group 20-24 years in Ramagere [Figure 4.2]. A fall in the number with increasing age even in the younger ages appears to be due to declining fertility. The absence of such a pattern for all villages at the younger ages imply a declining trend in fertility.[7] The age distribution of the villages suggest that Ramagere and Laxmipura have experienced a faster decline in fertility compared to the other two villages during the last decade. However, the age selectivity of the working population in Ramagere seems to be the cause for a peak in 25-29 age group.

The caste-wise age distribution present a confusing picture for ages beyond 20 years [Figure 4.3]. The reasons for this phenomenon can only be explained satisfactorily by differential mortality and migration patterns among various castes and in their different age groups which is possible only with a large data set. There, however, is a general trend of an initial rise and almost a steep fall in the proportion of population below 20 years of age excepting for the Low Castes for whom the

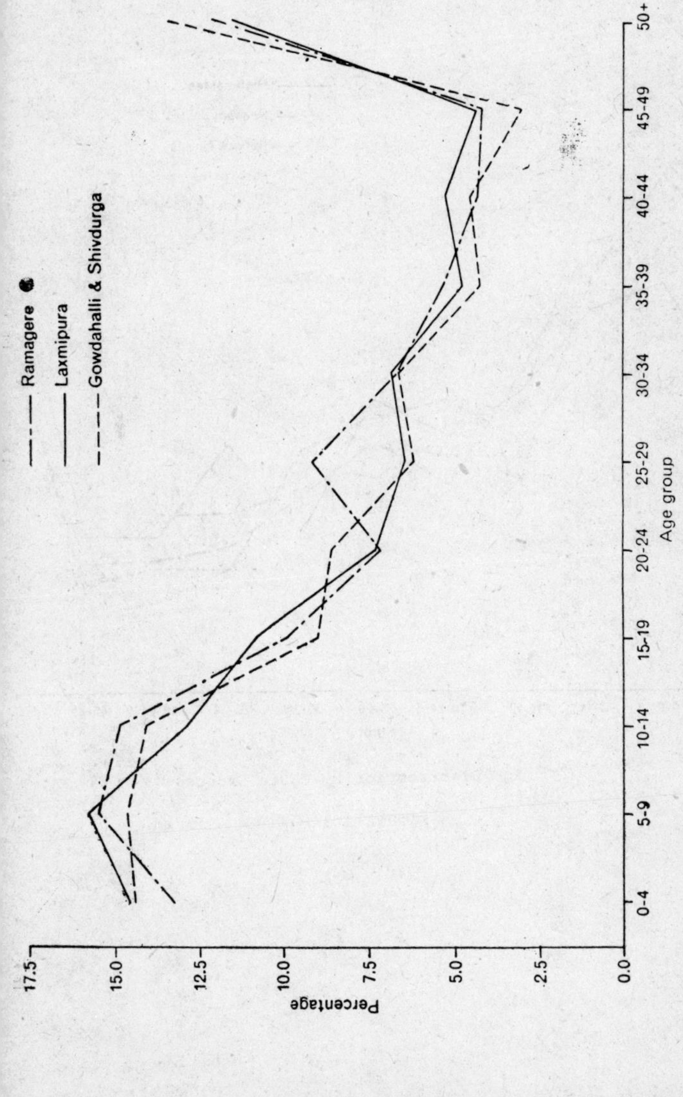

Age Distribution by Village

FIGURE 4.2

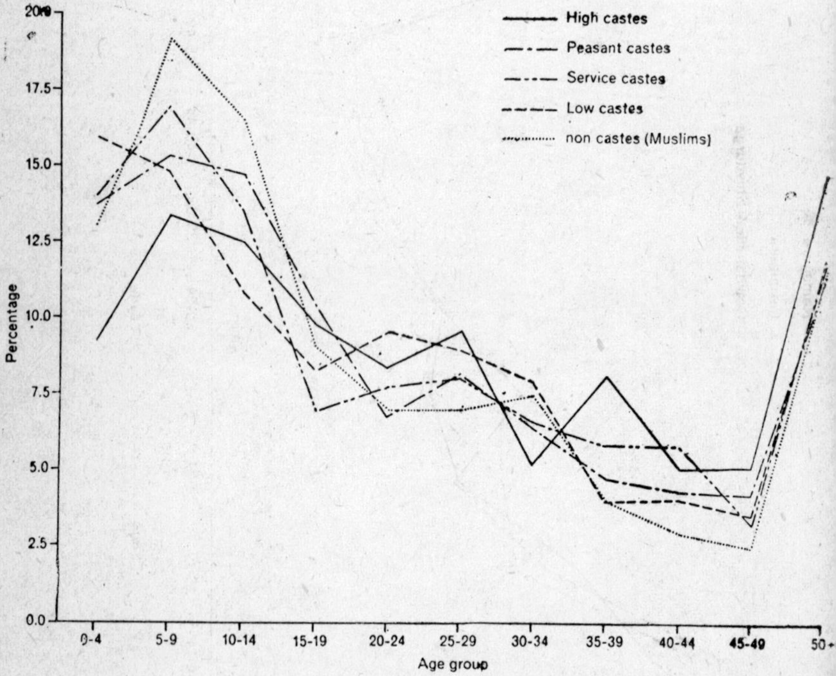

Age Distribution by Caste Groups

FIGURE 4.3

initial increase does not exist. For all the other caste groups the peak is found in the 5-9 years age group though it terminates at various levels. This indicate a trend toward falling fertility during the last decade or so. Among the Low Castes, the proportion of population in the 0-4 years age group is the highest when compared to any other caste group. This suggests differential decline in fertility among various caste groups. High Castes group appears to have acted first to restrict their fertility since about last two decades, and the rate of fertility decline also seem to be faster among them. The Low Castes have a relatively high infant and childhood mortality as compared to other castes in the area and the proportion of surviving children is the lowest for this group at 0.738. This could be a contributing factor for a distinctive age pattern for the Low Castes. But the age misreporting as well could be higher due to greater illiteracy among them.

4.3 Women and Marriage

A total of 707 women between ages 15-49 years were counted from among a total of 594 households belonging to all the four villages. Of these, 119 (16.8%) were single or unmarried, 532 (75.1%)[8] were found to be married, 17 (2.4%) were either divorced or separated and 40 (5.7%) were widowed.[9] Figure 4.4 persents the percentage distribution of all women aged 15-49 years according to marital status in five-year age groups. The percentage of single women in the age group 15-19 was 60.1 which fell steeply to 10.6 for the 20-24 group, then to 6.8 for the 25-29 age group. By the age 35-39 almost zero per cent remained never married. The proportion of widowed women increased substantially after the 25-29 age group. This emphasises the prevalence of universality of marriage in the area. Arranging the marriage of a daughter is considered largely as a matter of duty and responsibility by the parents and is a gauge of social prestige.[10]

The efforts of the parents are aimed at arranging the marriage of a daughter as soon as possible so as to avoid problems of achieving a marriage when she is older. Although there is a growing feeling among the population of Ramagere

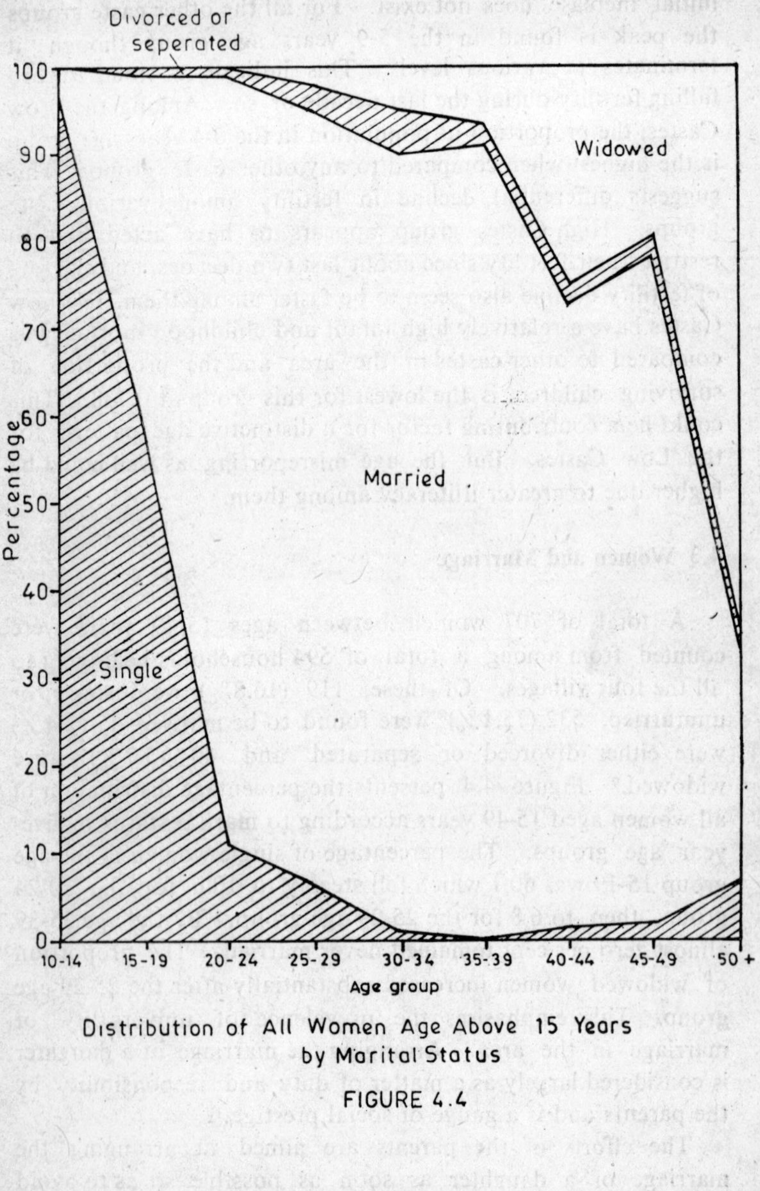

Distribution of All Women Age Above 15 Years by Marital Status

FIGURE 4.4

and Laxmipura that females need not marry until twenty years of age, they do not rule out the possibility of marriage at an earlier age if the boy has been chosen or the girl is wanted as a wife and daughter-in-law. The educated girls, who have at least attended high school, are marrying at a higher age than the uneducated ones mainly because the parents have difficulty in finding a suitable boy who should be educated as well. This problem is severe among all the communities of this area due to the practice of caste endogamy. Among Settys of the High Castes category in Ramagere the age at marriage for a few girls is substantially higher because they have a greater problem in finding a suitable boy from their own community. As this community is small in this area, finding a boy with a different *gotra*[11] and of a resonable distance in relationship is almost impossible, and, as a result, they have to find one from outside the village. Since this community in southern Karnataka is urban-oriented, convincing a boy and his parents to marry a girl from a rural background was reported to be difficult. To persuade a groom and his parents the girl's parents have to offer dowries and gifts more than the customary levels. Among a few Vokkaliga families of Laxmipura the age at marriage has risen to around 18 years. This is again because of the difficulties in finding a suitable boy of desired socio-economic and educational standards. Service Castes, Low Castes and the Muslims arrange weddings of their daughters early because it is easy to find a suitable match from the caste families who have relatively uniform social and economic standards. Among Muslims the practice of both cross and parallel cousin marriage system makes it easy to find a marriage partner. The Muslims of Ramagere are related to each other although in different degree, and a large proportion of the husbands and wives are found to be related to each other before marriage. Among the Scheduled Castes of Ramagere and Laxmipura the system of pre-puberty marriages is still prevalent. There is a considerable number of marriages performed while the bride is about eight or nine years old. Among the Scheduled Castes of Ramagere alone nineteen currently married women were married before they attained puberty. This practice was found to be prevailing among the High Castes especially the Brahmins and among the peasants during the 1940s and 1950s and 1960s respectively. Now this practice still exists among all the caste groups of the last two villages apart the Scheduled Castes of Ramagere and Laxmipura. In such cases the effective marriage or consummation takes place at a latter date after a second ceremony called *Sobana*[12] which is arranged a few days after the girl has attained menarche. Thus, in terms of age at marriage, the High Castes and some of the Peasant Castes seem to be in a transitional stage toward later female marriage for various socio-economic reasons. There were ten women aged forty years and above who remained single mainly because of physical and mental disabilities. The only exception was a Brahmin woman who worked as a high school teacher and remained unmarried as a matter of choice.

A caste-wise analysis of women aged 15-49 years who were not widowed, divorced or separated, showed that in the youngest age group of 15-19 years about 91 per cent of girls were still unmarried among the High Castes whereas this figure for the Peasantry and Service Castes was 70 per cent and 67 per cent respectively, and for the Low Castes this was at a very low level of 13 per cent. This is because of a high incidence of pre-puberty and early post-puberty marriages among the Low Castes of the area. For the Muslims this proportion was 45 per cent. The proportion single in the age group 25-29 years was highest among the High Castes at about 33 per cent and next highest among the Muslims at 16.7 per cent. For other castes this proportion was insignificant suggesting no movement of marriage to late ages. The proportion single for the women aged 30 years and above is negligible in this population including the High Castes. Thus there is a tendency only among the High Castes families to arrange the marriage of their daughters at relatively advanced ages but never beyond 30 years.

4.4 Fertility Levels

Various direct and indirect fertility measures have been calculated for the whole area as well as for the individual villages. Certain indices, which are based on one-year data collected retrospectively through the base line survey and the one-year continuous registration of the vital events, present the situation as it was found during the years 1980-81 and 1981-82 respectively. The rates derived from single year data on smaller populations may have a wide range of variation. It was found during a large-scale survey of vital statistics by the Bangalore Population Centre during 1976-78 that the birth rates for certain villages were as high as 65 per thousand population and for certain others the rates were as low as 20 per thousand population.[13] The vital rates may also vary considerably for the same village for the successive years. The following rates, however, have been calculated using the vital statistics for a two-year duration by pooling the data from the two systems mentioned above in order to reduce the sampling error. The figures presented below on the birth and death must, however, be treated with caution.

(i) Birth and Death Rates

The following are the results based on a retrospective survey with a one-year reference period at the start of the research work in the area. The reference dates used were from January 15, 1980 to January 14, 1981. These dates were carefully chosen so as to be the dates of important social occasion for the village people, so that the timing of the occurrence of vital events could be detected effectively. The famous festival of *Makara Shankaranthi* is celebrated on the fourteenth of January in most parts of South India and particularly in the study area. It is a celebration of thanks giving after a good harvest. The usual way of celebration is by decorating and parading the livestock especially bullocks, worshipping the holy cow, distributing sweets cooked from the newly harvested rice and offering to the Sun God. The competitive spirit of the celebration makes the festival prominent. But such a celebration is important only among the peasants and agriculturists who generally own land and livestock. Further, this celebration depends on the amount of yield and quality of crops in the preceding season. Because of the failure of monsoon during the last season and poor crops this occasion was only mildly celebrated only among a few households during the period of investigation. These days were just a fortnight latter than the days of another celebration and worship at the *Sri Subramaniya Ghati Temple* which is about 8 kilometers away from the research area. During the celebration a cattle fair is arranged where the cattle owners from all the surrounding villages, sometimes from villages as far as a hundred kilometers, gather for a week-long stay to buy, sell or exchange cattle and other essentials as well as to worship the deity. Practically, everyone in the study area, including the Muslims, remembers these events which was thus suitable to use as the reference date for the collection of vital events from the families of these villages. Thus, these two prominent occasions of the area were used as reference to help the people recollect the time of occurrence of the vital events.

The average birth and death rates have been calculated by pooling the two-year data (see Table 4.3). For the year 1980-81 the birth rate worked out to be 33 and the death rate 9.3 per thousand population. The birth rate for Laxmipura is lowest and the lowest death rate is in the village of Ramagere. Nevertheless, statistically there may not be a significant difference between villages as the sample sizes are small. For the same reason the discussion on the differentials in the birth and death rates by caste groups and other socio-economic variables are not appropriate due to small numbers. However, such differentials in cumulative fertility are discussed in subsequent parts of this chapter as this index has smaller sampling variation than the crude birth and death rates.

(*ii*) *Age Specific Rates*

The age-specific fertility rate (ASFR) and the age-specific marital fertility rate (ASMFR) for all the villages have been calculated using 1980, 1981 data and the average for 1980-81. Village level comparisons of the ASFR reveals the fact that the rate for the broad age group 15-24 years is highest in the grouped villages followed by Laxmipura and Ramagere [Table 4.4(a) and 4.4(b)]. But, the older women (25-44 years) in Ramagere have the highest age-specific fertility rate followed by the grouped villages and Laxmipura. The Laxmipura women in these ages seems to have a very low ASFR which is only 104. The ASMFR for women 15-24 years of age is

TABLE 4.3

Crude Birth and Death Rates for the Study Population
(i) Retrospective Survey 1980

Village	Mid-year population	Births	Birth Rate	Deaths	Death Rate
Ramagere	1932	65	33.6	19	9.8
Laxmipura	739	26	35.2	8	10.8
G. halli— S. Durga	472	17	38.0	5	10.6
All Villages	3143	108	34.4	32	10.2

(ii) Continuous Registration 1981

Ramagere	1957	66	33.7	14	7.2
Laxmipura	755	21	27.8	7	9.3
G, halli— S. durga	483	14	29.0	6	12.4
All villages	3195	101	31.6	27	8.5

(iii) Birth and Death Rates :
Average for 1980-81

Village	Birth Rate	Death Rate
Ramagere	33.7	8.5
Laxmipura	31.7	10.0
G. halli—S. durga	32.5	11.5
All Villages	33.0	9.3

highest in Laxmipura at 319 followed by grouped villages at 264 and Ramagere at 210 respectively. On the other hand, the rates for the women 25 years and above is highest in Ramagere followed by the grouped villages and Laxmipura.

TABLE 4.4 (a)

Age Specific Fertility Rates 1980-81

	Rama-gere	Laxmi-pura	G. Halli S. Durga	All
15-19	119	89	125	111
20-24	299	314	241	291
25-29	228	190	139	208
30-34	195	109	200	174
35-39	41	71	—	58
40-44	15	29	100	25
TFR	4.46	4.01	4.03	4.3
Broader Age Groups				
15-24	173	188	194	197
25-44	145	104	133	134

TABLE 4.4 (b)

Age Specific Marital Fertility Rates 1980-81

	Rama-gere	Laxmi-pura	G. Halli S. Durga	All
	300	286	250	288
	354	333	269	331
	265	210	147	236
	221	119	222	195
	44	83	285	64
	20	46	143	35
TMFR	6.02	5.89	6.58	5.8
	210	319	264	317
	168	123	150	155

The motivation for and practice of becoming pregnant at advanced ages seem to be relatively higher in Ramagere followed by the grouped villages. The couples in Laxmipura are found to have a greater motivation for pregnancies at early ages. Such a motivation fell steeply to the lowest level for women aged 30 and above in Laxmipura. This situation is also evident from a widespread practice of family planning by the women in Laxmipura. Many couples after having the desired or the sufficient number of children by 30 years decide to undergo tubectomy. Due to the absence of any such practice these rates are highest among the two grouped villages. The acceptance of tubectomies by the women in Laxmipura is a recent phenomenon which caught on particularly after 1975.

The ASFR and ASMFR for the village area has been compared with the rates provided by four different sources beginning from 1951 [Table 4.5(a) and 4.5(b)]. The comparative figures are the rates for the state as a whole and for the southern division of the state Karnataka. It can be interpreted that the emphasis on childbearing at early ages was greater in the study area during 1980-81 than in the other areas. Only a small number of women aged 35 years and above gave birth during the two-years period. This could be due to a chance factor that during the years of reference only a few of this age conceived to deliver a live birth during that period. This, however, need not necessarily be so, because it appears that the taboo on becoming pregnant while a woman is a grandmother is not very strong in the research area. Among certain communities, especially the Low Castes and Muslims, the older women who are grandmothers, at least to their daughters' children, do give birth to their own children. On the other hand, an increasing proportion of women who have the required number of children by 35 years or so have also accepted family planning. The widespread acceptance of the tubectomies in this area has reduced the chance for many women of begetting more children when compared with other areas of the state. The discussion of family planning and related issues in the research area are discussed in Chapter 6 of this thesis.

TABLE 4.5 (a)
Age Specific Marital Fertility Rates Compared with Figures from MPS, BPS and DRS

TABLE 4.5 (b)
Age Specific Fertility Rates

Age Groups	Karnataka South Rural Plain 1975 (1)	Karnataka South Rural 1971 Age Groups (2)	Karnataka South Rural Plain 1975 (2)	Karnataka South Rural Plain 1977 (3)	Research Area All Villages 1980-81 (4)		Karnataka South Rural Plain 1975(1)	Research Area All Villages 1980-81 (4)
15—19	277	134 (13—17)	282	265	288		88	111
20—24	293	271 (18—22)	295	363	331		213	291
25—29	302	265 (23—27)	286	313	236		207	208
30—34	170	212 (28—32)	179	146	195		157	174
35—39	157	148 (33—37)	142	77	64		97	58
40—44	61	81 (38—42)	39	9	35		44	25
45—49	—	39 (43—47)	—	—	—		10	—
50+	—	16 (48+)	—	—	—		—	—
TMFR	6.3	5.8	6.1	5.9	5.8	TFR	4.1	4.3
GMFR	222	—	237	—	—			
GFR	199	134	180	186	163			

1. Srinivasan *et al*, *op. cit.*
2. Census of India 1971, Series 14, Mysore, Part IIc(ii), Social and Cultural Tables and Fertility tables (p. 223).
3. Shariff *et al*, *op. cit.*
4. Data from four villages selected for this research.
5. Newsletter, Bangalore Population Centre, 1975, Vol II No. 3 p(6).

The age-specific fertility rate for the area, when compared with that of the state of Karnataka for the year 1975, reveals that the rate for the villages in 1981 for the age groups 15-19 to 30-34 years are higher than for the state. But, the rates for the succeeding age groups are lower than the rates for the whole state. This, however, suggests a pattern of childbearing in the early years of the marriage probably with short durations of spacing and then stopping the births by using family planning methods at more advanced ages. Reasons for relatively high level of fertility in the early period of childbearing are discussed in the following chapter while discussing the effect of education and family type on fertility. The comparative figures also suggest a moderate decline in Total Marital Fertility while Total Fertility has remained almost unchanged.

(*iii*) *Cumulative Fertility*

The forthcoming analyses are based on the pregnancy histories collected during the field work for all the *current married fertile* women of the research area. It is useful to briefly explain the concepts of Currently married and Ever married women as they are used in this thesis. Currently married women for our purpose are those married who were of ages between 15-49 years, living in a regular sexual union and fecund at the time of the survey. Thus the women who were infecund due to sterility and menopause are not included into this group.

The following criteria were used to identify women as sterile or having attained menopause. In the absence of any family planning acceptance, the women within a regular sexual union who have not conceived in the past sixty months were singled out as sterile.[14] To confirm the reported fertility status of a woman as one who has not attained menopause, aspects like duration since last conception, breast feeding and current menstrual status were used in conjunction. A few women thus identified who attained menopause or early menopouse were also excluded to arrive at the defined group of women. An important consideration, however, for including the women in this group was their current contraceptive status. A woman

TABLE 4.6

Mean number of Births and Living Children by Age of Mother

	15—19		20—24		25—29		30—34		35—39		40—49	
	No.	Mean	No.	Mean	No.	Mean	No.	Mean	No.	Mean	No.	Mean
Number of Women	43	—	109	—	107	—	83	—	50	—	54	—
All Live Births	20	0.47	175	1.61	309	2.89	378	4.55	261	5.22	309	5.72
Live Births (Sons)	10	0.23	97	0.89	164	1.53	178	2.14	130	2.60	167	3.09
Live Births (Daughters)	10	0.23	78	0.72	145	1.36	200	2.14	131	2.62	142	2.63
All Living Children	18	0.42	158	1.45	256	2.39	211	3.74	206	4.12	255	4.72
Living Sons	10	0.23	89	0.82	137	1.28	144	1.73	106	2.12	142	2.63
Living Daughters	8	0.19	69	0.63	119	1.11	167	2.01	100	2.00	113	2.09

who is less than 45 years of age and sterilized or if she is the wife of a sterilized man irrespective of the duration of sterilization were designated as currently contracepting and was included into this group of women. Past IUD users were not considered contraceptors in this analysis. Using these criteria we identified 446 currently married women from among all the ever married. Five women who were living in undefined categories of family types were removed from the present analysis.

The *Ever married* women in this study are those who have undergone the marriage ceremony irrespective of their involvement in sexual union. Thus, a girl who is ceremoniously or ritualistically married and has earned the identity of *wife*, though before puberty, is included in this category. The practice of pre-puberty marriages still exist to a certain degree among a few communities in the research area such women are culturally considered *Dharma Pathni*.[15] It is important to include them so that the effect of such a component can also be evaluated, however, the mean ages of marriage and effective marriage have been separately worked out. The widowed, separated and divorced women are, however, treated as ever married women.

The *mean number of children ever born* (MCEB) for women aged 40 and above is an approximate indicator of completed (past) fertility. Because of small numbers in the five year age groups after 40 years all women above 40 years of age have been grouped together in estimating this index of completed fertility [see Table 4.6]. The MCEB has worked out to be 5.72 and the *mean number of living children* is 4.72, indicating a loss of one child in the lifetime of a woman. It is noticed that the additional fraction to the mean number of children is low for women in the age group 35-39 and, 40 and above years compared to the younger ages. The highest addition is noticed between 25-29 and 30-34 age groups. The addition in the two other younger age groups, however, is also substantial (that is 1.14 and 1.28) respectively. The mean number of children currently surviving is 4.72 for women aged 40 years and, 3.74 and 4.12 for age groups 25-29 and 30-34 years respectively.

The means of children ever born and those who are living from the Mysore Population Study (MPS) and the Bangalore Population Study (BPS) are compared with means from the research area. The useful comparison is with the figures provided by the BPS in 1975. Leaving aside the women in age group 45 years and above there is a general trend toward a lower MCEB for the women in the study area. With regard to living children, the mean is substantially lower for the study area in the age groups between 25 and 35 years. (see Table 4.7). There seem to be a considerable underenumeration of the children ever born for the age group 45 years and above in both the MPS and the BPS. In this regard, the results provided by the present research are consistent and more reliable. The children ever born for women 45 years and above is 6 and the living children is 5.1 in the study area.

4.5 Differential Fertility

The following discussion is mainly concerned with differential fertility in the area. This is a preliminary analysis and is largely illustrative which is undertaken to explore various aspects of differential fertility before undertaking a better analysis using multiple regression techniques where controls over age and marital duration are used. The fertility indicators used are the mean numbers of pregnancies, live births and living children. Means by sex are also calculated for the live births and living children. The figures on proportions of surviving sons and daughters are useful to understand the mortality effect on the population.

The category of women considered for the analysis are the currently married women in the area. The results are presented separately for the villages and seven socio-economic variables. These variables are caste, type of family, annual income, land ownership, main source of income, education and use of contraception. The mean current age of women and the mean age at effective marriage[16] are also presented which in many instances explain the fertility differentials.

There were 446 women who were currently married and who were eligible for the collection of pregnancy histories.

TABLE 4.7

Mean Number of Children Per Ever Married Women by Age compared with figures from MPS and BPS

Age Groups	(a) Children Ever Born MPS 1951	BPS Area 1975	Research 1981	(b) Number of Living Children MPS 1951	BPS Area 1975	Research 1981
15—24	1.3	1.3	1.3	1.0	1.1	1.2
25—34	3.6	3.9	3.6	2.6	3.1	2.5
35—44	5.1	5.5	5.4	3.5	4.2	4.4
45+	4.9	5.2	6.0	3.0	3.7	5.1

MPS=Mysore Population Study
BPS=Bangalore Population Study

The mean age for all these women was 28.8 years[17] and the mean age at effective marriage 16.1 years. On average, each woman with a marital duration of 12.7 years had been pregnant 3.7 times, the mean number of children ever born was 3.3 and the mean number of living children was 2.7 per woman. The mean number of confirmed pregnancies which did not survive (all the pregnancy wastage and the dead children) was 0.76. However, 78 per cent of pregnancies resulted in live births who were alive at the time of survey. The sex ratio at birth was very close to unity which is reflected in the equal number of male and female alive births. On the contrary, the mean number of living sons was 1.4 which is slightly higher than the mean number of surviving daughters which was 1.3. The proportion of children surviving was 0.826 for all children, this was higher for sons at 0.850 and lower for daughters at 0.801 possibly suggesting a likelihood of a mild incidence of female child neglect.

(*i*) *Differentials by Village*

There are certain indications of the fertility differentials among the villages. The mean number of pregnancies in Ramagere and Laxmipura was almost the same, 3.6 and 3.5 respectively. For the grouped villages it was lower at 2.9. Nevertheless, the mean number of children ever born was

TABLE 4.8

Differential Fertility and Proportion of Surviving Children in Study Area

	Number of Currently Married Women	Mean Age of Women	Mean Age of Effective Marriage	Mean Number of Living Sons	Mean Number of Living Daughters	Mean Number of Living Children	Mean Number of Sons Ever Born
	(1)	(2)	(3)	(4)	(5)	(6)	(7)
All	446	28.8	16.1	1.4	1.3	2.7	1.6
Villages							
Ramagere	279	28.9	16.1	1.4	1 3	2.7	1.6
Laxmipura	104	28.8	16.2	1.6	1.2	2.8	1.9
S. Durga & G. Halli	63	27.9	15.8	1.2	1.1	2.3	1.2
Caste Groups							
High castes	39	30.2	18.0	1.2	1.2	2.4	1.5
Peasant castes	222	29.9	16.3	1.6	1.5	3.1	1.8
Service castes	52	28.7	16.3	1.2	1.2	2.4	1.5
Low castes	108	26.4	15.2	1.1	0.8	1.9	1.4
Non-castes (Muslims)	25	26.9	15.0	1.3	1.8	3.1	1.5
Type of Family of Current Residence							
Nuclear	296	30.4	16.0	1.6	1.5	3.1	1.9
Stem	86	25.0	16.6	0.9	0.9	1.8	1.1

Joint	21	27.6	15.0	0.8	1.3	2.1	1.0
Stem-Joint	27	26.7	16.7	1.2	1.0	2.2	1,4
Polygamous	11	23.7	15.3	1.0	0.5	1.5	1.2
Others	5	21.2	15.4	0.4	0.0	0.4	0.4
Annual Family Income							
Less than Rs. 5,000	310	28.2	15.9	1.4	1.2	2.6	1.6
Rs. 5,000 or more	136	30.1	16.6	1.5	1.5	3.0	1.7
Source of Income							
Agriculture	317	28.7	16.0	1.4	1.2	2.6	1.7
Non-Agriculture	129	28.9	16.4	1.4	1.5	2.8	1.6
Land Holding							
Landless or 0.5 acres	93	27.1	15.9	1.4	1.2	2.6	1.7
0.5 acres — 3.5 acres	233	28.8	15.9	1.3	1.3	2.6	1.6
3.5 acres — 6.5 acres	76	28.5	16.6	1.2	1.3	2.5	1.4
6.5 acres or more	44	32.4	16.8	1.6	1.6	3.8	2.3
Education of Women							
No Education	314	29.2	15.8	1.5	1.3	2.8	1.7
Some Education	132	27.9	16.9	1.3	1.2	2.5	1.4
Contraceptive Practice							
Non-contraceptions	358	27.8	16.0	1.2	1.2	2.4	1.5
Contraceptions	88	32,8	16.5	2,1	1,6	3,7	2,4

	Mean Number of Daughters Ever Born (8)	Mean Number of Live Births (9)	Mean Number of Pregnancies (10)	Proportion of Sons Surviving (11)	Proportion of Daughters Surviving (12)	Proportion of Children Surviving (13)
All	1.6	3.3	3.7	0.850	0.801	0.826
Villages						
Ramagere	1.7	3.3	3.6	0.856	0.799	0.827
Laxmipura	1.5	3.4	3.5	0.844	0.809	0.828
S. Durga & G. Halli	1.3	2.5	2.9	0.831	0.800	0.816
Caste Groups						
High castes	1.4	2.8	3.0	0.912	0.789	0.853
Peasant castes	1.8	3.7	3.8	0.880	0.827	0.853
Service castes	1.7	3.1	3.5	0.818	0.741	0.778
Low castes	1.2	2.6	2.8	0.757	0.717	0.738
Non-castes (Muslims)	1.8	3.4	3.4	0.868	0.936	0.906
Type of Family of Current Residence						
Nuclear	1.9	3.8	4.0	0.861	0.796	0.816
Stem	1.1	2.2	2.2	0.800	0.875	0.818

Joint	1.5	2.5	2.5	0.810	0.875	0.848
Stem-Joint	1.3	2.6	2.7	0.838	0.794	0.846
Polygamous	0.8	2.0	2.1	0.846	0.556	0.750
Others	0.0	0.4	0.4	1.000	0.000	1.000
Annual Family Income						
Less than Rs. 5,000	1.5	3.1	3.3	0.831	0.802	0.812
Rs. 5000 or more	1.9	3.6	3.7	0.891	0.801	0.844
Source of Income						
Agriculture	1.5	3.2	3.4	0.849	0.794	0.801
Non-agriculture	1.8	3.4	3.6	0.856	0.817	0.851
Land Holding						
Landless or 0.5 acres	1.5	3.1	3.3	0.848	0.827	0.838
0.5 acres — 3.5 acres	1.6	3.2	3.4	0.837	0.785	0.811
3.5 acres — 6.5 acres	1.5	3.0	3.2	0.856	0.829	0.842
6.5 acres or more	2.0	4.4	4.6	0.891	0.794	0.843
Education of Women						
No Education	1.7	3.4	3.6	0.832	0.791	0.812
Some Education	1.5	2.9	3.0	0.901	0.834	0.867
Contraceptive Practice						
Non-contraceptive	1.5	3.0	3.2	0.838	0.790	0.813
Contraceptions	2.0	4.3	4.6	0.879	0.837	0.860

higher for Laxmipura women at 3.4, followed by Ramagere which was slightly lower and the grouped villages at 2.5. The respective figures of the mean number of living children were 2.7 for Ramagere, 2.8 for Laxmipura and 2.3 for the grouped villages. All means for the grouped villages were relatively lower which emerges due to the relatively younger age structure of the currently married women in those villages. This is evident as the mean age of women in Gowdahalli and Shivadurga together was 27.9 years when compared to 28.9 and 28.8 respectively for Ramagere and Laxmipura women. In spite of the fact that women from the last two villages entered into sexual union at a relatively younger age (15.8 years) the mean duration of marriage was about half a year shorter than for the other two villages.

The sex differentials in case of the live births is noticeable among the women of Laxmipura where mean number of sons born alive was 1.9, and the mean for daughters is 1.5. On the other hand, for other villages the mean was slightly favourable towards females. There is a possibility, however, that these differentials are due to the small numbers involved. But the sex differentials in the mean number of living children rise interesting issues. In Laxmipura the mean number of living sons was 0.4 points higher than the mean number of living daughters, as in the case of live births. But, for other villages the mean sons, relative to mean number of daughters was lower in case of live births but turned out to be slightly higher for living children. This suggests the universality of son preference and a possibility of female neglect in those villages. The child survival of daughters was found to be lowest in Ramagere.

(ii) Differentials by Caste Groups

The mean number of pregnancies per woman by caste groups suggests a low incidence of pregnancies among the Low Castes, one pregnancy less than the highest mean observed for the Peasant Castes. But Low Caste women are the youngest having lowest mean age which is almost two-and half years younger than the peasant women. The striking difference was between the High Castes and the Muslims. The High

Caste women whose mean age is 30.2 years, the highest from among all the caste groups, have a mean number of pregnancy of 3, whereas the mean age for Muslim women was 26.9 years (3.3 years younger) yet the mean number of pregnancies is 3.4 per woman. A relative comparison of the Muslims and the Peasants in the population reveals the fact that Peasant women are as fertile as the Muslim women, who are on an average two-year older and have the highest mean number of pregnancies as well.

The High Castes and Peasants have mean ages which are higher than the average and the Low Castes and the Muslims have lower than the average. Service Castes have their mean age closer to the overall mean. But the High caste exhibit second lowest mean number of children ever born while the Peasants have the highest mean number. This seems to be due to : (i) the differences in age at effective marriage (almost 2 years higher for the High castes) and consequent differentials in marital duration between castes ; and (ii) the practice of deliberate control of fertility among the High Caste Hindus in contrast to the pronatalist attitudes of the Peasant Castes in the study area. Consequently, the mean number of living children is lowest for Low Castes at two children, a medium number of 2.4 for the High Castes and the Service Castes and a high number for the Peasants and Muslims of about 3 children. Child survival is also lowest for the Low Castes and highest of the Muslims. However, the proportion of daughters surviving is lower for all the Hindu castes while for Muslims it is higher than for sons ; the proportions calculated for Muslims, however, are based on only 25 pregnancy histories.

(*iii*) *Differentials by the Type of Family*

Another striking fact is the fertility differentials by type of family of current residence. The married women currently living in nuclear families are considerably older than those living in other family types ; therefore, the number of children ever born among the women in nuclear families is substantially higher. The joint and stem-joint families have a lower mean numbers of pregnancies, live births and living children and the women are on an average 3 to 4 years younger. A detailed discussion about the differentials by family type is treated separately in Chapter 5.

(*iv*) *Differentials by Income, Source of Livelihood and Land-holding*

The differentials in fertility for the two income groups is self-explanatory due mainly to the mixed effect of the difference in mean age of women and income. The women belonging to the families whose annual income is greater than rupees 5,000 are about two years older and are married at least one year longer than their counterparts in the other group. All the fertility indices retain a substantial difference indicating a higher fertility among the women of the high income group. It can also be inferred that the high income has little impact on the control of fertility in this area. The child survival especially for the sons is found to be higher among the families whose annual income is above rupees five thousand.

There, however, is only a slight difference in the mean number of pregnancies, live births and living children between the families who depend on agriculture and non agricultural occupations. There is also no difference in the mean age of the women between these groups. This strongly emphasizes the fact that age of the women and length of the marital duration are the two chief factors determining the levels and differentials in fertility.

The fertility differentials are compatible with the mean age of women for the categories in the land holding size, excepting for those who own between 4—6 acres of land. The women belonging to the families owing seven or more acres of land have a 19 per cent higher mean age than those in the landless category, though they have married one-year latter have a 39 per cent longer marital duration. All of these has enabled a 41 per cent higher fertility among the land owning women. This is fascinating because the general notion that the fertility among the poor (landless) is higher, does not appear to be true. On the other hand the evidence from this area is that both income and land holding has a positive relationship with fertility. For the middle land holding categories (4—6 acres group) have a 6 per cent shorter marital duration and also have achieved a 6 per cent lower fertility than the women in 1—3 acre category.

(v) *Differentials by Education*

A marked difference is found among the educated and uneducated group of the women in the area in their fertility. The mean age of the uneducated women is about one year lower than the educated, but the mean number of pregnancies, live births and living children are consistently higher. The educated women have 14 per cent lower marital duration coupled with a 20 per cent lower fertility suggesting a strong education effect on lowering fertility. Even the differentials in child survivorship is favourable for the educated group and more so in case of the son survivorship. All this suggests a relatively lower fertility and a greater capacity to keep the children alive among the educated women of the area.

(vi) *Differentials by Use and Non-use of Contraception*

The differentials by the use and non-use of contraception suggests that the women who are contracepting are on an average more than four years older than the non-contracepting women and have 1.4 more pregnancies, 1.3 more higher live births and an equal number of living children. The contracepting women have a 28 per cent longer marital duration (4.5 years) when compared to the non-contracepting ones, but have a 44 per cent higher fertility which strongly supports the hypothesis that the acceptors usually are older having many children. Thus the acceptors of the family planning methods are those who are much older and who also have sufficient number of living children especially sons. The mean number of living sons is 2.1 while the mean is only 1.6 for living daughters among the acceptors.

4.6. Multivariate Analysis of Fertility Differentials

(i) *Introduction*

The analysis presented above only partially help us to understand the contribution of the series of characteristics whose influence on fertility is to be determined. Secondly, we could not find out the cumulative effect of all the characteristics on fertility. Therefore, we proceed to further analyse the data to find out : (i) the extent to which the observed fertility differentials are maintained if differing background characteristics of the groups are controlled ? (ii) which one of the independent variables has a greater effect while the effect of other variables is controlled and (iii) the relative contribution of the various socio-economic and demographic variables to the total variance of the dependent variable ?

We attempt these by using the multivariate analytical methods. Multiple regression and multiple classification analysis are chosen as appropriate techniques to address these questions. These methods of analyses enable us to appraise the relative effect of the independent variables on the dependent variables. They also enable us to use all or many independent variables together in the analyses. In the following analysis we have in fact added a few additional variables to the regression equation. For instance, infant and child mortality are introduced as two different variables in the regression analysis and childhood mortality (infant plus child mortality) is used in the multiple classification analysis. The application of multivariate techniques in the demographic analysis is well documented (see for example Hermalin, 1975 ; Srinivasan, 1975). It has also been appraised that these techniques enable precision and summarization and yet retain the simplicity of original data.

A list of variables used in these analyses with respective measurements is given in Table 4.9. *Children Ever Born* (CEB) is used as the dependent variable which is a convenient measure of fertility for the data used. The independent variables reflect the social, economic and demographic aspects of the women while marital duration and age at marriage are the chief demographic variables. Since marital duration is known to have a nonlinear relationship with the number of children ever born, the square of marital duration is also introduced to account for this effect. The remaining variables (variables 5 to 14) represent the socio-economic characteristics of the population measured on either a nominal or interval (ordinal) scale. In view of the fact that decreasing levels of fertility may also be due to decreasing infant and child mortality, they are introduced as independent variables. These variables are treated as non-demographic, because their effect on CEB is both physiological as well as social involving decisions to replace the child lost and to insure for the anticipated infant or child death. Many studies have demonstrated a strong relationship between the work status of a woman and fertility. Since the detailed information on the work status of women is available, it was decided to include this variable in the analysis. Because almost all women reported household duties as their primary occupation, information on their secondary occupation is used to determine actual work status and to create a composite variable. A distinction was made to differentiate between work on own family farm and work outside home contributing monetary incomes. This variable is used in the analysis in four categories.

TABLE 4.9

Variables Used in the Regression Analysis and their Measurement

Variables	Categories and Measurements
1. Children ever born [CEB] (Dependent variable)	Actual number of live births
2. Marital duration [MDN]	Number in completed years calculated by substracting age at effective marriage from actual age of woman
3. Square of marital duration [MDNSQ]	Marital duration times marital duration
4. Age at marriage [AAM]	Female age at effective marriage in single years
5. Infant mortality [IMY]	Number of live births that did not survive till the end of twelve months
6. Child mortality [CMY]	Number of deceased children less infant deaths
7. Work status of woman [WORK]	Work status measured in four categories (1) Household work (2) Household and work on family farm (3) Household work and labourer (4) Work on modern jobs.

8. Level of family [LOFI]	Annual famlly income in three catregories (1)<—Rs. 3000 (2) Rs. 3000—5000 (3) >—Rs. 5000
9. Source of family income (SOFI)	Source of income from (1) Agriculture-(2) Labour or rural service (3) Non-agricultural
10. Type of family [FMLY]	Two categories (0) Simple (1) Complex
11. Caste groups [CASTE]	Muslims in reference category and four dummy variables for Hindu caste groups
12. Level of education of woman [EDN]	Three categories (1) Illiterate (2) up to 6th standard (3) 7th standard and above
13. Village of residence [VILG]	Group of smaller villages in reference categories and two dummy variables for t vo larger villages
14. Contraceptive status [FPUSE]	(1) Non-user (2) Current users

After deciding upon the variables to be included in the regression analysis, a matrix of Zero-order (Pearson's) correlation coeffieients was drawn to establish the degree of interdependence and check for multicollinearity to enter into multiple regression. It can be seen from Table 4.10 that there exists for instance a high degree of positive correlation between marital duration, or square of marital duration, and the dependent variable, indicating the dominating effect of demographic factor namely marital duration or age. Since age can be expressed as a linear combination of age at marriage and marital duration, its effect has been implicitly taken care of by these variables. Over half of the remaining coefficients are statistically significant but the correlations are not so high among the independent variables as to cause the problem of multicollinearity. Infant and child mortality shows a relatively strong and significant association with the dependent variable with correlation coefficients of 0.5 and 0.4 respectively. 108 of the total of 171 coefficients are significantly different from zero at less than the five per cent level. There, however, is only a low degree of interdependence among the independent variables themselves. Multicollinearity of a high magnitude in the range of 0.8 to 1.0 may create problems tn the regression analysis.

TABLE 4.10

Zero-Order Correlation Coefficients between Variables used in the Regression Analysis (all Currently married Women)

	1	2	3	4	5	6	7	8	9
1. CEB	1.0*								
2. MDN	0.7*	1.0*							
3. MDNSQ	0.7*	1.0*	1.0*						
4. AAM	—0.2	—0.3*	—0.3*	1.0*					
5. IMY	0.5*	0.3*	0.3*	—0,2=	1.0*				
6. CMY	0.4*	0.3*	0.3*	—0 1*	0.3	1.0*			
7. WORK	—0.0	0.0	0.0	—0.2=	0.1	0.1=	1.0*		
8. LOFI	0.1	0.0	0.1	0.2*	0.0	—0.1=	—0.4*	1.0*	1.0
9. SOFI	0.0	—0.1	—0.1=	0.1	—0.0	—0.0	—0.1*	—0.1@	0.2*
10. FMLY	—0.3*	—0.3*	—0.2*	0.1	—0.1=	—0.1@	—0.1*	0.4*	—0.2*
11. H CASTE	—0.1	—0.0	—0.0	0.3*	—0.0	—0.1@	—0.3	0.1=	0.3*
12. P CASTE	0.2*	0.1@	0.1=	0.1=	—0.1	—0.0	—0.1*	0.2*	—0.3*
13. S CASTE	—0.0	—0.0	—0.0	0.0	0.0	0.1	0.0	—0.2*	0.0
14. L CASTE	—0.1*	—0.1=	—0.1	—0.2+	0.1=	0.1	0.4*	—0.2*	0.0
15. EDN	—0.1*	—0.2*	—0.2*	0.2*	—0.1@	—0.2*	—0.3*	—0.2*	0.2*
16. VILRAM	0.0	0.0	0.0	0.0	—0.0	—0.0	—0.1	—0.1	0.4*
17. VILLAX	0.0	0.0	—0.0	0.0	0.0	0.0	0.0	0.1*	—0.3*
18. FPUSE	0.2*	0.2*	0.2*	0.1=	—0.0	0.1	—0.1	0.1=	0.0

	10	11	12	12	14	15	16	17	18
1. CEB									
2. MDN									
3. MDNSQ									
4. AAM									
5. IMY									
6. CMA									
7. WORK									
8. LOFI									
9. SOFI									
10. FMLY	1.0*								
11. H CASTE	—0.0	1.0*							
12. P CASTE	0.0	—0.3*	1.0*						
13. S CASTE	—0.1	—0.1@	—0.4*	1.0*					
14. L,CASTE	0.0	—0.2*	—0.6*	—0.2*	1.0*				
15. EDN	0.1	0.4*	0.1	—0.1	—0.3*	1.0*			
16. VILRAM	0.0	0.2	—0.0	0.0	—0.2*	0.2	1.0*		
17. VILLAX	—0.0	—0.1*	0.1=	—0.1	0.1@	—0.1@	—0.7*	1.0*	
18. FPUSE	—0.1*	0.1	0.2*	—0.0	—0.2*	0.2*	—0.0	0.2*	1.0*

Note : The variables are defined in Table 4.9. H CASTE=high castes, P CASTE=Peasant castes, S CASTE=Service castes, L CASTE=Low castes, VILRAM=Ramagere village and VILLAX=Laxmipura village.

* Significant at 0.00 level @ Significant at 0.01 level=Significant at 0.05 level

(*ii*) *Results of the Regression Analysis*

The data relate to 441 currently married women of childbearing age. The results of the regression analysis are represented in Table 4.11. The first column gives the list of variables, the second column gives the 'B' or raw (partial) regression coefficients and fourth column gives the 'Beta' or standardized regression coefficients. The raw regression coefficients represent the quantum of change (either positive or negative) in the dependent variable per one unit change in the independent variable while all other variables are held constant at the mean or controlled. The 'B' values, however, cannot be used to establish the relative strength or predictive power of the variables used because different variables have a different unit of measurement. 'Beta' coefficients on the other hand are the standardized coefficients. The 'beta' values indicate the number of standard deviation units change in the variable that would be predicted when a particular independent variable changes by one standard unit. In the forthcoming discussion we have used the 'B' values, because our aim is not to determine the relative strengths ; rather we want to know what contribution these variables make in explaining the fertility differentials. Column three in the above table provides the standard error of 'B'. "T' statistics are provided in column five and their levels of significance in column six.

All the independent variables included in the regression equation explain about 68 per cent ('R square' value of 0.679) of the variance in the dependent variable. However, many variables used in the regression equation have statistically insignificant effect on the dependent variable. Two demographic variables and two socio-economic variables are found to have independent statistically significant effect on the number of children ever born. Both, marital duration and the square of marital duration are significant at 0.00 level.

One can interpret from the 'B' values that little less than four years of marital duration will enable approximately one additional child birth. Both Infant and Child mortality are found to be important variables whose effect on the children ever born is significant at 0.00 level. The 'B' values imply that a high level of child mortality induces higher fertility.

TABLE 4.11

Multiple Regression Results, Dependent Variable : Number of Children Ever Born

Variables in the equation	B	Se B	Beta	T	Significance
(1)	(2)	(3)	(4)	(5)	(6)
Level of family income	0.002	0.001	0.060	1.892	0.06
Level of women's education	−0.017	0.119	−0.005	−0.146	0.88
Work status of women					
(Household [HH] in reserve)					
HH and work on family farm	0.135	0.208	0.027	0.625	0.52
HH and labourer	−0.057	0.242	−0.010	−0.236	0.81
Work on modern jobs	−0.279	0.437	−0.020	−0.639	0.52
Complex family (Nuclear=0)	−0.395	0.174	−0.072	−2.275	0.02**
Low Castes (Others=0)	−0.611	0.203	−0.105	−3.017	0.00*
Service Castes (Others=0)	−0.474	0.229	−0.062	−2.067	0.04**
High Castes (Others=0)	−0.564	0.278	−0.065	−2.027	0.04 **

Non-Caste Muslims (Others=0)	0.359	0.32	0.033	1.094	0.28
Infant mortality	0.841	0.102	0.151	8.243	0.00 *
Child mortality	0.886	0.135	0.203	6,545	0.00 *
Marital duration	0.291	0.033	0.925	8.716	0.00 *
Square of marital duration	—0.004	0.001	—0.387	—3.792	0.00 *
Women's age at marriage	0.006	0.034	0.005	0.163	8.87
(CONSTANT)	0.108	0.683		0.159	0.87

R Square = 0.679 Significant at 0.000 level

"B" is the raw regression coefficient ; "Beta" is the standardised regresstion coefficient ; and "Se B" is the standard error of "B". (†) Significant at zero per cent level and (††) significant at less than 5 per cent level.

Further the 'B' values also suggest a close to complete replacement for dead children. Each infant or child death seems to cause a 0.86 unit increase in CEB when the effect of all other variables is controlled for. It may, however, be argued that, in case of infant deaths, the biological effect through the interruption of lactation, the early onset of post-partum ovulation and the renewed vulnerability to conception can have a substantial impact on the birth of the subsequent child. On the other hand, such a biological effect is marginal if one is considering the effect of the death of children aged one year and above. It is clear from the raw regression coefficients that the replacement effect of child mortality (excluding infant mortality) is as high as that of infant mortality. The intention to replace a dead child are predominant while biological factors only contribute to speed up the birth of a desired child.

Even in this analysis caste affiliation of the women have retained an important bearing on fertility. Peasant Castes who are in the reference category have a high fertility, next only to Muslims. The lowest fertility is found among the Low Castes which can be attributed mainly to pregnancy wastage. This explanation is also true to a large extent for a relatively low level of fertility among the Service Castes. High Castes on the other hand have a relatively low level of fertility than the Muslims which is due to the intentional and voluntary control of fertility. Nevertheless, all castes excepting the Muslims have a significantly lower fertility compared to Peasant Castes.

Of the remaining variables only type of family present significant results. The fertility of the women currently staying in simple families is higher and on an average almost 0.4 children lower for the women in complex families. This suggests that the fertility among the women currently living in joint families is lower even when controlled for all other variables including age at marriage and marital duration and other socio-economic variables. It is, however, recalled that women living in joint families in the early period of their married life can be subfecund and also that the sexual behaviour is controlled by elders. Joint family may exert pressure on couples in the latter period of their stay to enhance fertility only to catch up the fertility levels of their counterparts in simple families. This aspect is clearly revealed in the discussion in Chapter 5 of this thesis.

Variables like the level of family income, the work status of a woman and the level of education have not demonstrated their effect on the fertility levels which is evident from their non-significant 'B' values. The only plausible answer for this pattern is that the mechanisms through which these variables are assumed to affect the fertility have not yet gained momentum in this area. This also indicates that in a changing traditional society the social values seem to supersede the economic values.

It was mentioned earlier that the total variance explained by all the variables put together was about 68 per cent as represented by the 'R square' values. It is interesting to note that only a few of these variables explain most of the variance. This is highlighted in Table 4.12 in which results of step up regression analysis are presented. Equations one to five contain various combinations of the socio-economic variables and the rest are the equations where one or more socio-economic variables are used along with the demographic variable marital duration. Essentially this exercise substantiates that the socio-economic variables have reasonably high predictive power in the absence of the demographic variable. Once the demographic variable namely the marital duration is introduced their predictive power falls steeply. All the five socio-economic variables considered in this analysis put together explain 52 per cent. On the other hand, marital duration alone explains 52 per cent of the variance. However, if all these socio-economic variables are used along with marital duration they add twelve per cent to the total explained variance. This exercise highlights the view that the socio-economic development in the area has only created milder yet an important effects on fertility.

(*iii*) *Results of Analysis of Variance and Multiple Classification Analysis*

Since most of the socio-economic variables involved are categorical in nature they could be effectively handled by multiple classification analysis and regression with dummy variables. Even though some of the variables are measured in interval scales, multiple linear regression can only be effective in detecting the linear relationship. In the absence of any prescribed pattern of relationship between the independent and dependent variables, multiple classification analysis becomes an useful device. However, this analysis can only be performed only when there is no interaction effect present between variables. Therefore, Analysis of Variance is first performed to detect the presence of interaction effect before proceeding to Multiple Classification Analysis. The following variables are used in this analysis : (A) *Socio-economic variables* : 1. childhood mortality (infant and child mortality), 2. type of family of residence, 3. levels of family income, 4. work status of woman, and 5. levels of woman's education. These variables are used as the 'factors' in this analysis. (B) *Demographic variable* : Marital duration is used as the demographic variable which is a covariate in this analysis.

All factors but for 'levels of education', and the covariate were found to be significant at 0.00 level. Level of education was found to be significant at 0.05 level. The effect of two-way interactions were found to be quite insignificant (see Table 4.13). High levels of significance and low level of interactions between the variables used provided encouragement to proceed to the multiple classification analysis. Table 4.14 presents the unadjusted and adjusted deviations in the mean from the grand mean of 3.29 children. It also presents the 'R square' values which is 0.594 when the adjustment is made only for the independent variables and 0.788 when it is adjusted for both independents and covariates. Thus, of the total of 79 per cent variance explained, twenty per cent is the contribution of all the socio-economic variables and the rest is the contribution of the demographic variables, age and marital duration.

However, one can see from the results that there are substantial variations among the subgroups of the variables as measured by the mean values. Variable Child mortality stands out whether one looks at the unadjusted or the unadjusted deviation. The noticeable fact is that even after controlling for the other factors and covariate, women who experienced infant and child mortality had 1.6 children more than those

TABLE 4.12

Multiple Regression Results for different Combination of the Variables used

Variables	1	2	3	4	5	6	7	8	9	10	11
Multiple R^2	0.23	0.32	0.33	0.38	0.52	0.52	0.60	0.63	0.64	0.64	0.64
Socio-economic					——Beta Coefficients——						
Variables											
Infant mortality	0.48	0.32	0.38	0.37	0.37		0.30	0.25	0.25	0.25	0.25
Child mortality		0.38	0.32	0.31	0.30			0.19	0.20	0.20	0.19
Work status of women			—0.08	—0.10	—0.12				—0.07	—0.08	—0.08
Type of family				—0.22	—0.22					—0.08	—0.08
Level of education					—0.08						—0.00
Demographic variables											
Marital duration						0.72	0.64	0.60	0.60	0.58	0.58
F statistics	133.4	103.7	70.8	64.9	52.9	480.2	334.4	252.0	192.7	156.6	130.2
Significance of F	0.0	0.0	0.0	0.0	0.0	0.0	0.0	0.0	0.0	0.0	0.0

TABLE 4.13

Results of the Analysis of Variance

Source of variation	Sum of Squares	df	Mean Square	F	Significance of F
Main effects (factors)	968.682	9	107.631	42.963	0.000
Child mortality (1)	556.286	1	556.285	222.049	0.000
Type of family (2)	190.246	1	190.246	75.940	0.000
Level of family income (3)	75.665	2	37.832	15.101	0.000
Work status of woman (4)	41.454	3	13.818	5.516	0.001
Level of women's education (5)	16.781	2	8.390	3.349	0.036
Covariate	714.046	1	714.046	285.022	0.000
Marital duration	714.046	1	714.045	285.022	0.000
2-way interactions	42.532	31	1.372	0.548	0.978
1 * 2	0.170	1	0.170	0.068	0.795
1 * 3	0.218	2	0.109	0.044	0.957
1 * 4	1.239	3	0.413	0.165	0.920
1 * 5	0.621	2	0.311	0.124	0.883

	2 * 3	0.147	2	0.074	0.029	0.971
	2 * 4	2.328	3	0.776	0.310	0.818
	2 * 5	5.706	2	5.853	1.139	0.321
	3 * 4	8.818	6	1.470	0.587	0.741
	3 * 5	12.429	4	3.107	1.240	0.293
	4 * 5	10.844	6	1.807	0.721	0.633
Explained		1725.261	41	42.080	16.797	0.000
Residual		999.587	399	2.505		
Total		2724.848	440	6.123		

TABLE 4.14

Results of the Multiple Classification Analysis

Grand mean=3.29				Adjusted for independents		Adjusted for independents + covariates	
Variable+category	N	Unadjusted Dev'n	Eta	Dev'n	Beta	Dev'n	Beta
CHILD MORTALITY							
No children dead	299	—0.86		—0.80		—0.51	
One or more children dead	142	1.82		1.68		1.08	
			0.50		0.47		0.30
TYPE OF FAMILY							
Simple families	304	0.45		0.48		0.18	
Complex families	137	—1.00		—1.06		—0.39	
			0.27		0.29		0.11
LEVELS OF FAMILY INCOME							
> RS 3000	188	—0.16		—0.51		—0.29	
RS 3000 TO RS 5000	118	—0.80		0.07		0.15	
<RS 5000	135	0.30		0.66		0.28	
			0.08		0.20		0.10

WORK STATUS OF WOMEN							
Household (HH) work	87	—0.46		—0.29		−0.07	
HH+work on family farm	215	0.36		0.29		0.13	
HH+work outside home	125	—0.11		—0.19		—0.09	
Work outside home	14	—1.58		−0.96		—0.69	
			0.17		0.13		0.07
LEVELS OF EDUCATION							
Illiterates	310	0.17		0.14		0.02	
1—6th standard	75	—0.08		—0.38		—0.18	
>7th standard	56	—0.86		−0.25		—0.15	
			0.14		0.08		0.04
Multiple R squared				.355		.612	
Multiple R				.596		.786	

Note : Covariate used is the marital duration.

who did not. Even though the likelihood that high fertility is the cause rather than the effect of infant and child mortality, its effect on fertility could be strong and substantial.

The type of family of current residence has the second most important effect on the dependent variable. On an average women living in simple families have a five per cent higher and those who live in joint family have a 12 per eent lower number of children ever born than the grand mean when the effect of all other factors and covariate are controlled for. This finding reinforces our arguments made above and in chapter 5 on family structure and fertility that the women living in joint families in the research area have lower fertility.

With regard to family income, it is interesting to note that women who reside in families with an income of less than rupees 3,000 have nine percent lower and the other two groups, namely family income of between Rs 3,000 and Rs 5,000 and above Rs 5,000, have 4 and 8 per cent higher mean CEB than the over all mean respectively even after the effect of other variables are controlled. The positive relationship of fertility with increasing income is a reality in this area. Such a paradox seem to emerge from the belief that the nutritious and health conditions of women increases as income increases which seem to reduce the pregnancy wastage resulting in the increase in average fertility. There are other mechanisms operating through changes in tastes and preference, increase in educational aspirations and value of children associated with increasing incomes of parents. There is a strong tendency in the research area for an investment in children both in quantity and quality. Especially among the self sufficient agricultural families, the desire that some children will take care of agriculture and some others will take to education and non-agricultural occupations who will add to family prestige and family income is growing which is fairly elastic with growing incomes as well. It also appears that the son preference is strongest among these groups when compared to others which keeps fertility at a relatively higher level with increase in current incomes.

The figures with regards to the work status of women are interesting. Women who work only on household duties and those who work on household duties and also on paid work outside the home have almost the same level of fertility which is very close to the over all mean. On the other hand those women who do household duties as well as work on their own family farm have a four per cent higher mean. The effect of work outside the home on regular employment is revealing for those women who reported that as the primary engagement. This group is small but they have a 21 per cent lower mean than the grand mean. One may, however, argue that those women who are engaged in household duties as primary activity, irrespective of their involvement in agricultural activities either on their own farm or as labourers, their fertility is not very much different. Only those women who work primarily on outside work (on modern jobs) demonstrate lower fertility levels. Thus it appears that the work on household duties or on farm and child bearing are compatible and the work in modern sector are not.

The effect of the education of the woman on the number of children ever born failed to show any systematic pattern. The mean CEB for illiterates is almost same as the over all mean. But the mean declines (8 per cent lower) for those women who have studied up to the sixth standard. Then, for those women who are educated beyond the seventh standard, the mean is almost 7 per cent higher. A detailed effort is made to find out the effect of education in combination to the family type in the subsequent chapter.

Although this analysis is too limited to be conclusive, it seems to be consistent with what may be regarded as the incipient stage of a fertility transition, where the effect of the sooio-economic variables are mildly felt. Thus, as was explained earlier, there are both endogenous and exogenous changes in the socio-economic standards of the population; neither of them are strong enough to leave an important effect on the levels of fertility or they are as yet not sufficient to enable a great change in the fertility levels of the region. Much of the fertility differentials in the area are explained by demographic variables alone. However, the questions regarding late marriage and contraceptive acceptance are not purely the demographic issues.

NOTES AND REFERENCES

1. Unlike for most states the 1941 Census data for the State of Mysore (Now Karnataka), were published.
2. The marriage arrangements in the villages causes migration where daughters move out to their husband's home mostly in a different village after marriage, and the sons who marry bring in their wives from other villages, thus, making a close to equal trade off leaving no great change in the population size of the village.
3. So far there is no convincing evidence to suggest an increase in the division of joint families in India. See also Caldwell *et al* (1984).
4. These ceremonies for the sons involve hosting a feast for all the people of the village or in larger villages at the least the people of the caste and kinship.
5. Only 45 per cent of the female children aged between 5 and 14 years were found to be in school compared to 63 per cent in the case of male children of the same age.
6. The horoscope is a document containing the time, day, date of birth and associated predictions professionally written by a Brahmin or other High caste priest at the time of the birth. This practice, however, is common only among the relatively High Castes and the urban residents in South India.
7. Mukherjee *op. cit.*, pp. 237-238, has also argued that the falling proportions in the 0-4 years age group for the country as a whole since 1960 seems to be explained by a slight decline in fertility.
8. In the 1961 Census this proportion was reported to be 78 per cent for South India consisting of four states namely Andhra Pradesh, Karnataka, Kerala and Tamil Nadu and a union territory namely Pandichery. The Proportion for the country as a whole was 83 per cent.
9. There is no incidence of legal divorce in this area. There were a few women who reported themselves as separated because they were staying in their parents' home for certain personal reasons. But on many occasions it was found that the husband visited the family periodically at least for a short time. Therefore, the women in the category divorced or separated are all cases of social separation. For further analytical purposes, the categories divorced, separated and widowed are grouped together.
10. There were only two instances in the recent past in Ramagere where the boys parents were not directly involved in arranging the marriages. However, the girls parents were responsible to ceremoniously perform the marriage to meet the required social sanction of marriage.
11. The *gotra* system which is widely practised in South India allows

a marriage alliance between two families of the one castes or sub-caste but a different subdivision or gotra with a fair distance in terms of the lineage and blood relationships. There may exist more than one gotra within one kinship group belonging to a common sub-caste. Therefore, we can speak of caste or sub-caste endogamy and gotra exogamy. This does not prevent marriages to close relatives where the relationship is through females and hence where the gotra is different. With in this pattern of marriage system, a man can marry to his sister's daughter.

12. *Sobana* is a ceremony that allows consummation of marriage to take place.

13. Bangalore Population Centre undertook an experiment to improve the vital registration system called the 'Dual Record System'. This project covered about 300 villages spread out in six districts of Karnataka. The experiment was conducted from early 1977 to late 1980, See for details Shariff *et al*, (1978, 1979).

14. Sterility in this discussion refers to both the primary and secondary sterility. A woman is regarded as a primary sterile if she has never conceived after effective marriage but continue to have a regular sexual relationship with her husband for at least last sixty months. Secondary sterile woman would have had at least one child birth after which time she did not conceive in the last sixty months.

15. Dharma Pāthni means a wife recognized by religion and the society.

16. Since there still is a practice of pre-puberty marriages in the area particularly among the Low Caste Hindus, the age at effective marriage is considered as a better event. All the currently married women were asked to give the age at the firsl sexual union between her husband within marriage.

17. Mukherjee *op. cit.*, p 191, has calculated the mean age for currently married women in India various zones from 1901 to 1961. For the South zone, the mean age was 25.83 in 1901 remained almost constant until 1931, and consistently increased thereafter. He has presented a mean age of 26.66 years for the currently married women of the south zone in 1961.

5

Family Type and its Relationship with Fertility

5.1. Family Type

(i) Introduction

The family is the basis of Indian society. A part from being a social institution, it is the residential, reproductive, productive and consumption unit. It is, therefore, the nucleus of the economic, demographic and social activities. These activities aim at creating incomes to be shared and distributed among the members of the family, procreating and nurturing the next generation to adulthood, and extending protection and shelter to the older generation who have passed beyond the reproductive age. Ordinarily, a person acquires membership of the family by birth, marriage or adoption. The nature of the various relationships and the relative influence of each of the member of the family keeps it as a coherent social unit. As a residential and reproductive unit, the family is subjected to considerable attention in demographic researeh. In a peasant society, like that of study area, the family is a complex institution with numerous functions operating through strong extended ties with the wider social institutions of kinship, clan, caste and the village. It is assumed in the following discussion that the structure of the family largely determines the functions of the individuals within it. While the family in India is exposed to the influences of modernizing economic transformation ; that is changes from a familial to a labour market mode of production, increasingly secular influences of education on the family's division of labour and the intergenerational role relationships, it is also being subjected to both structural and functional disintegration resulting in the erosion of the family's extended relationships and accompanying functions. Because the forces of modernization and education are filtered through the family before they affect individual behaviour, the study of family type become an issue of fundamental importance.

(*ii*) *Importance of Family Structure in Understanding Fertility Behaviour*

In the discussion below, the aim will be to study the nature of the extended (complex) family system through a study of family or households structure. The joint or extended family, which is often referred to as an institution in itself, is considered to be one of the cultural factors favouring high fertility. The theoretical formulations for such a hypothesis were advanced by Lorimer (1954 : 201) and Davis (1955 : 34-36). These formulations about the effect of family structure on fertility postulated the presumed role of the extended family in augmenting fertility. Lorimer based his proposition on the characteristics of the extended family and its socio-economic functions which require the services of many people. Davis explained this in terms of an institutional structure[1] favouring high fertility as a necessity to match a high mortality situation in developing countries. They also assumed that the costs of rapid childbearing would be absorbed by the extended family rather than the parents alone.

Following these formulations many others attempted to systematically study the relationship between fertility and family structure in general, and fertility and the extended family system in particular (Nag 1975, 1965 ; Bebarta 1977, Driver 1963, Burch and Gendell 1970). However, there is no consensus to support the proposition put forward by Lorimer and Davis. Much of the evidence on the fertility effect of the the joint family seem to be contradictory and inconclusive (Caldwell *et al* 1982c). Elsewhere, Lorimer himself speculated that the extended family system may not necessarily stimulate high fertility (1954 : 247),[2] and hence that the fertility in the extended family system may not be higher than in other systems. Nag (1967) also argued that lower coital frequencies in the extended family may in fact counteract the fertility increasing tendencies. Freedman (1968), on the contrary maintained that, due to periodic fission in the joint family resulting in nuclear families, fertility will be lower, but fertility will be lower still in nuclear families. In the Indian situation also the association between family type and fertility is a matter of controversy as there are studies which support both the positive and negative relationships between them. The correlation between family type and fertility does heavily depend on the relationship between development of modernization and family structure.

The analytical discrepancies in the study of family structure seem to arise from two interrelated issues : (i) the lack of a concise and standard definition of the family, and (ii) the lack of consensus on the categorization of family types. This has allowed researchers a great deal of autonomy in categorising family types. An attempt is made in the following to explain the family and family structure in the study area without going into the debate on the functional and structural aspects.

The 'family' ordinarily refers to the members of the household who are related to each other. The United Nations has adopted the definition of the family as "those members of the households...who are related, to a specific degree, through blood, adoption or marriage" (1973 : 337).[3] The emphasis is on the interpersonal relationships between the members of a household. Thus the term family enables us to identify and recognize individuals within a household as distinct persons, where their functions are observed, and their power and authority is evaluated. Nevertheless, in the study area the functional boundaries of a family often appear to go beyond the dwelling place or outside the household. Residential patterns alone do not lead to an understanding of the social structure or the order of kinship, descent and marriage. At best they provide an index of the boundaries of the internal structure of the domestic groups (Fortes. 1958 : 3). Since in in India a family is based on the principles of marriage, sex segregation, caste endogamy and patrilineal relationships, generally the dimensions of the family extends, beyond the place of residence. To be concise the family appears to be an organization of imaginary limits consisting of related persons of a certain degree who ordinarily live within the boundaries of a household.

For analytical quantification the limits to a family demand demarcation. The following hypothetical example helps in this regard. Let us start with a domestic group consisting of a reproductive couple with children. This is a nuclear or conjugal family. Once children reach marriageable age the parents are obliged to arrange their marriage.[4] In the patri-local (virilocal) system the daughter after her marriage leaves her parents' house to join her husband.[5] The family in reference still remains nuclear. In the meantime a son who reaches marriageable age brings in a wife who may live with her parents-in law. The patriarchal system ensures that, 'a wife will reside with her husband if he, or whoever has jural authority over him, has unrestricted rights over her sexual and economic services and her reproductive powers, and children will reside with those who have similar powers over, and the concomitant responsibilities towards them' (Fortes *op cit* : 4 ; See also Paige and Paige 1981). The addition of the daughter-in-law makes the family a 'stem family' consisting of two couples belonging to different generations. At a later date the younger couple may move to a separate residence for reasons like crowding, arrival of another couple,[6] rift between the family members especially the mother-in-law, and the daughter-in-law or simply the intention to live separately. Under these circumstances, in spite of the formation of a separate household (structural separation), strong relationships continue to be maintained with the family of orientation which keep both the families so close as to make it difficult to distinguish functionally between the two. Therefore, there is considerable speculation as to whether the newly formed family of the kind mentioned above can be called a conjugal or nuclear family at all (see for example, Kapadia 1959 : 73). Goode (1963 : 243), however, rejects this argument on the grounds that if this definition is used it will make even all western families 'Joint families'. The continued relationships in this context are usually the mutual rights and obligations, emotional, social and economic interdependence and required consultations for decision-making. The family orientation always tries to exert its control over the subordinated family to maximize its power and prestige as well as to ensure support in the future days when the couple is old. Such relationship, however, depends on the strength of the continuation of filial ties, transfer or extension of relative power and authority and the level of social and economic interdependence. All of these relationships depend on the composition of the families and their cultural and traditional strengths, wealth, social prestige and pattern of the division of family property and the family. This kind of physical separation of members of the original family eventually decreases the intensity and frequency of social contact to the extent that the integration becomes weaker after a period of time (Goode 1963 : 247).

It is ordinarily held, that it is the subdivided family which subordinates to the family of orientation to receive help and protection from the other. This was so because the division of the joint property used to take place much later than the separation of the living arrangments. It is the timing of division of joint family which is important, especially whether the division is before or after the patriarch death. Though it appears that there is no hurry for the division of the joint property after the death of patriarch (Caldwell *et al* 1984), among the land owing families, the sub-division of land is taking place even before the death of father because the father himself intend to do a just distribution of the joint property thus avoiding a confrontation between sons over the property rights. Such a division becomes much easier if there are no daughters of marriageable age. Among the landless and trading communities of the area the division of family and other estates occur at the time of a marriage especially when a second or subsequent son gets married. Nevertheless, in the recent times it appears that the effort of the family of orientation is to keep control over the newly formed family after an inevitable consequence of the division of the family, because the newly formed family possesses a greater economic potential due to the relative young age pattern of the male members who are economically more active.[7] The two families, however, project their independence through separate dwellings, cooking food separately, having different budgets and maintaining personal independence. In the meantime the conjugal bond between the husband and wife strengthens, and there emerges a pattren of co-operative and even independent decisions with regard to many issues like the frequency of coitus, abstinence and the regulation of the wife's visits to her natal home.

On the other hand the elders intend to control such matters as purchases, sales, marriage, fertility, and celebrations which are traditionally the business of old. In the extended family system, help from other elder relatives is required in matters like mate selection, raising funds for the marriage and for marriage arrangements. Subsequently, aspects of the timing of sexual intercourse of the newly weds, bride's visit to her parents' place and various kinds of post-marriage sexual abstinence are controlled by the older parents or the eldest women in the kinship. When the child is born the child care is regarded a collective task of the older women and the mother. Apart from these matters, the major religious and ancestral celebrations are also controlled by the old parents. Thus, even after the division, the older parents try to keep control over some or all of these, although their relative influence by then is weak. Threfore, the study of the extended family relations becomes essential to the study of fertility and fertility decision-making. Some of these aspects are further discussed in chapter 7 and 8 of this thesis.

Freedman (1961-62 : 51) and Burch and Gendell (1970 : 232) have advocated studies at the societal level as appropriate to establish the relationship between family type and fertility. This calls for categorising societies based on the extended or nuclear family system. But the caution advanced by Goody (1958) and by Nag (1975 : 29), is that, though a particular family type is preferred, it need not necessarily be the norm, because of the developmental cycle through which the family passes so that its structure is subjected to voluntary and involuntary transformation. Therefore, the predominant family type need not necessarily have the greatest influence on the social system. This is true in the case of south India. Though it is the nuclear family which dominates numerically, it would be wrong to this society as nuclear oriented at the societal level because of the greater influence of the extended family system on the entire society. Such an approach seems to be advisable to establish the relationship between the family systems and fertility, but for our purpose of understanding decision-making patterns yet another approach is required. The differences in family type within a given society and culture seem to influence the fertility decision-making in independent households. We are interested in investigating how couples behave in a given socio-cultural environment of the family which are the micro-cultural elements, rather than of the whole society. It is well recognized here that these micro-cultural elements are in fact derived from the macro-cultural or societal elements of the prevailing culture. We are also interested in identifying who, among so many relatives and kin, are responsible for the family decisions. Therefore, in the following we discuss in detail various types of the family found in the study area and identify examples to understand the decision-making patterns.

(iii) Discussion : Family Type in the Study Area

The families in the study area are divided into two major categories, namely Simple and Complex, which are further sub-divided into different sub-types. The categories are based on the structure and relationship between the family members and the generation differences. See Table 5.1 for the family type categories and respective definitions found in the study area. Tables 5.2 and 5.3 present in detail the incidence of family types by village and major caste groups respectively.

In the research area as a whole, the simple (nuclear) type of family predominates. Seventy per cent of rhe families are simple in which 65 per cent of the total population lives, however, only 40 per cent of all households are intact nuclear. Another eight per cent of the families have either a single person or unrelated persons in them where only two per cent of the population lives. The remaining 22 per cent are complex families in which thirty-two per cent of all population lives. A little less than three-quarters of all complex families are stem, and about one quarter are joint or stem-joint families. However, only 9 families or 7 per cent of all complex families are polygamous in nature.

TABLE 5.1

List of Family Type Categories and their Structure

TYPE OF FAMILY	FAMILY COMPOSITION
SIMPLE (NUCLEAR) FAMILY TYPES	
1. Intact nuclear	* Husband, wife and unmarried children
2. Extended nucler	* Above family plus other unmarried, widowed of separated relatives who have moved into the family
3. Residual nuclear	* Couple without children, single parents with children
COMPLEX FAMILY TYPES	
STEM FAMILY	
4. Intact stem	* Two couples of different generations
5. Extended stem	* Above family plus other unmarried, widowed or separated relatives
6. Residual stem	* One intact couple, one of the spouses of another couple belonging to a different generation and their children with or without other relatives
JOINT FAMILY	
7. Intact joint	* Two or more couples of the same generation and their children
8. Extended joint	* Above family plus other unmarried, widowed, or separated relatives
9. Residual joint	* From among the couples, one of the spouses in one couple is dead

STEM-JOINT FAMILY

10. Intact stem-joint	* Three or more couples of different generations and their children
11. Residual stem-joint	* Above family with one of the spouses of a couple dead and other relatives may or may not live with them

POLYGAMOUS FAMILY

12. Polygamous nuclear	* Man with two or more wives living at the same time with their children
13. Polygamous stem (none in our area)	* Above family plus another couple of different generation with or without relatives
14. Polygamous joint	* Two or more couples of the same generation and at least one male having more than one wife

OTHER TYPE OF FAMILY

15. Single persons	* Single person
16. Non-family	* Persons living together who are unrelated
17. Other	* Any other type not mentioned above

Three-fifths of the simple families are structurally categorised as 'intact-nuclear', they are simplest in structure and dyadic or conjugal in nature. These families are the result of a disintegration of complex families. This type is just one stage in the family's development cycle. Another one-fifth of simple families are the 'nuclear-extended' type, so categorised because of the presence of an extra related person who is unmarried, widowed or separated.[8] Such relatives have moved into the intact nuclear family to make it an extended type. Fifty-seven or 66 per cent of such families acquired this status when the relative was one of the parents of either the husband or the wife, in this area they are most frequently husband's parents. A little over three-quarters were widowed mothers and in about one-quarter of cases they were widowed fathers. The remaining one-fifth of all simple families are 'nuclear-residual' where a widow lived with her unmarried children, or a couple lives with no children sharing residence with them.

Of all the complex families, three-quarters were found to

be 'stem', in which about 20 per cent of the total population lives. 56 per cent of these are of the 'intact' type consisting of two couples belonging to different generations, the common combination is a older couple living with a married son, his wife and children, together with other unmarried children of the older parents. Another one-tenth of the stem families are of the 'extended-stem' type because of the presence of either an old parent or other relative living with the intact stem family. However, the remaining 34 per cent of the stem are designated as 'residual stem'. The family becomes a residual stem type if one of the spouses of any of the two couples dies or split away from an intact-stem family. The most frequent pattern in the study area is that in which one of the older parent dies leaving behind the widowed spouse who lives with the younger couple. The living spouse in about three-quarters of such instances were widowed mothers and a little over one-quarters were widowed fathers. The difference between the residual-stem type of family and the extended nuclear type is that in case of the former the widowed parents do not move into live with the younger couple, as is the case in extended nuclear families.

In the study area there is a common practice that the old parents, frequently the widowed mothers, move periodically among the families of different sons who live separately. Although this is not an ideal arrangement, it is an effective system which ensures care and support to the old and the responsibility is shared approximately equally by all the sons and in some cases the elder brother of the old woman. The widowed mother may also shift her residence to extend support and train the daughter-in-law during her pregnancy and child birth. Because this practice is common, the prevalence of extended-nuclear families is higher than the residual-stem type. The differentiation between these two types of family is emphasized because the comparative status of the older parent or other relative is lower in the case of the extended nuclear type. Frequently, they are the very old mothers staying with the youngest son. This is because a widow would have had both good and bad experiences while living with her older sons and her expectations are still higher from the sons who have more recently established a new family. The old mother also feels obliged to train the younger daughters-in-law in the craft of family management and living so as to fit into the prevailing culture of the village. The young daughter-in-law also need help in child care and household work which motivates the couples to have a old woman at home. There is a tendency among a greater proportion of younger couples to be better educated and occupationally diversified. As a result, they appear to have a better capacity to support the old dependents as well. However, the presence of a member of the older generation in the nuclear-extended family is not a major force in family decision-making. But, in the case of the residential stem families the older generation seem to have relatively greater capabilities for influencing the younger couple in certain matters like child care (for instance, deciding about the type of medical treatment for an ailing child), enforcing customary as well as post-natal sexual abstinence and the matters relating to certain aspects of household budgets. More often than not such relatives own their share of property or individual wealth which the young are interested in aequiring at a latter date or when the relative dies. It is the existence of this property that explains the fact that a old widow or widower manages to stay within a family. However, the sequal to the above discussion is that the stem families are the families in transition which may eventually transform into more nuclear families or may consolidate to become joint or stem-joint families which eventually may also be transitional.

'Intact joint families' as a category of family type are those where two or more couples of the same generation live together, as in the case of two married brothers who live together with their wives and children. There is only one family in the study area where two married sisters live together along with their husbands, while there is no example of a family in which a married sister shared residence with her brother's family. If other unmarried, widowed or separated relatives join a joint family, the family becomes an 'extended joint' type, whereas the death of one of the spouse makes it a 'residual joint' type. Most complex families in the area are the 'stem-joint' families, in which two married brothers live along with their wives and children, and with both parents.

Only 2.7 per cent (4.5 per cent of the population) and 2.6 per cent (5.8 per cent of the population) of all families in the area are identified as joint and stem-joint respectively. The residential and living arrangements of these families are more a matter of voluntary choice and desire rather than a part of family's developmental cycle. These families are found among the peasants who have large amounts of lands which are being operated as a kind of industry.[9] The economics of scale of the land management is the main reason for the existence of such families. However, some of the male members of these families disclosed that they have met with difficulties in managing a family of such a structure and size, and speculate that their families may split sooner or latter. The heads also feel that it is the division of work and assignment of tasks along with the sensitive aspects of the distribution of resources that threaten the family solidarity. The Panchayat Chairman of Ramagere is also a head of a huge joint family of twenty six persons. His son is the only person who has reached the Pre-university level education in this family, but it is increasingly becoming difficult for the head to provide funds for his son's future education not because the joint family cannot afford it but because it amounts to unequal distribution of the family funds. The same reason is advanced by him for he being not able to buy a motorcycle which is now essential for his movements. His headship of the joint family was one of the attributes which helped in he becoming the Chairman and a continued headship is essential for him to remain in village politics, at the same time he feels that the family division is going to come sooner or latter. In some other joint families the complains are about certain male members of such families who are increasingly taking undue advantage of either spending family funds on personal pleasures, like frequently visiting towns, spending money on recreation and hotels, or that they do not contribute regularly and substantially their productive services or money to the joint family. Nevertheless, one striking fact among most of these families is that the heads need not necessarily be the oldest male member of the family ;

they can be younger but would have demonstrated in the past their skills and expertise in making better judgement and decisions regarding the family affairs. The status and role of women among these families are carefully ranked and duties are allocated to respective individuals. The system works on rigid rules and values. The scope to satisfy individual needs is non existent among these families. The most important characteristic of such families is their economic stability and higher income levels which appears to be the main driving force to live together.

The incidence of polygamous families is negligible in our area : 1.5 per cent of all or 7 per cent of complex families are identified as polygamous in which at least one man had more than one surviving wife (only two in our villages). The decision to bring in another wife ordinarily originate from the childlessness of the first wife. However, there are exceptions to this rule. At least in one Peasant family, the husband confirmed that he brought in a second wife to satisfy his parents' demands to marry the girl of their choice, while the first marriage was an unarranged event. The husband from another Scheduled Caste polygamous family reported that the earnings from two wives were handy and also that he enjoys certain non-working days and there is sufficient money left for his daily drink. In yet another instance the man was forced to marry the younger sister of his wife because of the exposure of his extra-marital relationship with his sister-in-law. There is no instance of polyandry in the study area.

It is clear from the above discussion that the predominant type of family in the research area is 'nuclear' and the common type of complex family is the 'stem family' which is a consequence of the development cycle. Family in this area is subjected to a process of cyclical change ; as a result it is transformed more frequently into the nuclear type followed by the stem type. The transformation to a complex family as a result of the developmental cycle of the family is found to be rare and the existence of a real joint family depends more on a voluntary choice to live together with an intention of either keeping the land intact or to save the labour time of adult females among the families who sell labour for daily wages. These aspects are further investigated below in this chapter.

(iv) Intra-village Differentials in Family Type

While the incidence of family types among the villages follow a similar pattern as discussed above, there are certain intra-village differentials worth examining. Although nuclear families are numerous among all the villages, the incidence of this type of family in the grouped village category (Shivadurga and Gowdahalli) was only 59 per cent compared to 69 per cent in Ramagere and 71 per cent in Laxmipura. The complex families are found to be in a greater proportion (26 per cent) of all families in the last two villages followed by 23 per cent in Ramagere and only 19 per cent in Laxmipura. The stem families are relatively predominant in Ramagere where the proportion was 79 per cent of all the complex families followed by Laxmipura with 65 per cent and only 41 per cent in the last village category. Thus it appears that the practice of living in joint and stem joint families is still strong in the smaller villages where traditional values still persist and family is the main source of labour to the family agriculture, whereas the people prefer to live in nuclear families in the larger or more developed villages. The people of Ramagere, which is a diverse and relatively heterogenous village, have a lower preference for living in joint and stem-joint families as far as residential and economic relations are concerned. While single-person families are most numerous (24 in number) in Ramagere, they are proportionately a little lower than the percentage found in Laxmipura. But the characteristics of these single persons are totally different between villages. While most of the single persons are the officials working in various institutions in Ramagere, they are widowed or separated persons in Laxmipura. This is because the old persons in Ramagere are successful in demonstrating their usefulness and contributing monetarily to the family through child care, leaf plate making and small business which is not the case in other villages.

In Laxmipura, a purely agricultural and relatively better off village, the evidence of the distribution of families according to structure is contradictory to the general notion, that the extended families are characteristics of the land-owing groups (Kolenda 1968 : 342). A recent study present highest prevalence of nuclear families in Mandya district while comparing with two other districts namely Dakshina Kannada and Dharwad. Mandya district is predominantly a rice growing area and also that it has the lowest proportion of landless when compared with other districts mentioned above (Rao *et. al* 1982). It is, however, not the land in isolation that guides the preference to live in a particular type of family but it works in conjunction with the levels of income. The trust in the fertility of land and promising yields in Laxmipura has provided the primary desire among the people of that village to live independently. The contributing factor is that the peasants of this village have adopted modern methods of agriculture to cultivate certain cash crops. Most families in Laxmipura grow cash crops like sugar cane, grapes, watermelons, flowers and vegetables in the lands having access to irrigation. They hire outside labour and rely relatively less on the family labour. Epstein (1962 : 177-178) has found in two South Indian villages, not far from the study area, that the introduction of cash crops created competition between the components of families resulting in the breaking of kinship ties. There is a mistaken emphasis in this remark, as the kinship ties do not break due to such changes ; on contrary they survive and strengthen because of the economic opportunities to be maximized. What seems to happen is the structural division of families without affecting drastically the familial bonds and kinship ties. For example, the three tractors owned by the rich farmers in this area are allocated on a preference basis, although for a price, among immediate relatives before hiring out to the non-relatives and farmers outside the village. Another example is that, since the major source of irrigation is the electrically operated pump irrigation and also that relatives own land adjacent to each other, it requires an extraordinary faith and co-operation among kin and relatives while sharing water. A separate living arrangement, competition between them and a strict accounting system in their dealings is a way of life which is compatible with the

TABLE 5.2

Distribution of Households by Family Type and Village

Type of Family	Ramagere		Laxmipura		S. Durga—G. halli		All villages	
	N	%	N	%	N	%	N	%
NUCLEAR	251	69.0	99	71.2	63	59.2	413	69.6
Intact	143	39.3	58	41.7	39	42.9	240	40.4
Extended	57	15.7	24	17.3	6	6.6	87	14.7
Residual	51	14.0	17	12.2	18	19.8	86	14.5
STEM	65	17.9	17	12.2	10	11.0	92	15.5
Intact	38	10.4	11	7.9	3	3.3	52	8.8
Extended	7	1.9	1	0.7	1	1.1	9	1.5
Residual	20	5.5	5	3.6	6	6.6	31	5.2
JOINT	5	1.4	4	2.9	7	7.7	16	2.7
Intact	3	0.8	0	0.0	3	3.3	6	1.0
Extended	1	0.3	3	2.2	3	3.3	7	1.2
Residual	1	0.3	1	0.7	1	1.1	3	0.5

STEM-JOINT	10	2.7	2	1.4	3	3.3	15	2.6
Intact	7	1.9	2	1.4	2	2.2	11	1.9
Residual	3	0.8	0	0.0	1	1.1	4	0.7
POLYGAMOUS	2	0.5	3	2.2	4	4.4	9	1.5
Nuclear	1	0.3	3	2.2	3	3.3	7	1.2
Stem	1	0.3	0	0.0	1	1.1	2	0.3
OTHER	31	8.5	14	10.1	4	4.4	49	8.2
Single persons	24	6.6	8	5.8	2	2.2	34	5.7
Others	7	1.9	6	4.6	2	2.2	15	2.5
ALL TYPES	364	100-0	139	100.0	91	100.0	594	100.0

TABLE 5.3

Distribution of Households by Family Type and Caste Groups

Type of Family	High Castes		Peasant Castes		Intermediary Service Castes		Low Castes		Non Castes	
	N	%	N	%	N	%	N	%	N	%
NUCLEAR	42	65.6	201	69.8	59	75.6	91	67.4	20	69.0
Intact	22	34.4	121	42.0	33	42.3	53	39.3	11	37.9
Extended	11	17.2	44	15.3	10	12.8	19	14.1	3	10.3
Residual	9	14.1	36	12.6	16	20.5	19	14.1	6	20.7
STEM	10	15.6	44	15.3	10	12.8	24	17.8	4	13.8
Intact	7	10.9	24	8.3	4	5.1	13	9.6	4	13.8
Extended	0	0.0	6	2.1	0	0.0	3	2.2	0	0.0
Residual	3	4.7	14	4.9	6	7.7	8			
JOINT	0	0.0	8	2.8	0	0.0	6	4.4	2	6.9
Intact	0	0.0	1	0.3	0	0.0	4	6.0	1	3.4
Extended	0	0.0	4	1.4	0	0.0	2	1.5	1	3.4
Residual	0	0.0	3	1.0	0	0.0	0	0.0	0	0.0

STEM-JOINT	1	1.6	8	2.8	3	3.8	2	1.5	1	3.4
Intact	1	1.6	5	1.7	2	2.6	2	1.5	1	3 4
Residual	0	0.0	3	1.0	1	1.3	0	0.0	0	0.0
POLYGAMOUS	0	0.0	6	2.1	0	0.0	3	2.2	0	0.0
Nuclear	0	0.0	5	1.7	0	0.0	2	1.5	0	0.0
Stem	0	0.0	1	0.6	0	0.0	1	0.7	0	0.0
OTHERS	11	17.2	22	7.3	6	7.7	9	6.7	2	6.9
Single	11	17.2	16	5.6	3	3.8	3	2.2	1	3.4
Others	0	0.0	6	1.7	3	3.8	5	4.4	1	3.4
ALL TYPES	64	100.0	289	100.0	78	100.0	135	100.0	29	100.0

nature of rural families. The modern developments in agriculture, the intermediary achievements in education and the increase in living standrds appear to strengthen the kin relationships rather than destory them. An apparent increase in the division of family with an increase in agricultural modernization and overall development in fact originates from yet another phenomenon namely decline in mortality. As more children survive to reach their adulthood and the old survive to a higher age, the family splits increase in number and they become inevitable consequence without affecting the familial bonds and kinship ties.

(v) *Caste Differentials in Family Type*

The following analysis of the caste differentials in type of family has to be treated with a certain degree of caution due to the small number of families in the Non-Caste (Muslims) category. However, the analysis is meaningful because of a substantial representation of other caste categories. Most numerous of all in the caste groups is the 'intermediary-Peasant Castes' followed by 'Low Castes'. There is, therefore, a heavy influence of these castes on the overall population. A greater tendency is found among the 'Service Castes' followed by the Peasants and 'Non-Caste' to live in nuclear type families. The 66 per cent of the 'High caste' families which are nuclear represent the lowest proportion. Among them, the incidence of the complex families is also lowest ; only 17 per cent of all their families are complex in structure. This is because the proportion of the High Castes living in the single-person households is the highest. One-quarter of the families each from the Low Castes and the Muslims are found to be complex in nature, which is the largest of the proportions for the caste categories. The lowest incidence of jointness is found among the Service Castes followed by the High Castes : 91 per cent of the complex families among the High Castes are 'stem' in nature and there is only one true joint family from among their total of 64 families. The jointness among the Low Castes who are economically low as well, is relatively high although most (73 per cent) of these are of the stem type. However, the complex families other than the stem type are also highest among the Low Castes of this area. This finding from our research area again refutes the generalization made by Kolenda. *op cit* that the joint families were least charateristics of the untouchables. It is possible, however, that change may have occurred more recently due to acceleration in various types of social and economic change.

In the study area, there are various reasons which can be put forward to explain the low incidence of jointness among the High Castes and a releatively high incidence among the Low Castes. The Brahmins families are the disintegrated families left behind due to a consistent stream of out-migration of the youth from Ramagere. Relatively better educational standards and a readiness to move enabled the Brahmin youths to settle in towns and cities in modern jobs. The persons left behind are the old and often widowed parents on one hand and the Brahmin officials who have come to Ramagere to work in the village level institutions on the other. The two Brahmin complex families consist of two brothers living together along with their children, and even in them the elder of the brothers is a widower. Another major caste included in the High Castes group is the Setty (vaishyas). They are the traders, large businessmen and the money lenders living in Ramagere. They strongly believe that the success of their trade and survival lies in the capacity of individuals rather than the whole family. They also believe that each male member of the family can manage a business of his own. Because of this reason we find that even the unmarried sons manage their own shops and independent businesses, after marriage they are more likely to live in a nuclear type of family and yet retain strong ties with the original family. The only caste among this group which has a tendency to live in large families is the Lingayat but they are too small in number to distort the overall behaviour of this caste category.

In contrast, all the individual castes included in the Low Castes category are poor and many are landless. They live in a separate colony of huts and face a shortage of housing as well. Since all adults and many children of both sexes work as labourers, they have uniform daily incomes. Their life style and expectations in life are not far-reaching. This characteristic, though not necessarily contributing to it, does not hamper their desire to live together. There is a feeling among this section of the population, perhaps the result of a latent emulation of the High Caste behaviour of the past, that it is beneficial to live together. For them, there are certain immediate benefits of living together. Since all work outside home and sometimes travel outside the village, it is always beneficial to leave at least one woman behind on household duties. In a joint living this arrangement works without much loss of wages for the family as a whole. Further, this arrangement helps during illness and disabilities. Another contributing reason for a high prevalence of complex families among Low Castes in Ramagere is the success of the government sponsored *Janatha Housing Scheme* in that village. The allocation of a site and funds for construction is done by a high official at the taluka on the recommendation of the village panchayat. The village panchayat's recommendation on the other hand is based on the assessment of the housing shortage and associated problems faced by the applicant's family. Therefore, many of the Scheduled Castes and other Low Castes live in crowded conditions in small huts and the applicants from such families have a greater chance of getting a Janatha House allotted. The reason appears to have created a spurious tendency among the Low Castes of Ramagere to live together. Because of all these reasons, the propensity to live together among the Low Castes is relatively high : 32 per cent of their families in Ramagere are found to be in complex families which is the highest proportion for any group in the area. One other village study has discovered that joint families were more prevalent among Harijans in Tamil Nadu (see Matthews, 1979 : 67-68 and 89).

The chief obstacles for the joint family living in this area seem to emerge from the diverse individual desires, differing attitude to life, relative differentials in the individual incomes and contacts with outside persons both in and outside village. Peasants in this regard have occupied an intermediary level. Seventy per cent of their families are nuclear, 22 per cent are large, and only 7 per cent are classified as other types. There, however, is a difference between the peasants of Laxmipura and their counterparts in other villages. The incidence of both nuclear and joint living patterns is lowest for the peasants in Laxmipura while a large proportion of 12 per cent, are categorised as 'others' (all single persons). Since there is no single-person family among the peasants of the last two villages the proportion in both nuclear and joint type is relatively higher.

In summary it can be said from the above discussion that, (i) the incidence of jointness is higher among the lower castes and economically poorer section of the population of this area ; (ii) High Castes have responded with a preference for living in the nuclear type of family ; and (iii) the peasants of Laxmipura have a greater proportion of single families as well as stronger motivations to live in nuclear families while the peasants of the smallest villages prefer to live in complex families.

A contradiction, however, arises if one looks into the figures on the family type by annual income and size of land holding. There are equal number of families distributed between nuclear and complex family types for the annual income category of 'rupees ten thousand and above'. The respective proportion for the land holding category 'families owning seven acres of land and above' is 44 and 56 per cent. This anticipated result does not contradict our conclusion because these categories constitute a selected group of families which in fact is the result of jointness rather than the other way round.

5.2 Relation between Family Type and Fertility in The Study Area

(i) *Fertility Index Used in the Analysis*

The fertility index used in this section to explain the relationship between family type and fertility is the *mean number of children ever born* (MCEB). This measure of fertility seems to be less appropriate for such an analysis than the use of age-specific current fertility, like the age-specific fertility or marital fertility rate. This is for two reasons : (a) Current fertility may explicitly reveal the differences if they exist among various family types. In other words, the effect of simple or complex domestic units will be evident in current fertility as an immediate effect which may be more trustworthy if controlled for the duration of stay in particular family units. On the other hand, in case of the MCEB which is in fact the cumulative fertility of a woman's total duration of marriage, the possibility of such a woman having lived in more than one type of family is so great that the fertility differentials cannot be associated with a specific current family type. (b) The completed family size of a woman, irrespective of her current affiliation to a particular family type, may end up at the same level, or inappreciably different, because a majority of women at some stage of the developmental cycle may reside and bear the effects of different family types.

But due to the limitations of data in terms of its size, the use of the age-specific rate is not attempted in this study. Instead the current cumulative fertility index, namely MCEB, is used for following reasons : (a) As opposed to the argument presented above it is worthwhile to search for the differentials in cumulative fertility by type of family if some kind of control is established over the effect of the dynamism in family. (b) The differentials, if they exist, in completed or current cumulative fertility, they are more forcefully established. Current fertility does not completely explain the lasting effect of family type influences gathered along the way of the family's developmental process. There are reasons to believe that the norms evolved during the stay in complex or simple families may be carried on, later to display their effects latently, by which time the couples may have moved to the next phase of the family cycle. (c) By introducing controls over age and the duration of marriage it is possible to investigate the impact of family type on the fertility patterns at different age levels of the women.

(*i*) *Findings : Family Type and Fertility*

In the following analysis, the grouping and re-grouping for age and family type categories is done deliberately and freely. This is for two reasons ; firstly, to find out the variations from different combinations of women whose characteristics terms of various dependent and independent variables used are meaningful, and secondly, to minimize as far as possible the effect of fluctuation due to small size, particularly where there are less than ten cases in a category. The currently married women identified from all the four villages have been distributed into fourteen specific types of family category. This is presented in Table 5.1 and clearly reveals the predominance of women living in nuclear families. For the sake of convenience in presenting data, the family types have been re-grouped into two main categories. While doing this, the women belonging to category 'Others' have been excluded. All women in categories 1, 2 and 3 are grouped as women living in *simple* family type and the rest are grouped as those living in *complex* families. The word complex instead of joint or large is used here only to indicate the presence of at least one more adult member who, as we will see later, is likely to be involved in the decision making procsss in the family.

Sixty-nine per cent of all the currently married eligible women lived in the nuclear or simple family type while only 31 per cent lived in non-nuclear or complex type of family at the time of the survey. The age distribution of all women follows the pattern of an inverted curve but towards the younger age groups. However, instead of a peak, the curve is rather flat on the top. The mean age of all the women is found to be 29 years, the women in simple families are on an average 1.5 years older while their counterparts in complex families are 1.8 years younger. Probably the most important issue in this discussion is that of the proportion of women in younger and intermediary reproductive ages found in different residential systems. It is clear from Table 5.5 that the proportion of women aged 15-19 years is almost two-and-a-quarter times higher in complex families. The combined proportion for the first two age groups is found to be 53 per cent in the complex type. This proportion is important for our analysis because such a pattern is attributed to the cultural factors prevailing in this area. It is to be expected because in a large number of cases in rural areas the sons after marriage choose for virilocal residence. This is one of the rules of family formation in the Indian sub-continent with the exception of a few com-

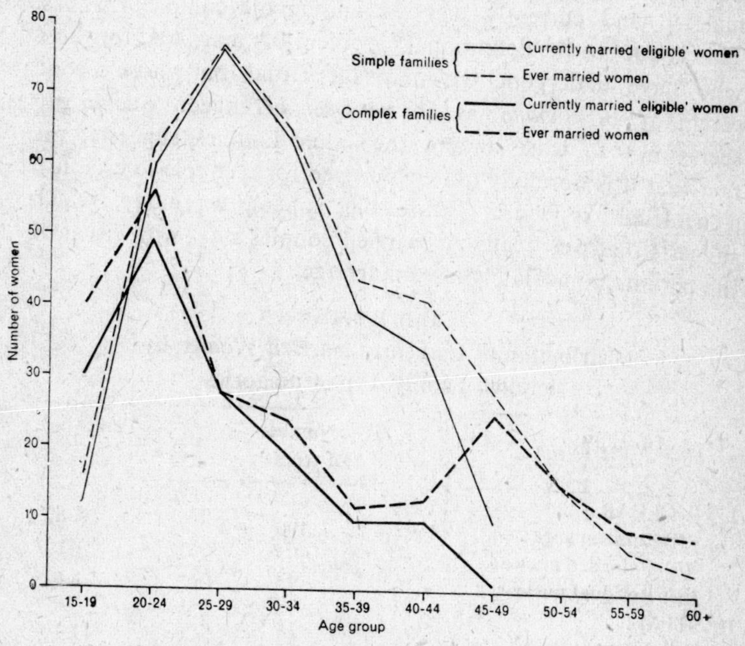

Distribution of All Ever-Married and Currently Married Women by Family Type of Current Residence

FIGURE 5.1

munities in Kerala and the north-eastern provinces where the matrilineal family systems exists at least in a weak form.

Figure 5.1 is plotted two show the distribution of ever married and currently married women, both as defined in Chapter 4, according to the residential affiliation to simple or complex types of family. In the younger age groups one notices a considerable gap between the segments of ever married and currently married among the complex families. This is due to the definitional problem of marriage, for those who have undergone the marriage ritual but whose second ceremony or *Sobana* has not yet been arranged. Such a gap seems not to exist among the simple families, suggested the fact that it is normally not encouraged for a couple to establish a neolocal residence before the sobana ceremony, which suggests that practically all married couples stay with either of the parents immediately after marriage.

TABLE 5.4

Distribution of Currently married Women by detailed Family Type Categories

Type of Family	Number of women	Percentage
I. NUCLEAR		
(i) Intact nuclear	196	43.9
(ii) Extended nuclear	75	16.8
(iii) Residual nuclear	25	5.6
II. STEM		
(i) Intact stem	52	11.7
(ii) Extended nuclear	8	1.8
(iii) Residual nuclear	26	5.8
III. JOINT		
(i) Intact joint	7	1.6
(ii) Residual joint	12	2.7
IV. STEM-JOINT		
(ii) Intact stem-joint	2	0.4
(ii) Residual stem-joint	21	4.7
V. POLYGAMOUS		
(i) Polygamous nuclear	6	1.3
(ii) Polygamous stem	8	1.8
(iii) Polygamous joint	3	0.7
VI. OTHERS		
(iii) Others	5	1.2

TABLE 5.5

Percentage Distribution of Currently married Women by Age and Family Type

Age Groups (years)	All Women %	N	Per cent in simple family
15—19	9.2	41	31.7
20—24	24.3	107	57.0
25—29	24.0	106	75.5
30—34	18.8	83	78.3
36—30	11.4	50	82.0
40+	12.3	54	81.5
All ages	100.0		68.9
Average age	29.0		30.5

Note : Average of women in Complex families is 27.2.

It is also clear from this graph that the curve for women in simple families starts from a lower level for both groups of women when compared to the complex families even in absolute numbers. The shape of the curve reveals that women immediately after marriage live in complex families where ordinarily there will be an old woman, most frequently the mother-in-law of the bride, which is evident from a second peak at the end of the curve for the ever-married women of the complex family type. By age 25 or so the daughter-in-law split away and move into simpler conjugal types of families which is represented by a steep increase in the number of women aged between 20 and 34 years, the peak is found for the women in age group 25—29 years. Elsewhere in Chapter 8 we have calculated from a selected sample of families that on an average a couple stays for nine years immediately after marriage in the extended (stem or joint) type of families before permanently establishing a nuclear household. However, this duration is only six and half years if all the families of the area are considered.

In the following discussion, we will look into variations in fertility by age and family type. This helps us understand not only cumulative fertility but also completed fertility and the tempo by which the fertility levels are achieved. The first panel in Table 5.6 present the fertility index by shorter age groupings. The age standardized MCEB is substantially greater among the women in simple families in all age groups but for the last category of 40+ years. There is a steep and disproportionate rise in fertility for women above forty years of age living in complex families. This discrepancy may be due to the small number of women in the age groups 35—39 and 40+ years. However, the age standardized MCEB for women of all ages retain a substantial differential of 0.7 child per woman favouring women in simple families. To eliminate the effect of small numbers the ages were regrouped into only three broad age categories which are presented in panel two of the table. From this it is fairly clear that the fertility in the younger ages is considerably higher for the women in simple families whereas the older women in complex families seem to catch up ending at almost same level of completed fertility as the case among the older women of simple families. Thus the older women living in complex families seem to retain a greater motivation for reproduction at least to reach the level of their counterparts in simple families. Younger women living in simple families may experience a higher coital frequency than their counterparts living in complex families, while the frequency of sexual intercourse may increase for women in complex families after a period of time by which time the women have entered the higher age groups. Another way of looking this phenomenon is that it is because of the past high fertility that the old women enter into complex (stem) families and not because of stem family that they have high fertility in later part of the married life. This argument, however, supplement the above explanation and partiallly explains the movement of a couple out of the complex family.

To obtain an additional comparison, the ages are further re-grouped to only two groups which are presented in panel three of the table. Even here it is clearly evident that the reproduction among the older women living in complex families is quite high. The table confirms the fact that women living in complex families are subject to the strict and closely supervised enforcement of norms and taboos relating to abstinence and prolonged breast feeding practices which is believed to increase

TABLE 5.6

Mean Number of Children Ever Born to Currently Married Women by Age and Family Type

Age Groups (years)	Simple MCEB	Simple N	Complex MCEB	Complex N	Complex Stem MCEB	Complex Stem N	Complex Joint MCEB	Complex Joint N
(i)								
15—19	0.9	13	0.3	28	0.5	22	0.2	6
20—24	1.9	61	1.3	46	1.3	34	1.3	12
25—29	3.0	80	2.6	26	2.6	11	2.5	15
30—34	4.7	65	4.0	18	3.8	11	4.3	7
35—39	5.3	41	4.4	9	4.3	6	4.7	3
40+	5.6	44	6.6	10	8.2	5	5.0	5
All Ages	3.7	304	2.3	137	2.1	89	2.6	48
Standardized MECB	3.7		3.0		3.1		3.0	
(ii)								
15—24	1.7	74	1.0*	74	1.0*	56	1.0*	18
25—34	3.8	145	3.2*	44	3.2*	22	3.3*	22
35+	5.5	85	5.6*	19	6.2*	11	4.8*	8
(iii)								
15—29	2.4	154	1.7*	100	1.6*	67	1.8*	33
30+	5.2	150	4.9*	37	5.0*	22	4.6*	15

* Standardized by age within the respective age range against simple family type

N-Number of women

the chance of child survival. The younger women in a complex family may experience only irregular sexual unions because of the shortage of space, poor housing and the presence of many others at home. But as the couple grows older, they assume new responsibilities, acquire relatively enhanced powers and a greater say in decision-making in family matters, and by that time, as a consequence, also acquire increased privacy and better living arrangements.

Another argument, supplementary to the above finding, is that the women (men as well), irrespective of their living in a specific type of family, express a preference for a certain level of desired family size which is uniform. This seems to be highly rational in view of two important issues, one relating to sex preference and the other being a result of fairly high levels of infant mortality. Two sons and a daughter is the most preferred combination of living children in the area. Given an equal probability of the birth of a male or a female child, on an average five live births may well be needed to achieve this (for more on this aspect see May and Heer, 1968 and Krishnamoorthy, 1974). There still is a possibility that a child of the preferred sex will not survive until adulthood because of high infant mortality of around 110 per thousand live births in this region. Therefore, couples tend to have more than the desired number of children to attain the minimum number of children preferred of each sex. A considerable difference in the desired family size argument presented above and the level of desired family size reported by surveys arises from conceptual variations. The concept of desired family size presented above includes the risk of child loss before reaching adulthood, whereas survey results often give the impression that only living children are being referred to. Thus it seems that at least at a sub-conscious level the desired family size exerts a greater influence on the completed fertility of the women than any other attributes, socio-economic or otherwise.

Page (1977 : 85) has demonstrated the usefulness of decomposition by marriage duration of fertility schedules. In our analysis too, marital duration is an important variable which partly explains the differentials in the tempo of the fertility by age and between family types. The following analysis is aimed at bringing in the role of marital duration in determining the levels of fertility. Table 5.7 which presents age standardized MCEB by age and marital duration supports the proposition presented above. Among the women living in complex families and who have been married for less than five years the standardized MCEB is half of the level found among their counter-

TABLE 5.7

Mean Number of Children Ever Born to Currently Married Women by Age, Marital Duration and Family Type

Age Groups (years)	Marital Duration 0-5 years MCEB	N	5-9 years MCEB	N	Above 10 years MCEB	N	All MCEB	N
(I) Simple Families								
15—24	0.8	23	1.8	43	3.8	8	1.7	75
25—34	0.5	2	2.2	22	4.1	121	3.8	145
35+	0.0	0	0.0	0	5.5	85	5.5	85
All Ages	0.8	25	1.9	65	4.6	214	3.7	304
(II) Complex Families								
15—24	0.0	45	1.8	29	0.0	0	0.9	74
25—34	2.0	1	2.4	12	3.5	31	3.2	44
32+	0.0	0	0.0	0	5.6	19	5.6	19
All Ages	0.4	46	2.0	41	4.3	50	2.3	137
standar—dized MCEB*	0.4		1.9		5.2		2.9	

* Standardized against the Simple family type.

N-Number of women

parts in the simple families. But the women of 5-9 years marital duration irrespective of family type exhibit the same level of MCEB which is possible either by speeding up births through the deliberate reduction of the length of birth intervals by the women belonging to complex families or that certain women with higher fertility have moved into the complex families which is least likely in the research area. This demonstrates two facts : firstly, that the status and role of married women slowly changes with time and the couples tend to become less influenced by external pressures and more motivated to take their own decisions, with regard to coital frequency, abstinence periods and length of breast feeding ; and secondly, that other members of complex family themselves may encourage couples to accelerate child bearing, because by then relatives would realize that the young couple is lagging behind in child bearing. The application of the *reference group hypothesis* is appropriate to this situation. There is a strong tendency among the village people to watch and scrutinize what neighbourers do and the reference group acts as a consultative body. The intentions to accelerate or decelerate the rate of family growth are the reflections of the behaviour from other couple of the same generation, most often from their own married brothers and sisters and near kin of same ages. The fertility of women belonging to complex families who are married for longer than ten years is higher in the research area. Nevertheless, the grand mean number of children ever-born is just 2.9 for the women in complex families when compared to 3.7 for the women in the simple families.

The education of women appears to have a considerable impact on their reproductive behaviour in combination with the type of family in which they live. Illiterate women living in simple families have a clear edge over women in all other categories at any age in their level of achieved fertility, and the tempo of change in fertility is highest among the illiterate women living in complex families who catch up to the level of their counterparts living in simple families (see Table 5.8). The fertility level of literate women appears to be moderate and the achieved level is significantly lower when compared with their counterparts in the illiterate category. Nevertheless, the literates who live in complex family demonstrate higher fertility over their sisters living in simple families in age groups less than 25 and 25 to 34 years. This paradox is difficult to explain, yet two issues provide a clue in understanding the situation. Firstly, the infant and childhood mortality for those literate women who live in complex families could be lower, because besides the benefit of mother's education, there will be other experienced people helping in child care activities including quicker response to illness and other child problems. (see Table 4.8, in which it is found that the proportion of sons and daughters surviving is substantially higher among the educated women). Secondly, the elders are less likely to enforce traditional abstinence and prolonged breast feeding periods on the educated daughters-in-law in which case the fertility in early periods will be higher compared with those educated women in simple families who face the opportunity cost problem as well as the problem of securing support during pregnancies. A relatively low fertility of educated women living in simple type of family appears to arise not only from the fact that they have less support from others but also that the motivation to control fertility is higher.

TABLE 5.8

Mean Number of Children Ever Born to Currently married Women by Age, Literacy and Family Type

Age groups	Illiterates		Literates	
	Simple	Complex	Simple	Complex
<25 years	2.1	0.7	1.1	1.6
25-34 years	3.9	2.7	3.3	3.8
> 35 years	6.1	5.8	3.9	4.2

* Figures are standardized against the total women within the respective age groups.

In the following we provide a pattern of age, age at marriage and education and portion of women living in different family types which helps in understanding the above discussion. As mentioned elsewhere, the practice of pre-puberty and early marriage still dominates many families across the cross-section of the population. The 589 ever married women are distributed according to their current age and age at marriage in Table 5.9. Age at marriage is broadly categorised into two : 'pre-puberty or immediate post-puberty marriages before 14 years of age' and 'post-puberty marriage after 14 years of age'. Fourteen years is assusmed to be the age at which girls ordinarily attain puberty. We found that thirty per cent of younger women aged less than 30 years, and 37 per cent of older women aged 30 years and over were married at an age

age less than 14 years of which a substantial proportion of marriages were arranged before the bridge attained puberty. There is a slight decrease in the proportion of early marriages as evident from the above percentages, although there are substantial changes as to who are more likely now than in the past to arrange early marriage in terms of their caste identity. Interestingly over five-sixth of all those who had early marriages were illiterates in contrast to only two-thirds who got married after 14 years of age. The younger women in the early marriage category are the ones who are likely to continue in complex families longer and also experience low fertility while young. On the contrary, women who get marry later are releatively more likely to be educated and less likely to continue in complex family structure for long but are more likely to have experienced relatively higher fertility in young ages before they move into simple family structure. A supporting explanation is that the couples who get marry at younger age are closely guarded and guided, and the sexual intercourse is in fact arranged by the elders especially when the girl has recently attained puberty. Such wives are generally less knowledgeable about sex, they are shy and governed by female modesty which reduces the frequency of coitus and consequently reduce fertility at younger ages (Rindfuss and Morgan 1983 ; See also Nag, 1972). Nevertheless, at the very early period after puberty the women are known to be subfecund, and the effect of complex family living may start only after the woman has acquired normal reproductive capabilities. Although 34 per cent of all marriages were performed before the age of fourteen and a substantial proportion was pre-puberty marriages, it appears that there is a slow increase in the age at marriage. It has also been observed from the marriages which were arranged during the course of field work in the area that the boy and the girl had already met and loved each other before the marriage ceremony. The average age of these brides was far more higher and the age differential between husband and wife was substantially lower. This suggest that there is a change towards an increase in the aspects of sexuality of young which is known to speed up fertility in the early period after marriage. If the age at marriage of the girl is above twenty years it is logical both on the part of the couple as well as others to ensure births sooner and at shorter intervals.

Although this analysis is not sufficient either to reject or maintain the hypothesis that the extended or joint family system encourages high fertility, it is an attempt to provide a consistent pattern of relationship between fertility and family type. This analysis, however, puts forward issues which have to be further investigated.

TABLE 5.9

Distribution of all Ever Married Women by current age and age at marriage

Age at Marriage	Current Age	
	Less than 30 years	30 years and over
All Ever Married Women	305	284
1. Number of women who had pre-puberty or immediate post-puberty marriage before 14 years of age	96	106
Per cent literatres	15.7	13.2
Per cent currently living in Simple families	41.7	63.2
2. Number of women who had post-puberty marriage after 14 years of age	209	178
Per cent literates	34.5	26.4
per cent currently living in simple families	48.1	61.2

NOTES AND REFERENCES

1. Davis explains that under the extended family system, marriage occur early, the young woman is pressurised to bear many children as soon as possible, the couple is motivated to have many offspring early because they raise the family's social status and the cost of child rearing does not fall on parents alone. All these favour a high fertility.
2. Lorimer acknowledged the fact that the extended family, if disasso-

ciated from the emphasis on competitive relations or values, does not enforce pressures towards high fertility.

3. This definition, adopted by the United Nations in their publication 'Determinants and Consequence of Population Trends Vol. I,' heavily draws upon the definition given by Burgess and Locke (1953).
4. Practically all the marriages in rural south India are negotiated and arranged by the parents or the elders in the family partly because of the traditional practice of transfer and exchange of wealth, money and gifts of a substantial value and quantity, and also in an effort to keep the purity of caste endogamy. The arranged marriage has other results as well : for instance, the ability to choose the new daughter-in-law and to make more effective the control of the younger generation.
5. Daughters after marriage lose their membership in the parental house. They become members of the husband's family on marriage where they are expected to live, serve and, if required, contribute to the new family. This feature is characteristic of the patrilineal family. But the daughters are allowed periodically to visit their natal homes on certain occasions like child birth, marriage of other relatives, celebrations and rituals.
6. There however, is no standard norm or rule as to who of the two or more married brothers move out of the extended family. This arrangement largely depends on the emotional and economic obligations between the couples belonging to older and the younger generations. Yet there appears to be a tendency where the oldest married brother stays while others move out.
7. Many couples belonging to the newly emerged nuclear families are relatively better educated and work in non-traditional occupations thus securing better incomes.
8. This category appears to be a stem type of family in its structure but functionally it will be misleading to categorize it as stem family for reasons discussed in the following. This is the main reason as to why the proportion of simple families are higher in the research as classified by the investigator when compared with the proportions normally provided by others. See for example Reddy (1978), who presents the proportion of nuclear families to be 57.3 per cent. In fact in Table 5.2 if we add 14.7 per cent, the proportion of nuclear-extended to that of all stem we get a total of 30.2 per cent stem families which is almost equal to the proportion provided by Reddy, and we will also have the proportion of all simple families to be 54.9 which are close to his figures. Reddy's figures are for a larger area of the southern Karnataka, however, it is not clear whether he excluded the single person families and families in unclassified categories from the nuclear family category.
9. The argument is that the people choose to live together to keep the land area undivided.

6

The Family Planning Programme in the Research Area

A brief overview of the family planning programme in India and in the state of Karnataka is presented in Appendix I. What follows is a worm's eye view of the people's perception, their reaction and related issues of the family planning programme in four south Indian villages selected for this study.

6.1 People's Perception and Societal Norms Regarding Family Planning

Normally, family formation in this area is governed by physiological and cultural rules. Pregnancy and child birth are regarded as physiological phenomena which are controlled and regulated by cultural and spiritual norms. The family planning programme which intervenes in the tempo and size of family formation does not fit into either the biological or the cultural frame of rules. Rather it is visualized as an exogenous factor. Ordinarily, rural couples perceive contraception as unnecessary, unnatural, inconvenient, disruptive, expensive and dangerous. In over thirty years the family planning programme has no doubt done much to popularize the small family norm at the societal level, yet there seems to have been only a mild impact on the cultural values associated with uninterrupted pregnancies and consequent births. The view that family planning is essentially an administrative and medical programme still persists. Accepting contraception as a behavioural issue (Marshall, 1972 : 3), it seems clear that ineffective practice and non-acceptance is the result of a pervasive attitude that family planning is artificial and that it interferes in the natural process (Gould, 1969). Nevertheless, a woman having many children born within short intervals have always been subjected to shame, but if she has many sons among these children she is applauded. The practice of couples abstaining from sex after birth in the early period of married life is not necessarily a means for prolonging the duration between successive births rather it is to safeguard maternal and child health.

In the study area abstinence periods are enforced upon couples by the elders and certain couples practice it when they are old. There are various kinds and different periods of abstinence, such as the period between the marriage ceremony and *sobana*, abstinence during the days of *Ashada*, one of the months in fall season, and many other short durations spread all over year particularly during festivals and on certain specific dates. The traditional abstinence taboo is also imposed on couples for a person ranging from a few days to many months after a death in the family or kinship network. The reasons for abstinence are many. It supposedly is helpful in timing the birth of a child : for instance, to avoid the birth of a child during the peak agricultural season or a period when the child is more likely to be susceptible to certain diseases and ailments like measles, chicken pox, diarrhoea and eye infections. The role of abstinence as a means for increasing the birth intervals in an effort to minimize the risk of infant death and also debilitation to the mother was also identified (see Caldwell *et al*, 1982a). It is believed to work as a control to limit the conjugal bond from strengthening between the husband and the wife which is seem as a threat to authority and future support to the older generation. However, every facility is made available for the newly wedded couple to have privacy especially to ensure a pregnancy anticipating the birth of male child. The couples who have a large number of children and who are skeptical about the use of modern contraceptives also reported a predominant practice of sexual abstinence more as a matter of religion and tradition. Nevertheless, the women from this group of couples were often old and nearing menopause.

A section of the population still employ one argument or another emphasizing the value and use of an additional child. The current practice of contraception in the area is found among 20 per cent of the currently married women, yet contraception is considered a rich man's comfort. The following views highlight this issue :

> Before my tubectomy operation I would have managed to eat *Ragi balls* and *Chilly curry*, but after the tubectomy I have to eat good and nutritious food. As we cannot afford such good food, it is difficult to perform hard work. [Ramagere, case 164]

> Tubectomy and family planning is a luxury for the rich. They can afford to take care of their health, avoid hard work and eat nutritious food. They also take long periods of rest after delivery and the tubectomy operation. [Ramagere, case 312]

Accepting family planning especially tubectomy is considered a serious form of health hazard which is expensive to control. This impression among some sections is true because a tubectomized woman spends more money on her health than what she receives as free medical aid and incentives. Because of complications, at least seven women have spent over two hundred rupees on travel to various hospitals and medicine, within few weeks of sterilization in Ramagere.

Family planning is identified by both males and females of the area as *hengasara operationau*, which literally means female operation (tubectomy). A few people who have favourable attitudes towards family planning nevertheless believed they would have difficulty in accepting contraception. The following behaviour is normally considered essential but difficult to follow if one is accepting tubectomy : (a) increased nutrition both before and after sterilization is essential but beyond their reach ; (b) a substantial duration of rest from work, especially from outside and manual labour, is essential but not practicable ; and (c) a relatively long period of post-sterilization sexual abstinence is desirable. Concern about the consequences of the latter two issues was expressed frequently by the husbands of the eligible women.

It is possible to list certain norms regarding contraception which have been derived from over two decades of family planning history in the area especially in Ramagere. The norms presented below are drawn from the case-histories and an effort is made to describe the beliefs which are found at large among the people of the community.

1. People perceive family planning as a means for limiting family size and the concept of spacing is absent from their understanding. In a way people consider the acceptance of family planning as an end in itself rather than a means to plan future births and the well-being of their children. Temporary family planning methods are viewed as inappropriate for the community needs and requirements, whereas sterilization is thought to be a resort finally adopted. Non-terminal methods are believed to be unreliable, troublesome, inconvenient and harmful. The use of the condom is shameful and subjected to ridicule if known by others and the IUD is regarded as extremely harmful. These methods, while in use, lead to a feeling of detachment and embarrassment between the conjugal couple. The exceptions were a couple who endorsed the use of the IUD for spacing births and two other husbands who used condom so as to be able to resume coitus sooner after child birth. There are a few other irregular condom users in Ramagere. The husband whose wife did use an IUD for spacing purpose is a college educated Lingayat and is a teacher in the local high school [Ramagere, case 217]. The decision to accept an IUD after the first birth was taken by the husband on the advice of doctors after experimenting with safe period, oral pills and condom. The IUD was

expelled only three weeks before the interview in order to bear another child anticipating a birth of son while the first child is a daughter. The husband's concern was whether to continue with the IUD or go for sterilization after the birth of a son. He complained that the health personnel including the medical doctors glorify the advantages and do not provide sufficient knowledge about the relative disadvantages and post-operative complications of various methods.

The condom users are intermediate caste Hindus involved in small trade who are exposed to the outside world. They live in conjugal families and have relatively few relatives in this village [case histories 258 and 75]. They did confirm that they use condom not with the intention to stop a conception nor to space the next child birth, but that it was convincing for both the husband and the wife to resume coitus sooner without risking the believed danger of spoiling the breast milk. This phenomenon highlights the change in the attitudes of the young about the sex and traditional abstinence. Nevertheless, a method which is believed to interfere with normal sexual activity seems inappropriate particularly in this community where women have little control over men's sexual behaviour. Terminal methods are convenient to these people as they put to rest the issue once for all, but the decisions regarding the acceptance of a terminal methods are the most difficult and pass through various phases which are described in Chapters 7 and 8.

2. Contraceptive intervention is normally discouraged for those couples who do not have at least two sons and a daughter because of the fear of the woman becoming sterile and some of the children dying. This fear originates because all the family planning methods are suspected of causing permanent incapacity to procreate similar to the effect of tubectomy and vasectomy. Such a feeling is the result of an overemphasis on the stopping of future births because of defective communication by the family planning programme. Overemphasizing the advantages of tubectomy on one hand and granting women the status of target population in itself is a defective approach, instead of providing information on a range of family planning methods already available and

making family as the target of the programme. While these misconceptions are present in the cross-section of the population it is found predominating among the Low Castes of both Ramagere and Laxmipura and among all families in the remote villages.

3. A common stipulation among the people is that a woman below twenty-five or above thirty-five years of age need not seek tubectomy or any other method. A young woman undergoing tubectomy is believed to take a greater risk of her life whereas a woman above thirty five is already old and is unlikely to conceive any more. It is the cash incentive scheme which attracted older women to contracept ; otherwise it was unlikely that they would have accepted tubectomies. Some older couples resort to abstinence because of the belief that it ensures the physical and spiritual wellbeing of the couple and also helps to avoid births in old age. But accidental births due to the failure of abstinence are not regarded as unwanted.

4. The general feeling in the population is that it is convenient if a woman undergoes tubectomy during her post-partum period. This avoids the problem of her taking additional rest from work and seeking help once again from relatives during the operative and post-operative periods. On the other hand programme personnel normally advise that the child should be sufficiently grown before the woman undergoes sterilization, and they prefer the child to be at least three months old. However, the majority of the sterilizations in the area are performed in the post-partum period mainly because the women undergoing tubectomy already have a large number of surviving children.

5. The IUD is rejected as a family planning method because of the rumours concerning the after-effects. The wife of a famous state level politician who is an Ediga is referred to by all others in Ramagere as an example (Ramagere, case 325). This Ediga woman was one of the first few to accept the IUDs in Ramagere in mid 1960s. Because of a close political and agriculutural affiliation between the Ediga and Balagiga castes, this early example of IUD acceptance was immediately followed by many Balagiga families and a few other Peasant Castes.

But practically all in the village say that the woman died from cancer which is believed to have been caused by the IUD. The IUD was expelled after a fairly long duration of use, when the woman was reaching menopause. Her son whose wife is tubectomized, reported that she died of cancer not attributable to her past use of the IUD. But the rumours against the IUD are widespread and people have repudiated it. Two other reasons for a decline in IUD acceptance are : (a) that the past acceptors complain of a high incidence of back and spinal ache which apparently kept many women out of work for many days ; and (b) that the IUD is belived to cause extra-menstrual bleeding, which makes them unclean for a longer period than the normal duration and unable to perform household duties especially cooking. In this area it is noticed that a menstruating woman spends most of her time outside home, either in the back yard and in the veranda or front court yard. It is, however, observed that in Ramagere there are some couples who are the potential users of the IUD, they are the educated and belong to bureaucratic and elite groups of the village. During the field work none was found to be a current IUD user in Ramagere. The Vokkaliga couples of Laxmipura and others in the remote villages were never impressed with the usefulness of the IUD largely because the idea did not enter these villages due to the absence of a leader in accepting IUD and demonstrating its advantages or disadvantages. Note that there are some Vokkaliga, Golla, Kuruba and Bovi families in Ramagere but none took a lead in accepting the IUDs which probably would have taken the message of IUD to other villages being discussed.

6. For men, using the condom is inconvenient because of its repetitive and sexually dependent nature. They also fear that if it is known by others they will be ridiculed. Procuring the condom from a local store is associated with shame and embarrassment. Condoms are sold for a nominal price in two of the local stores which started selling them at the initiation of a research project undertaken by the Bangalore Population Centre during 1978-1980. The shop owners could not identify majority of the buyers because they were the outsiders, but for a few bureaucrats living in Ramagere who were irregular

buyers. Shop owners, however, felt that it is a sensitive issue to discuss about the buyers identity because accordingly they were morally bound to be discreet on the issue. Though a small number of husbands confirmed that they did use the condom, none said that they used it regularly or use it as a family planning method. Condom users also expressed that they have problems of privacy and disposal of used condoms. Apparently, the motivation to use the condom for some husbands originated from the fact that they can resume coitus sooner after childbirth, reducing the expected abstinence period. It appears that the use of condom by some couples has lessened their fear of spoiling the breast milk and the consequent effect on the suckling child when coitus is resumed early.

7. A voluntary preference for accepting vasectomy does not exist in the society, the more so because of the widespread belief that matters relating to reproduction are women's business and men should be free from them. Even women endorse this idea and consider that women alone should undergo sterilization. Women cherish a sense of sacrifice by offering themselves to undergo tubectomy thus feeling responsible for saving their husbands from the danger of illhealth or impotency which threatens the ability to earn and affect family income. For instance one tubectomized woman expressed her sense of sacrifice as following :

> *Nau hange hogudu hinge hogudu, gandasarana yake tundare koduodu* : We (the wives) are the sufferers either that way (having too many pregnancies) or this way (getting tubectomized), then why should we put men into trouble (of vasectomization). (Ramagere, case 164)

Such women are regarded as disciplined and good housewives. The belief that men become both physically and sexually weak after vasectomy is very strong and the vasectomized males feel shy to admit their vasectomization in public. Such beliefs about the vasectomy are widespread across the country and are different only in relative emphasis and interpretations, for example Poffenberger 1964 and Misra *et al* (1982 : 115) present similar facts from the rural parts of Gujarat and Uttar Pradesh states respectively. However, some of the vasectomies during the 1960s were performed on people of Ramagere and of the region who were lured by huge offers of monetary incentives which made vasectomy unpopular among the population. During the mass vasectomy drive of the 1960s, additional incentives were offered from the Taluka Development Board and voluntary agencies, apart the normal cash incentives given by the state family planning programme. The gross monetary incentive per vasectomy was as high as rupees one hundred, about $20.60 in 1964.

8. There is no history of an official programme meant to popularize oral pills in this area. Nevertheless, family planning including the IUD is closely linked with the health programme, and the concept of a pill which is identified with modern or allopathic medicine is easily acceptable to the population provided it is not to be taken continuously or recurrently. A continuous and regular administration of oral pills is regarded as a prolonged medication which provides women a sense of sickness. Rural people, especially women, have only a vague knowledge about the oral pill ; they believe that the pills are to be taken only once or twice to avoid a pregnancy. Because of this kind of ignorance and people's desire to use simple and uncomplicated contraceptives the quacks and sometimes irresponsible health workers prosper by selling a variety of pills of unknown origin or composition purportedly of a contraceptive nature but which are probably useless and sometimes dangerous to health. There are two very recent instances in Ramagere and one in Laxmipura where the wives used such pills. A Balagiga wife (Ramagere, case 297) desired to stop more children and contacted a Brahmin herbalist who periodically visited Ramagere. She, without the consent or knowledge of her husband, bought three courses of pills (manually made) and after self-administration of two courses she fell sick. The husband explored the cause of sickness and destroyed the final course of medicine and instructed her not to think of even limiting children in future. In yet another instance (Laxmipura, case 14), the female health worker supplied with six modern pills for a price and assured the woman that she will not conceive after she consumes them.

This respondent held that oral pill is not an effective contraceptive because she conceived even after taking those pills. The tablets provided by the female health worker appear to be a drug used for menstrual regulation. Nevertheless, based on the frequency of enquiries made with the investigator about the availability of the oral pill even by many Scheduled Castes and Muslims it can be indicated that there is a unprecedented demand for simple contraceptives in the rural areas.

9. There is incomplete knowledge about the legality and availability of the medical termination of pregnancy through government dispensaries. But there is a considerable demand for the termination of pregnancy which is evident from the disclosure by a local registered indigenous medical practitioner[1] that on average three to four women or their relatives approach him each month to have their pregnancies terminated. Apparently it is only rarely that he has come across a premarital or extramarital pregnancy. Generally, the expenditure necessary to receive the *free* Medical Termination of Pregnancy services from a government dispensary is considered to be higher than the amount local practitioner charges for similar services. It is also believed that the local practitioner will be more discreet than the dispensary staff where more than one person will know about the matter. This practitioner claims that he is capable of effectively aborting a pregnancy in the early stages of gestation of less than four months through an oral administration of local herbs. The conventional reports of illegal abortions performed by quacks and *dais* using un-hygienic and non-medical means were not found in this area.

The above discussion raises some of the intricate problems involved in the success of the family planning programme in this area. Some problems originate from loopholes in the implementation of the programme and some from a lack of understanding, poor knowledge and ignorance of the people. It is, therefore, worthwhile to single out the issues concerning the programme in general and its approach in particular, and to evaluate its working in rural society. Less emphasis is given in this discussion to the organizational and implementational problems of the programme than to the problems found at the village level which are discussed in the social context.

6.2 History of The Acceptance of Family Planning Methods in The Area

It has been mentioned elsewhere in Appendix I that there were many phases by which the Indian family planning programme was introduced and when experiments were extensively carried out all over the country. Traces of these experiments are found especially in the largest of the villages. Some surviving early acceptors still live in Ramagere. They are the acceptors of vasectomy popularised during 1966, who incidentally belong to the poorest section of the community. All but one are Scheduled Castes, while the other is a Vokkaliga. Accordingly, they underwent vasectomy in a state of sheer ignorance and misguidance by the self-appointed family planning workers.[2] All vasectomy acceptors even today complain of ill-health and express dissatisfaction. Because of the attractive package of acceptor incentives a few of the poor were tempted to accept vasectomies. In reality the intentions behind the introduction of incentives are questionable. Incentives to some extent worked as a substitute for the requirement of the diffusion of knowledge and information regarding family planning and for a genuine demand.

Starting from 1965, the propagation of the intra-uterine device (IUD) intensified during the late 1960s and early 1970s in the area. The acceptors were Edigas, Balagigas (both classified as Peasant Castes) and the Brahmins in Ramagere. But the majority of acceptors had expelled the IUDs by 1973-74. Major setbacks for the IUD acceptance were apprehension and side-effects. Slowly IUDs gave way to tubectomies which became popular during the mid-1970s. Indeed, tubectomies with higher cash incentives appealed to past IUD users; the cash incentive for IUD acceptors even in 1981 was equal to only 3 Rupees or about 40 per cent. This trend of method-specific acceptance and a fast retreat from the IUD is found only in Ramagere, while in Laxmipura neither vasectomy nor the IUD were ever popular. The extension of family planning and its acceptance has been negligible in the two small villages even up to 1981. It was during the intensive information and service campaign of the Emergency that tubectomy was widely employed in the two large villages.[3] In fact, family planning was adopted for the first time by the people in a big way in Laxmipura where by 1981, 31 per cent (41 per cent of all tubectomies in the research area) of currently married women had accepted tubectomies compared to only 16 per cent (58 per cent of all tubectomies) in Ramagere. There is only one tubectomized acceptor from among the women of the remote villages. She underwent tubectomy after having delivered all her three children in Bangalore hospitals where she got exposed to modern and urban ideas. She now lives in Gowdahalli and her experience with the village people is interesting which is thus narrated

> Now that I am tubectomized and live in this village, I have to listen to different stories from different people each day. Even if I get a headache or fewer people suspect and attribute them to tubectomy. There is none who can understand, none have ever tried even to use an IUD. (Gowdahalli, case 4 ; Note that she has a sense of pride and feeling of innovativeness of her tubectomization.)

that she stays in Gowdahalli and even if she gets a headache or fewer other women of the village attribute them to tubectomy and they do not consider her as one among them. Nevertheless, the emphasis of the official programme is on popularizing terminal methods, and information on alternative methods is scarce in the area. This situation is true of the rest of country as well (Vicziany, 1982a, 1982b).

6.3 Village Levels Workers, Their Work and Responsibilities

Family planning is one of the well known government programmes in the area, Unlike programmes concerning agricultural development, rural banking electrification, dairy development and the like, the family planning programme seems to have reached most families in the area. The Female Health and Family Welfare Worker[4] is the most popular official among the local population. Even children identify her and know of her general functions. She normally wears a white *sari*[5] while at work, and visits couples in their own homes. Male health and Family Planning Worker[6] has no distinct identification in terms of the colour of his dress, but at least in one village he is more popular than the female worker. This is due to his relatively long working relationship with the people of that village. He is, widely known in this village as a 'doctor' and not as a para-medical worker. This aspect of the identification of the health and family planning personnel assumes importance in the diffusion of family planning based on community extension approach, in which case interpersonal communication is of absolute importance. One of the major objectives of the extension approach is allaying apprehension about the after-effects of contraceptive methods and convincing people that contraception and sexual life are compatible, which is known to be possible through interpersonal communication. In fact communication in rural areas is effective only through personal communication. Since the recruitment of health personnel is centralized it is only rarely possible to recruit a worker from the same or a neighbouring village who will be known to the local people. Hence the aspects of identification of the health personnel by the population and rapport building by the worker are essential elements of the family planning programme. Such an identification is a precondition to what is termed 'homophily' which has been identified as essential for the effective diffusion of family planning on a large scale (Rogers, 1971 : 210).

All the four villages chosen for this study are covered both by female and male workers. The largest of the villages is the working headquarters of one male and one female worker. The female worker is attached to a dispensary in this village manned by a medical officer. She has her living quarters attached to the dispensary. She is administratively controlled by the Block Health Centre at the Taluka headquarters. This worker is expected to visit households in this village during afternoons on certain fixed day of the week to provide maternal and child health services, and to propagate family planning among the couples. The FHW who works at Ramagere is a High Caste Hindu and comes from a neighbouring state. However, she has learnt the local language over time and effectively communicates with the people. She is a married woman having a son aged about one year who stays with his father in a different town. The Female worker is assisted by a *dai* who used to be a traditional midwife in this village. The functions of the *dai* are not well defined but she seems to help the female worker in all her duties. People address the female worker as *nursamma* or the nurse. They have varied opinions about her work responsibilities, and also have varied levels of satisfication from her service.

The formal appointment of *dai*, a local lady who is expected to help the FHW is a most recent scheme of the family planning programme. Before her association with the FHW, the FHW was responsible for the primary extension activities of the programme, she used to employ various methods and use different social network in order to select the most responsive couples for the advice on family planning. This included getting clues from the previous FHW and the MHW of the village as to the nature of people, consult and update the 'target couple register' maintained at the sub-centre, contact the formal and informal village leaders and undertake house to house visits. But it is observed that since the appointment of *dai* most of these functions are being delegated to her and the FHW has assumed a role of supervisor. This result is bound to happen even in other villages because, the *dai* being a local lady, is not only vulnerable to the FHW's pressure but also acceptable to the villages especially if she was involved in traditional practice of village attendant or *dai* even before her appointment. It is in Ramagere that the institutional deliveries[7] are higher but more than three-quarters of them were attended by *dai* not the FHW who is more qualified and the MCH is her prime responsibility. At least in Ramagere this is the situation and the FHW is able to avoid most of her original duties presenting herself as another higher official in the government bureaucracy. For instance when she visits a village the *dai* carries her official records and FP and MCH kit consisting of the basic instruments and medicine and conduct deliveries.

The male worker is directly attached to the Block Health Centre situated at the taluka headquarters and administratively is not responsible to the medical officer who works in the village dispensary. He is a native of this village and lives in his own home in a joint family. Apart from his normal duties, he also takes care of his family agriculture. He is recognized by all the adult members of the community as a health worker. The male worker is responsible for various preventive health schemes at the village level, and is also expected to motivate and provide family planning services to the people. But he admitted that he rarely devotes time to the propagation of family planning because of a preoccupation with other, functions. Nevertheless, the largest cluster of households having sterilized women is found around his home in this village.

The next largest village, Laxmipura, is regularly visited by both a female and a male health worker. They do not stay in this village as their headquarters is a neighbouring village. The male worker has been associated with this village for a very long time. The main person responsible for a satisfactory family planning performance in this village is the male worker. He does not distinguish family planning as a separate and distinct function from his normal duties. He needs no exclusive and extra visits to villages to motivate and propagate family planning. The key for his success in achieving the family planning targets lies in his approach to motivating people through his good work on preventive health schemes and also the distribution of simple medicines and first aid services. He gives importance to the follow-up services to the sterilized women which indeed has increased the credibility of his service to the people of this village. Thus the level of acceptance of family planning (tubectomy) in this village is due to two reasons. Firstly, the social homogeneity in the village has encouraged people to follow the elite or innovators of the village. Secondly, trustworthy services were conveniently available for those who had decided to accept family planning through the male health worker (service agent) in whom the people of this village have a high degree of confidence. The aspect of homophily between the community and the health worker is of prime importance for a programme based on the community extension approach. Some people, particularly the women from Ramagere, said that, beause the approach and behaviour of workers in that village is highly impersonal and business-like, they fear to receive maternal and child health, and family planning services from them as sometimes it is offensive because of their disregard for the values people hold. The Ramagere women also face difficulties in receiving follow-up services from the dispensary because of lack of a good referal system from the field workers. This is largely true of the behaviour of the higher health officials whose interaction with the population is far from desirable from the view point of the villagers. For instance a group of sterilized women said :

> If we go on our own to the dispensary for the treatment of children or for follow-up service, we have to pay for the services in spite of showing the sterilization card ; therefore, we *catch* the female health worker who took us for tubectomy through her we get free post-sterilization and follow-up services. (Ramagere, four tubectomized women residing in the neighbourhood, and case 235).

Two other villages fall in the non-intensive area of the health scheme. Ordinarily a health worker is expected to cover intensively 3,000 to 5,000 population living in one or more villages. A few villages peripheral to this area are also attached to the worker who is asked to cover them regularly at longer intervals, like a fortnight or a month. Therefore, the two smaller villages are situated in the non-intensive area of the health and family planning scheme and are only rarely visited by either a male or a female worker. Thus the level of service and supply of health and family planning facilities are low. A strong negative correlation between the distance from the serviee centre and health and family planning supply has been shown by Chandramouli and Guruswamy (1979) which is found to be true in the study area as well.

Since the introduction of the multipurpose health programmme on an experimental basis in 1978, the functions of the paramedical village level workers are well defined but remain same in priority as was the case in the past. The new scheme emphasizes co-operative work between the male female worker. In principle it is highly desirable that both workers chart out a co-operative work schedule, but it is unlikely to work for various reasons. In spite of the high priority given to family planning, the female worker finds it useful to combine maternal and child health and family planning activities. On the other hand the male worker has to either combine his preventive health care duties with family planning or work exclusively on family planning during a particular visit. These differences is sex-specific work priorities, which emerge from the nature of the work itself, have not permitted a co-operative work schedule in the area. Secondly, inter-personnel differences appear to come in way of co-operative work. Another factor which worked as an obstacle to co-operative work is the imposition of targets to be met independently by the workers. Thus there is no co-operative activity of the male and female worker in the implementation of the health and family planning programme in the study area.

The male and female supervisory staff is expected to co-ordinate the work input and improve the work output of the workers at the grassroots level. However, there was hardly any occasion when the supervisory staff worked at least in the larger village during the investigators stay in the village excepting when the investigator requested the female supervisor to visit the village for an interview with her. This is because the field workers and supervisory staff generally meet at least once a month at the block level staff meetings and thereafter they may again meet during family planning camps at various places. Because of these meetings a visit to the village is felt to be unnecessary by the supervisory staff. Thus the role and contribution of the supervisory staff in the co-ordination of work of the village level workers and in the extension activity of the propagation of family planning and MCH programmes is negligible.

Apart from the above mentioned field and paramedical staff there is a medical officer who is responsible for the running of the medical dispensary in Ramagere. The dispensary was sanctioned in 1968 but rarely functioned for want of accommodation and a doctor willing to work in the village. The establishment of the dispensary was made possible because one of the residents of Ramagere emerged as an important politician at the state level. In fact he donated a large area of land at the entrance to the village for the construction of a dispensary building which is yet to start for want of money to meet the construction costs. However, when the new sub-centre building was constructed in 1977 under the India Population Project scheme the dispensary was established in one of the sub-centre rooms and a qualified medical doctor was appointed. He does not, however, reside in the village, which is ordinarily expected of him. He travels daily from the town twenty kilometres away. People have mixed feelings about him because he belongs to the Scheduled Castes category and yet is a highly educated person. However, major complaints against this medical officer came from his own community people that they are subjected to prejudice when they approach him for medical treatment. Because of this, many travel to the town to receive medical treatment which involves substantial expenditure in terms of transport and loss of wages. The Scheduled Caste colony in Ramagere is on the other side of the road where the new health centre is located. Yet people from this locality do not make use of the facility mainly because the medical officer either prescribe medicine which has to be bought from a chemist of town, or because he sells medicine for money. Because the annual supply of medicine through government channels does not last for more then a few months, the medical practitioner has no other way for dealing with the situation. Yet the practitioner can very well use his own discretion to prove free medical treatment to the Scheduled Castes and other poorer sections of the community rather than to the rich land owners and other bureaucrats which he is obliged to do for personal reasons. In one instance, the medical practitioner refused to provide free treatment to an infant suffering from diarrhoea and this child happened to be the son of a Scheduled Caste woman. The Scheduled Caste community in both Ramagere and Laxmipura are critical about the present medical officer while no other community feel this way.

The Medical Officer is not trained in the technical and social aspects of family planning which is essential for a medical officer to help propagate the family planning programme in rural areas. Family planning was listed last when he was asked to list his work priorities. He devotes all his working time to curative duties for the people who visit the dispensary. He generally does not visit a home unless it is an emergency and is paid for. During non-working time he is not accessible because he does not reside in the village. He only passingly communicates about family planning to some woman who visits the dispensary for treatment. Since there is a total absence of an organized effort to contact people, it appears that the responsibility for the diffusion of family planning through interpersonal communication largely rests with the female workers of the area. The male worker only partly becomes involved in fulfilling this responsibility.

6.4 Diffusion of Family Planning

The most important difference between the tubectomy acceptors among the villages is that the early acceptors in Ramagere were past IUD users. They were also impressed with the incentives which were viewed as windfall income and this was a stronger emotion than their feeling of need, whereas all in Laxmipura were new acceptors of family planning. Nevertheless, acceptance became popular only among the High and Intermediary-Peasant Castes of these villages. If one explains that the people belonging to these two caste groups have a favourable attitude and have understood the need for family limitation it is only a partial answer. Couples from these castes have acquired relatively better knowledge and awareness due to easy access to family planning information mainly from inter-personal communication and through the mass media. In Ramagere the presence of the official population has ensured greater attention to the government programmes and has also contributed to increasing the level of awareness among certain groups of the population. It is obligatory on the part of the officials to speak favourably about the family planning programme and they get extra incentives for sterilization acceptances. In the absence of effective mass media channels (radio is not effective in chanelling family planning information in these villages) and the inability of the mass media effectively communicate with the rural masses[8] the extension activity by the village level programme workers is found to be decisive ; in spite of the fact that the diffusion of information is late, inaccurate and incomplete (Nan and Burt, 1975-76). Nonetheless it is noticed that workers tend to provide selective services to selected families and groups of people. Indeed they seem to have good reason to do so. Because of the imposition of the monthly targets, recurrent evaluation of work achievements for non-performance, workers inevitably cover the most responsive families. A relatively favourable response from the High and Intermediate-Peasant Castes is a result of better rapport achieved through intensive coverage of couples belonging to these caste groups. This issue to be emphasized here is that there is some demand for fertility restriction and the control of family size among all sections irrespective of caste and class differences excepting among some Low Castes and Muslim families. The poor feel the need due to relatively greater economic pressure and others feel it in an effort to increase the standard and quality of life through better education and nutrition, and to enhance social prestige. The following views will highlight this argument.

> In 1971 when we accepted tubectomy the harvest was poor, and it was difficult to secure labour work as well. Many went for tubectomy acceptance not only to avoid births but also to receive incentive money. For us it was becoming difficult to feed these children and the eldest son had to leave school. [Ramagere, case, 255]

> It is easier to water one tree than to water ten of them. In the past the preference was there for many children out of which they used to secure pride and water, but that has proved to be wrong. These are the people who are suffering now and feeling economic pressure because of small land holdings. [Ramagere, case 152]

> Who knows how the future will be. It is wiser to be careful, have fewer children, take a good care of them, provide better education and good health. [Ramagere, case 304]

> The decision for my daughter-in-law's tubectomy was taken

by my son, and I had no reason to oppose that decision. I underwent eight births and of them, only this son saved the family from disaster. What is required is a wise son and one need not have too many children to get one. [Laxmipura, case 74]

Why then have the couples forming the poor section so far not accepted in equal proportion to others? The answer is the inaccessibility of knowledge, restricted communication, and a low level of FP diffusion. It may, therefore, be useful to mention briefly the channels, networks and speed of information flow, and communication strategies in these villages. As we have discussed elsewhere, a village is a unit consisting of various subgroups formed due to social stratification whose social intercourse is determined by standardized social norms. The basis for the social stratification is caste affiliation and in the recent past occupational differences seem to have operated to create often overlapping groups. Any information either to help protect or to enhance the interest of the associates within the group flows freely and swiftly, whereas any extension of this information to other groups is controlled by aspects of caste hierarchy, inter-caste and inter-group competion, rivalry and the extent of interdependence. However, subject-specific information may flow between groups. For instance, information concerning the availability of loans from the local co-operative credit society may not be diffused outside a specific group ; on the other hand information that the celebration of a particular deity is being arranged on a particular date, is freely communicated. Similarly, a particular kind of information may flow faster than another depending upon the sensitivity of the issue. Other criteria usually followed for social interaction are based on the age and sex of carrier and receiver.[9] The standard norm is restricted communication between sexes, between low and High Castes and between older and younger men. These relationships between people also determines social intercourse.

Family planning information is generally considered sensitive because it is related to sex. It follows a sex and age specific track of diffusion and does not flow freely between groups. The carriers of information from among the people of village, themselves have limited knowledge about the merits and demerits of a particular kind of family planning; therefore, they fear that advising and propagating the issue may have detrimental results because of the unknown risk involved. If the carrier is not already a village leader, a status usually ascribed rather than achieved, then he is subjected to suspicion as well. He runs the risk of being described by others as 'one who is trying to push himself to prominence and impress the bureaucrats'. There were five relatively aged males who normally advise the acceptance of contraception to those people who had occupational and traditional contacts with them. Nonetheless, two of these five were political and community leaders, one was a local practitioner and the others were government officials.

The IUD was the first method to be propagated through the extension approach among these villages during the mid 1960s. The family planning workers were selective in approaching families because of the initial feeling that the hard core group might disregard and reject advice. It was easier for workers to approach high and intermediary castes. The information thus diffused did not flow between groups and the acceptors were from various exclusive communities. Tubectomies, too, were propagated following the same criteria. The belief which exists even today among the block and village level health officials that high incentives will attract many from the poorer sections is not wholly true. Incentives seem to have helped motivate such couples who had at least some knowledge about methods and who had realized the usefulness of limiting family size. But the incentives scheme has also helped in depreciating the quality of the family planning acceptors who became acceptors to receive the windfall income. Along with the IUD and tubectomy even the maternal and child health and other health services have been provided for a selected group which seems to have created differentials in accessibility to health and levels of infant and child mortality. Other reasons for a differential coverage by the health workers are social and personal factors. For instance, the caste of a worker largely determines his status in relation to the community. A high caste worker is less likely to work intensively among the Scheduled Castes, whereas a low caste worker will not be acceptable to the high caste community. This is true of Ramagere and Laxmipura where the health worker rarely visit the Scheduled Castes colonies. Aspects like affection and friendliness between workers and certain families also contribute to create differentials in diffusion in family planning and the provision of health services.

Family planning is a matter which has to reach many of the target couples and so secure best results. In the past, younger married women were least accessible to both female and male health workers because the elder family members disapproved of youngsters being provided with knowledge of family planning at an early period of family formation. Family planning information is believed to increase the sexuality of youngsters, both before and after marriage which is regarded by the community as unnecessary. Other sources of communication were also limited because of community contact. Outside family contacts were restricted within kin or caste groups and women were expected to meet and interact only with women. Outside information reaching a family undergoes a process of filtration and is often not communicated to the younger women. In the rural area husband-wife communication is weak in the early period of marriage. Such weak husband-wife communication may not continue to prove a hindrance to contraception in this area, because the conjugal relationships are now appearing to be in a process of change towards increased affection and interdependence (see also Conklin 1973). Nevertheless, there is a requirement that husband has to declare his consent in writing before a woman is tubectomized which makes a wife dependent on her husband for a decision. Only when a woman is sufficiently old and has many children does she get opportunities to receive services of modern health care and family planning on her own and by that time she is also more likely to live in a simple family setting where the mutual interdependence is enhanced. Even the intra-family communication involving the woman improves and the conjugal bonds strengthen when the women is sufficiently old. However, the increase in the channels of outside information. other than from the health workers, depends upon the role of women in household decision-making. Such factors have created an unbalanced diffusion of an innovation in the rural areas. Nevertheless, an increasing number of present-day younger women are exposed to information on family planning because they could not escape the pursuit of female workers. Such exposure has been relatively easy when women visited their parents' home during pregnancies. Relatively higher education and exposure to modernization have also contributed to this process.

There are wide differentials in the communication strategies between the villages as well. Ramagere, a relatively open village, and Laxmipura a progressive village, have an equal advantage over the other remote villages with regard to the accessibility of information on agricultural and rural development including family planning because of wider village networks (See Marshall 1971). Because of the economic prosperity among the large villages the possibility that there are some innovators who would experiment with the new ideas is certain whereas in the remote villages such innovators are rarely found. The emphasis is on the aspect of the effect of demonstration from the same cultural and social group within a village which is the most familiar social institution. This was the main reason why dairying did not develop in the small villages while it was taken to in a big way by the families of the large villages. Other constraints originate from their distance from road network, and inaccessibilities to mass media like newspaper and radios. Some of these aspects of differentiated patterns of communications between progressive and non-progressive villages are well discussed by Shankariah (1969).

6.5 Cluster Pattern in Family Planning Acceptance

In the research area two kinds of cluster patterns have been observed with regard to sterilization acceptance. We have already mentioned that caste affiliation plays a major role in determining access to health and family planning information and services. But the cluster patterns have emerged in two different settings. Firstly, it has been found that the influence of those acceptors who are close relatives[10] me is strongest upon other eligible women in encouraging them to use contraceptive innovations. This pattern is a selective effect of the 'satisfied customers' syndrome. Frequently the example of a sister, brother's wife, husband's sister or husband's brother's wife who may have already accepted family planning is followed by younger women. This pattern we may name as the 'kin cluster pattern of acceptors'. The second type is 'neighbourhood clustering', in which most acceptors are found to live in a close proximity. These tuto pattern often overlap because in the rural areas relatives ordinarily live close together. However, these cluster patterns support the hypothesis that the diffusion of family planning information is relatively more effective within a homogeneous group through interpersonal communication. These clusterings provide an opportunity to study in detail the origins of information and channels of communication within a group and the decision-making pattern. The hypothesis is that there seems to be a locus (nucleus) within these clusters which is responsible for diffusing family planning information among cluster members. An extension of this argument is that the diffusion strategy of the Indian family planning programme cannot penetrate the society uniformly, whereas the satisfied clients seem to demonstrate the usefulness of an innovation acceptance and actively encourage members of specific groups.

The theories concerning social stratification are largely used to identify coherent groups and investigate differentials. Because such groups arc identified using wide parameters, like sex and the caste system in India, one encounters difficulties in implementing action-oriented ideas or programmes. Secondly, the social strata are mainly identified from the viewpoint of social distribution and less attention is given to finding out common features within the group. A departure from this approach is warranted with a view to investigating uniformity or what one may call social adhesiveness within groups which creates cohesiveness. Analysis of this kind in a rural society normally results in a large number of smaller groups, indentifiable using kinship and geographic attributes as parameters. A similar observation is made by Taeuber (1958) on Japanese society :

Whatever the external relations with the more extended kin group it is among the small group, of the people living together that relations are closest and more frequent (p 104).

Among such groups it is easier to locate a locus which controls subject-specific behaviour. One may do so because he is more knowledgeable and may have already experienced certain gains from the acceptance of innovation. Within a group there may be different nuclei of control depending upon areas of expertise. For instance, the ritualistic authority may rest with an old woman whereas the decision to install an electrically driven water pump may be taken by the younger son. The practical application of the identification of such smaller groups based on the principle of accumulation and adhesiveness is its ability to pinpoint the origins of decisions and diffusion of information flow regarding issues family planning. The family planning programme is based on the community extension approach emphasizing door-to-door-interaction with the people. But an evaluation of this approach has confirmed that the sheer size of the community has made it impossible to achieve this aim. The fact which has so far either not been thought of or been ignored is that the rural social setting offers an easy way to contact the community through influential relatives who are not necessarily the community leaders.

6.6 Acceptors, Non-Acceptors and the Discriminating Characteristics

In the following section we attempt to find out the differences between the characteristics of family planning acceptors and non-acceptors. These facts can easily be highlighted by a discriminant analysis using the data gathered from the research area. We counted eighty-eight couples currently contracepting. Only six of them are those where the husband is vasectomized. All others are tubectomized women and none use other contraceptives though some reported past use of the IUD. The proportion of acceptors classified by eight socio-economic characteristics is presented in Table 6.1. Five

TABLE 6.1

Percentage of currently married women classified as Acceptors and Non-acceptors by selected characteristics

Characteristics	Percentage acceptors	N (=100%)	Level of sig. (Chi square, DF, P)
Total	19.7	446	
Age of women			
<—19 yrs	0.0	43	
20—24 yrs	6.4	109	
25—29 yrs	22.4	107	44.16, 5, .000
30—34 yrs	27.7	83	
35—39 yrs	38.0	50	
40 yrs	27.8	54	
Village of residence			
Ramagere	19.7	279	
Laxmipura	30.8	104	21.00 2, .000
G. Halli—S. Durga	1.6	63	
Caste affiliation			
High Castes	28.2	39	
Peasant Castes	25.7	222	
Service Castes	19.2	52	19.64, 4, .001
Low Castes	6.5	108	
Non-Castes (Muslims)	15.0	25	
Level of household income			
<Rs. 3000/year	15.7	191	
Rs. 3000—Rs. 5000/year	20.2	119	Not sig.
Above Rs. 5000/year	25.0	136	
Major source of HH income			
Agriculture	21.0	210	
Agl. and other labour	13.4	157	8.59, 2, .014
Non-agl. occupations	29.1	79	

Household's land holding			
Landless	17.2	93	
< 3 acres	18.5	173	Not sig.
3—6 acres	16.2	117	
Above 6 acres	31.7	60	
Women's occupation			
Only household (HH) duties	24.1	87	
HH+work on family farm	22.2	216	Not sig.
HH+work as labourer	12.5	128	
Work on modern jobs	20.0	15	
Women's education			
Illiterate	15.0	314	
Studied till 6th Std.	32.9	76	15.56, 2, .000
7th std. and above	28.6	57	

of the variables, namely the age of the woman, village of residence, caste affiliation, major source of household income, and woman's education are found to have a significant relationship with acceptance. However, a notable fact is that the woman's education and village of residence have a demonstrable effect on acceptance, while these factors were found to be less important in explaining fertility differentials (see Chapter 4). The demographic variables, age and parity, retain their strong effect on acceptance as in the case of fertility. On average, the current acceptors are found to be five years older than non-acceptors, and have 1.4 extra children of whom one child is almost invariably a male. The age specific mean number of sons and daughters and mean number of dead sons and daughters are presented for acceptors and non-acceptors separately in Table 6.2.

It is interesting to know what are the most important distinguishing characteristics of the acceptors and non-acceptors? In other words, how well can one discriminate these groups by their characteristics? The answer to this question can be sought by undertaking a discriminant analysis

TABLE 6.2

Number of Live Born Sons and Daughters and Proportion Dead for the Currently married Women

Age of Women	Number of Women	Boys Born	Boys Born Mean	Boys Dead	Boys Dead Mean	Girls Born	Girls Born Mean	Girls Dead	Girls Dead Mean
NON-ACCEPTORS									
15—19	43	10	0.233	0	0.000	10	0.223	2	0.047
20—24	102	83	0.814	8	0.078	78	0.765	9	0.088
25—29	83	112	1.349	20	0.241	107	0.955	25	0.301
30—34	60	118	1.967	19	0.317	164	2.733	33	0.551
35—39	31	77	2.484	16	0.516	87	2.807	27	0.564
40+	39	125	3.205	21	0.539	99	2.548	22	0.871
All	358	525	1.467	83	0.232	545	1.522	118	0.330
ACCEPTORS									
15—19	0	0	0.000	0	0.000	0	0.000	0	0.000
20—24	7	11	1.571	0	0.000	2	0.286	0	0.000
25—29	24	48	2.000	6	0.250	42	1.750	8	0.333
30—34	23	57	2.478	9	0.391	39	1.696	5	0.217
35—29	19	53	2.790	5	0.263	47	2.474	7	0.368
40+	15	41	2.733	4	0.267	43	2.867	9	0.600
All	88	210	2.386	24	0.273	173	1.966	29	0.330

which is possible using the available data. Initially eleven characteristics were used to run a stepwise discriminant analysis. The characteristics were : marital duration, woman's education, village of residence, caste affiliation, family type, level of annual household income, number of living sons, number of dead infants, and number of children dead who were above one year of age. Data on a smaller number of women was selected to be used in the discriminant analysis. Only those women (both acceptors and non-acceptors) who had two or more living children were selected to be included in the discriminant analysis. Thus a large number of women having one child or no living children were excluded. The selected group includes 209 non-acceptors and 78 acceptors from among a total of 446 currently married women.

Five of the eleven characteristics used in the analysis emerged as the important discriminating variables. These variables were selected by the stepwise discriminant run (a standard SPSS programme) after meeting the default stipulation of a minimum value of 'F' for inclusion of 1.0. The results are presented in Table 6.3. The overall discriminating power of these variables is reasonable as judged from the Wilk's lambda value of 0.888, and canonical correlation of 0.334. The chi-square values associated with these are also statistically highly significant. Infant and child mortality (a variable not selected in the discriminant run) seem to have least discriminating ability because there is only a negligible difference in the infant and child mortality experience between acceptors and non-acceptors of this group of women. However, the category number of living sons indirectly accounts for the effect of mortality among children.

The standardized discriminant function coefficients present the relative importance of the selected variables in the discriminant function (see panel one of Table 6.3). Woman's education is the most important characteristic, followed by caste affiliation and number of living sons. Marital duration and family type of current residence are found to be least in their relative importance. The coefficients for family type suggest that a woman currently living in a nuclear family has

TABLE 6.3

Results of the Discriminant Analysis to classify Couples as Acceptors and Non-acceptors of Family Planning Methods

(1) Discriminant Analysis

Variables*	Wilk's Lambda	Discriminant Function Coefficient Unstandardized	Standardized
Marital Duration	0.893	0.034	0.240
Number of Living Sons	0.897	0.270	0.319
Family type	0.894	0.610	—0.245
Woman's education	0.934	1.058	0.702
Caste affiliation	0.907	0.423	—0.440
Constant		0.278	

(2) Classification Results

Actual Group	Predicted group membership (Percentages) Non-acceptor	Acceptor	Total number of Women
Non acceptor	69.9	30.1	209
Acceptor	37.2	62.8	78

Canonical Correlation=0.334 ;

Wilk's Lambda=0.888, Chi-square=33.4, D.F.=5, Significance=0.0

Centroids of groups : Non-acceptor=—0.216, Aceeptor=0.578

* See Chapter 4 for details on the groupings of these variables.

a greater probability of contracepting than a woman in a joint family.[11] This interpretation is illustrative because the real effect of the family type has to be related to the duration of stay in a particular family type. Similarly, if the women belong to lower levels in the caste hierarchy or if they are Muslims, they are less likely to accept contraception. A higher level of education of women and a greater number of surviving sons are associated with increase in level of contraception. In short the results suggest that the higher the education of a woman is, the higher is the caste to which they belong and have sufficient number of living sons, such women are more likely to accept sterilization with an intent to stop births of more children. The length of marital duration and the type of family of current residence facilitate the family planning acceptance.

The predicted group membership, with the derived discriminant functions, are shown in the second panel of the table. Almost 70 per cent of non-acceptors and 63 per cent of acceptors are correctly classified. However, the misclassification for non-acceptors is relatively higher than for aceeptors. This suggests that there is larger homogeneity among the acceptors than the non-acceptors. This is quite understandable because the non-acceptors tend to vary widely in their reasons for not accepting a family plannlng method.

It is evident from the above analysis that a woman's education and caste affiliation are the most important discriminating attributes in the research area. Therefore, there is large segment of population who do not bear these attributes and are less likely to accept family planning in this rural society. The fact that a woman's education is a powerful discriminating variable suggests that the intention often associated with determination originates from the woman who wants to accept family planning. Applying the argument that the supply of services, information or otherwise, are relatively easily available to these women, the demonstration effect leads to immediate results. The advantage to this group is ever more self-reinforcing in terms of better maternal and child health and other health facilities as well. In contrast, the women belonging to other groups are disadvantaged both because of inaccessibility, either due to restraint or lack of workers' attention and lower demonstration effect.[12] A large segment of the population is still apprehensive about seeking either modern or allopathic medicine and the demand for maternal and child health service is small. Trust in the healing effect of *mantras* and *yantras* is still great, particularly for certain types of childhood diseases and ailments (Caldwell *et al*, 1982a : 702-703). One respondent said :

> . . .my father and forefathers were traditional healers, the treatment was effective, although I do not know much about this kind of traditional medicine I have a strong belief in its ability to cure illness. I also believe in magic. [Ramagere, case 197]

Local herbs are available either free or at negligible cost compared to costs (costs incurred to meet transport and some times payment to the practitioner) to secure allopathic medicine. Maternal and child health services extended to the door steps are *suspected* to be a precursor to the announcement of a family planning message as opposed to the *intentions* of the programme implementators. In fact, accepting MCH service is viewed as granting the health worker a right to insist on the use of contraception. Therefore, there is a need to rethink and modify the extension strategy to suit the independent needs of the larger segment of the community by splitting maternal and child health from the family planning programme or through the specialization of work responsibilities. The scheme and model of the alternative strategy is, however, outside the scope of this thesis. The son preference is strong among all the sections of the population, therefore, there is a need also to emphasize the value of daughters through increasing the standard and role of female education, increasing female participations in various formal and informal occupations and control of the practice of dowry system.

NOTES AND REFERENCES

1. There is a system in the state of Karnataka, like many other states in India, that the practitioners of traditional medicine such as *Homoeopathy* and *Unani* register themselves as medical practitioners with a special institution, namely the Association of the Practitioners of Traditional Medicine. Thus, though they are not recognized as qualified medical practitioners, they receive recognition as practitioners of traditional healing and medication.
2. The cash incentive scheme for motivators induced many field workers to recruit non-officials as their agents who supplied clients from around the area. This was one of the main reasons for the success of vasectomy camps dvring the mid-1960s.

3. In the 19-months period between late June 1975 and mid-January 1977, India was ruled in a state of national Emergency. For an account of the family planning programme during the Emergencey see Panandiker *et al.*, (1978) and Gwatkin (1979).
4. The Female health and family welfare worker will be referred to as 'Female worker' in the following text. She was earlier known as an Auxiliary Nurse Midwife or ANM.
5. The *sari* is a commonly accepted dress for the south Indian adult women.
6. The Male health and family welfare worker will be referred to as 'Male Worker' in the following text. He was earlier known as a Health inspector or Block Health Worker. Another name for them was Family Planning Health Workers.
7. Institutional deliveries are those deliveries which occur either in a hospital or a dispensary, or that a qualified health personnel is present in case of home deliveries.
8. Poffenberger and Poffenberger made an unprecedented attempt to fill the gap in the research about the effect and role of mass media among rural India population. and expressed reservations about the effect of the mass media (including radio and news paper) to bring about rapid social change (1971 : 41)
9. A similar observation is made by Poffenberger (1968 : 761) while studying the resistance to family planning in a north Indian village.
10. Sisters and brothers' wives of either of the couple are regarded as close relatives.
11. This analysis is based on the current residential status of couples and not on the life time residence criteria. A detailed analysis of the life time residential criteria is undertaken in Chapter 8 where it is proved that the acceptance rate is higher for those couples who had experienced an extended living immediately after marriage. Nevertheless, the differences in the approach to investigating a similar phenomenon help us to understand the merits and demerits of using current residential status versus the life cycle approach.
12. The demonstration effect of innovation acceptance is ordinarily spread across the cross-section in a community but any action as a consequence is only rare and slow. Our concern in this argument is that innovation diffusion has to create immediate response and consequent action.

7

Fertility and Family Planning Decision-Making : Dimensions and Supports

7.1. Introduction

In this chapter we discuss issues concerning fertility and family planning decision-making. In the first part the discussion is on the origin of the theories on decision-making which are subsequently modified to fit into the cultural context of the research area. The second part presents the conceptual framework of the present work and the third part attempts to describe in detail the pattern of decision-making by the marital dyad within the changing dimensions of the extended family system. This chapter is essentially a background to the analysis undertaken in Chapter 8.

(*i*) *Origins of the Concept of Fertility Decision-making*

The qualitative study of fertility behaviour is of recent origin in demographic literature. Since the late fifties the emphasis in research has moved more towards explanatory issues of demography. This shift was the result of contributions to demography by writers from other disciplines mainly economics, psychology, anthropology and sociology. The focus of investigation has shifted toward the social, economic, cultural and psychological aspects of fertility behaviour, and the interest in exploring behaviour from different kinds of social groups with differing cultures, family and kinship systems and individual tastes and preferences grew steadily. It can be predicted that as the socio-demographic differentials in fertility decrease and are controlled, individual factors will attain increasing explanatory power. Therefore, a study of the decision-making process which is better understood at the individual level will help to predict future fertility behaviour of a particular group or set of people. This necessitates different methodological approaches and analytical techniques.

The theoretical framework for fertility decision-making has been provided by economists, particularly Leibenstein (1957) and Becker (1960). They employed a micro-economic model using the economic theory of the consumer choice to explain fertility decisions. The unit of analysis used was an adult or a a couple or a family. Becker's analysis was essentially the analysis of decision-making under resource constraint. The underlying assumption that couples make the family size decisions for the whole reproductive period only once, led to a static model to explain fertility behaviour. Leibenstein (1974) emphasized marginality, especially the decision to have an additional child given that the family already had three or more children. He refined the concept of rationality and emphasized that one need not assume that the entire realm of fertility behaviour embodies rational calculations but that only one decision at the 'critical juncture' in one's life is rational. Later, others attempted to modify and refine this model but retained the consumer theory model and its assumptions as the base (Easterlin, 1969 ; Namboodiri, 1972, Turchi, 1975). All these researchers have assumed a process of rational maximization of utility which is fundamental in their analyses.

A major criticism against the economist's approach to fertility decision-making is of the maximization aspect of utilities. Leibenstein (1977) himself has rejected this hypothesis ; instead he prefers to call this 'selective rationality'. Simon (1957) argued that the human behaviour is not the one set for maximization but is just 'satisfying'. Wolpert (1954 : 537) has considered human goals to be multidimensional and in his view optimization or maximization is not the criterion. Namboodiri (1980), although endorsing the idea of maximization, considered lifetime maximization hypothetical and unreal. For him, an individual maximizes at a particular time the possible utilities ; thus rewards are measured in terms of immediate costs and sacrifices. Udry (1983) has recently demonstrated the validity of the sequential decision-making model using micro-models, and emphasized that the best predictors are the intervening variables which are distinct from those used in the macro-models. These intervening variables are the individual experiences and circumstances special to each individual.

The assumptions generally made in the micro-economic approach seem to oversimplify much of reality, especially its application to developing countries. The decision-makers are in a world of ignorance and confusion because of *imperfect knowledge*, and their goals are multidimensional, in which case they are willing to compromise to achieve some level of all goals instead of maximizing only one, because of the absence of perfect substitution. However, for them certain goals have priority over others. For the important ones they accept a non-maximized utility or even tolerate a negative utility in accordance with the direction of endogenous and exogenous forces. For instance, a couple, may choose to produce children until they get a son irrespective of the number of daughters they already have. The socio-psychological benefits and satisfaction parents get by having a son may be still higher than the costs and dissatisfaction from the large number of daughters whom they already have.

The matter of uncertainty is decisive. If the immediate goal of a couple is to have a child, they indeed expect to obtain a child who will grow and live at least till the parents' death. In the presence of high infant and childhood mortality, achieving this goal is uncertain and the decision-making process may change accordingly. The concept of rational choice is central in the consumer choice analysis of the micro-economic model, yet it is a vague and nuclear concept when applied in practice. Within this model, if a consumer chooses to have an *inferior good* it is irrational. The model also assumes that the income effect on the inferior goods indicates a decline in their demand. Yet this approach cannot explain a situation where the parents choose to have a child under a regime of low child survivorship : a child exposed to a high infant mortality situation is considered here an example of 'inferior good'. The economic theory of fertility does not consider children 'inferior goods.' On the contrary, the distinction between wanted and unwanted children is identical to the distinction between *good* and *inferior* goods. In reality, however, parents may choose to have many children rather than none so as to end up at least with some surviving children. What sounds theoretically a highly irrational decision is the most widely observed decision in practice.

A departure from a pure economic approach seems to be essential to reveal the actual process and pattern of fertility and family planning decision-making. This approach does exist which borrow extensively from the works of psychologists, anthropologists and sociologists besides those of economists. For instance, Easterlin (1973, 1975) used the psychologist's approach to describe tastes for children versus material goods. In contrast, Backman (1978, 1983) and Hass (1974) have successfully applied the psychological decision-making theory to explain fertility behaviour in the western countries. Recently Hull (1983) and Conklin (1981) have followed the lead of Blood and Wolfe (1960) in using a sociological approach to describe the individual level decision-making patterns from anthropological nature of data. We have also chosen this approach to the study of decision-making because of its ability to present the actual pattern rather than a discussion of hypothetical situation. This approach helps to reveal the actual process and pattern of fertility and family planning decision-making in the developing countries. This approach, however, does not disregard the contribution of micro-economic theories rather they can be used along with the theories from psychology, anthropology and sociology.

(*ii*) *Nature and Dimensions of Decision-making*

The following is a brief discussion on the nature and dimension of decision-making in the context of rural Indian society which eventually is developed as a framework for the analysis of fertility decision-making. In doing so we depart from the conventional economic framework of fertility decision-making and employ a psycho-social model which is practical and well suited model for our objective. This model is then used to explain two overlapping kinds of demographic decision-making : (a) decision-making with regard to either having or postponing the birth of child ; and (b) decision making for limiting the number of children and family planning acceptance.

To understand the decision-making process it is important to know two aspects in advance : the first is the nature of decisions and the second is the environment in which such decisions are made. Decisions are distinguished between 'active' and 'passive' (Hollerbach, 1980 ; Leibenstein, 1981). Passive decision-making is said to be a decision taken by individuals or couples in accordance with the internalized social norms regarding appropriate behaviour on the basis of their assumptions regarding the partner's attitudes (Hollerbach, 1980 : 6) ; or according to Leibenstein (1981 : 386), passive decisions involve routine or day-to-day behaviour. Therefore, most decisions in a family are passive. On the contrary, active decisions are infrequent and are based on communication, power and disagreements between the actors involved. The active decisions are warranted because they involve the choice of a specific alternative or behaviour which is identified by the psychologists as a 'process of elimination' of aspects of different alternatives. According to Leibenstein, if an event is so strong as to create sufficient impact on the dicision-maker, he becomes activated and stimulates an active decision process. An active decision is required to achieve goal maximization under at least two different circumstances : (a) when an individual is incapable of balancing the pros of a particular pattern of decisions by his past experience, perhaps due to ignorance, insufficient knowledge or just incapacity to make innovative decisions, and (b) when the nature of the problem itself is grave enough to include or necessitate a combination of forces from different criteria as well as from varied persons.

Hollerbach (1980), while attempting to formulate a theoretical framework on the relationship between decision-making and power in families, categorized six power bases which have been identified by French and Raven (1960) and Raven, Centers, and Rodrigues (1975). They are (a) legitimate power, (b) referent power, (c) expert power, (d) informational power, (e) reward power and (f) coercive power. Using these models, she discussed the importance of communication in categorizing decisions to be active or passive. Accordingly, a chance agreement and concurrence in decision is based on stereotyping or projection rather than direct communication which is said to be characteristic of early fertility decision-making. Similar views are found in the works of Hass (1974) ; Hill, Stycos and Back (1959) ; Kammeyer (1971) ; and Yaukey, Griffiths and Roberts (1967). This, however, is described as due to similarities in husbands, and wives' beliefs, values and attitudes emerging through commonly shared socialization thereby internalizing or accepting norms defining appropriate fertility behaviour (Hollerbach, 1980 : 6). In the rural Indian context we will add another characteristic similar to the above, that there exists an implicit and conditioned behaviour which also encourages stereotypic events. These are internalized moral imperatives with negative sanctions for the violators of the norms. For instance, normative influences condition newely wedded women to bear sons as soon as possible.

Nevertheless, the essentials in understanding the process of decision-making is identifying, (a) the issue or problem which has to be decided, (b) the persons who are affected if the decision is taken, (c) the existence of knowledge about alternative or complementary decisions which could be made, (d) the required knowledge and motivation on the part of the decision-maker about the means and options of a particular decision to be made, (d) the perceived costs and benefits involved in the process of decision-making, and (f) the environment, the social, cultural and power context, and the conventions which are immediately available, under which a particular decision has to be made.

7.2 Framework of Decision-making Analysis

In figure 7.1 we present a simple schematic model which attempts to present the process and stages involved in fertility and family planning decision-making. Backman (1978 : 61) constructed a schematic model of fertility decision-making suited to western countries, this model is modified and extended by the investigator to be able to fit into the socio-cultural aspects of the society found in the research area. The present model assumes that : (a) the basic decision-making unit is the marital dyad which is a frequent unit where the impact of decision-making is felt, (b) the decisions regarding fertility regulation and family planning acceptance are identical and pass through a similar process, (c) the family planning method couples choose is only sterilization (reference is made to temporary methods when found essential), and (d) the sequence of extra-couple influence is normally consistent.

(*i*) *Schematic Model of Fertility and Family Planning Decision-making*

The figure is broadly split into three parts based on the importance, strength and type of relationship between the members participating in the decision making process. The primary unit, which can also be interpreted as the primary stage, of decision-makers is assumed to be the marital dyad. The impact of the fertility or family planning decision is directly felt by the couple, especially the wife. It is observed that the ultimate effect of such decisions rest on biological parents and it is only among a very few families which are categorized as joint (structural as well as functional) that the impact is distributed across the other members of the family. It has, however, been argued in the subsequent part of this Chapter and Chapter 8 that the practice of both kin and affine providing various kinds of supports to a couple and their children, such as providing clothes, shelter and even education is widespread. Such supports although appear to be cultural practices, they are noticed to be provided on the request and demand from the biological parents especially the mother. Thus it can be attributed to be one of the planned strategies of parents for child management. This system is not the same as saying that the child care and rearing responsibilities are shared by the extended kin. It is found in Ramagere that the young widows and separated women who have children are

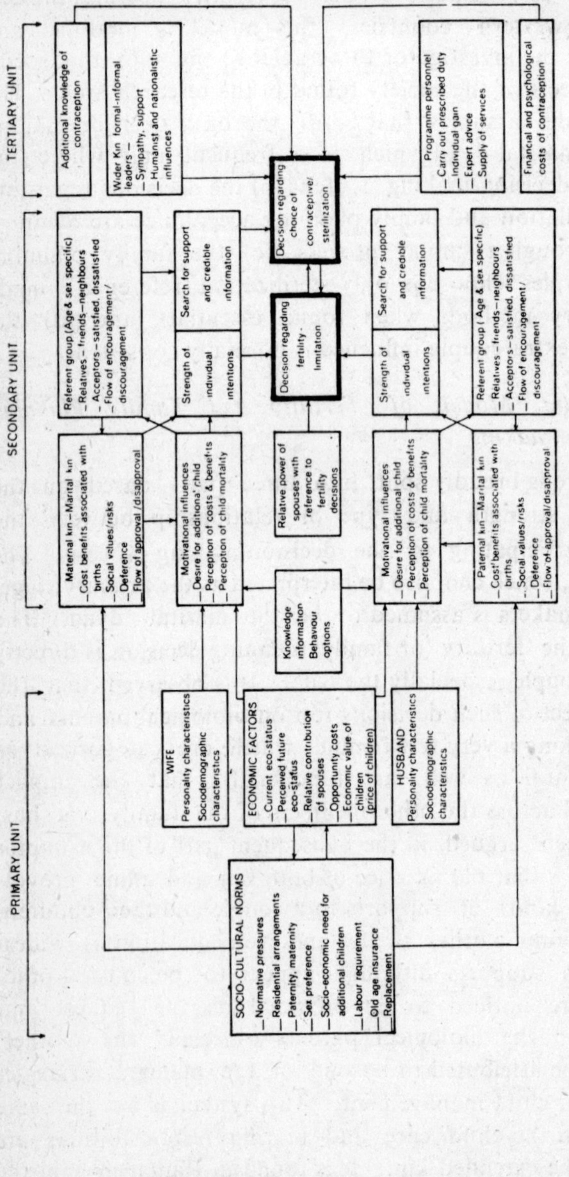

A Model of the Influences of the People Involved in Fertility and Family Planning Decision-Making

FIGURE 7.1

largely left alone responsible for their children although some kind of support is offered for their living by immediate relatives.

Nevertheless, normative, economic and informational factors influence the husband and the wife independently through their personalities and socio-demographic characteristics. Cognitive understanding of the perceived costs and benefits, fear of child mortality and the health status of the dyad provides a framework in modelling individual behaviour. Individual motives are treated as focal, rather than peripheral, to the description of decision-making within the extended family system which is governed by positive or negative incentives. At some stage in the reproductive span due to the pressure of many children, or the ill health of one of the couple, the issue of fertility regulation becomes activated to be appropriately decided upon. Initially the behaviour is almost always of a passive or routine nature leading to events which are regarded as normal by the community. Meanwhile, the motivations, desires and perceptions regarding additional children may reach a stage where they explicitly express intentions initially to the spouse which may later be revealed to others; and the extra-couple influences flow in from the extended family and kin group.[1] The initiation and first suggestions of family planning need not always originate from the couple, as there are occasions where the mother-in-law herself has suggested her daughter-in-law for a tubectomy. Other members who may normally initiate the process of decision-making are the woman's mother, her elder brother or sister, husband's elder brother or sister and his sister-in-law.

In the meantime the decision-makers especially the couple have begun to observe referent group behaviour and may even have established contacts with them for advice and support. A mixture of dos and don'ts, consolations and apprehension, persuasions and threats, satisfactions and dissatisfactions will be communicated by all others to the decision-makers either independently (frequent) or together (sometimes). This phase of extra-couple interference is regarded in this model as the second unit (second phase) in the process of decision-making. The degree of outside influence at this stage depends partly on the power partly on credentials of the specific person who intervenes in the process. The nature of the extended family influence in such affairs is spontaneous and forceful because it is expected that the younger generation is bound by morality and deference. On the other hand, the referent group's is sought mainly as expert advice, believed to be authentic and trustworthy. The referent group in the study area is almost always a group of couples who are the acceptors of family planning methods and also that they are either close relatives or neighbours mostly of the younger generation. The extended family and kin group influence by culture is authoritative whereas the referent group influence strengthens individual's intentions and increases the knowledge and credibility of information. While the extended and kin pressure can be both discouraging and encouraging, the referent group's influence seems to be always favourable and encouraging. In this stage there occur events of give and take, or 'bargaining', between various actors in the decision-making process if their intentions are contradictory in the first stage. There also occurs a bargaining between the couple, either independently or together, and other extended family members. During this stage, additional elements which are discussed in the 'tertiary unit' will start intervening in the process to facilitate the decision either against or for the issue.

Once the decision about whether or not to have additional children is favourably discussed, the person or persons involved in the process may decide to seek advice, additional information and sometimes from the village leaders. This is a tertiary unit (tertiary stage) in the model. Nevertheless, the decision to limit fertility or the decision not to have another child is possible in the second stage itself. Thus the third stage is optional. But, in the study area advice of experts or at least their support in providing services is frequently sought and appear to be essential. Nevertheless, the decision to control fertility and the decision to accept family planning methods are almost always taken at the same time. In fact there are instances when the decision to accept family planning precedes and activates the intention to restrict fertility.

7.3 Supports to the Fertility Decision-Making

The following section deals with those situations and supports which facilitate a particular pattern of decision-making. It has been argued that a different pattern of decision-making has evolved in which women are prominent and affines provided both direct and indirect support. The men have an intermediary status and kin appear to be losing their traditional authority over the young.

(*i*) *Socio-Cultural Norms*

The cognitive process of an individual is primarily influenced by the social environment of a specific culture. Normative limits forbid the reproductive partners to postpone the first few births. Early paternity and maternity are valued most as a means to gain social status and recognition, and the sex combination of children helps determine the direction and level of social status. The sequence and timing of births, especially those of sons, are decisive to achieve not only economic mobility but also to ensure future security for living and the continuation of the family. Because of the common practice of virilocal residence immediately after marriage, these norms assume greater importance and the perception that the bride is young and inexperienced provides greater authority to the parents-in-law in controlling reproductive behaviour. Since female age at marriage is still low in this area the cognitive understanding of the couple, especially the wife, is highly restricted and the family normally allows only limited access to outside information.

The pronatalist social norm appear to have been evolved over years in an effort to keep the subsistence level of living from depreciating. The considerations are not only the continuation of the lineage and attaining social status, but also to ensure a sufficient labour supply for subsistence agriculture in future and to ensure old age support. But it would be inappropriate to conclude that the demand for children is the derived demand for child labour. The norms have also been evolved with regard to the desired number of boys and girls as opposed to the desired number of total children.[2] In the presence of high infant and childhood mortality, the replacement of a dead child is the inevitable consequence of such norms.

Nevertheless, certain aspects of social control over the timing of marriage, prescribing the sexual behaviour of the newly wedded couple, the timing of the birth of a child and regulating the breast-feeding practices as well as restricting the atmosphere for a congenial growth of affection between spouses are important in the Indian context. These pressures are still strong even on the people living in neolocal residences although there are differentials in the extent influence and such influence are weakening over time. The support and pressures from the natal home of the bride, which encourage frequent births in the initial periods appear to weaken over time because they fear that there could be more demands of care and support from a pregnant daughter threatening their economic well-being, especially when there are many daughters. However, the scope for the development of the individual cognitive process is heavily controlled by social and cultural norms.

The individual motivations acquire prominence slowly along with an increase in age and status of couples. Since normative pressures, both expected and experienced, are related to age and parity, as age or parity increases the pronatal pressures decrease and antinatal pressures seem to increase and for higher parities no uniform trend of normative consensus can be found (Fried and Udry, 1980). Norms do exist discouraging repeated births with short intervals and against births of children to those women who are still fecund when their daughters or daughters-in-law are pregnant. Situational aspects like health and economic considerations also induce pressure in either postponing or limiting future births which are frequent when the couple already have many children and the woman is sufficiently aged. Such motivations, nevertheless, depend entirely on the level of information and knowledge, and the availability of services which include traditional practices. Sexual abstinence and induced abortion, performed by quacks, were two such services.

(*ii*) *Economic Factors*

Economic issues create important forces which affect fertility and fertility decision-making in the area. Current and perceived economic status normally help in evaluating the costs, benefits and quality of children. In spite of the fact that the relative costs involved in bringing up a child are only marginal, the important reasons given by the people as to why they intend to limit the family size are economic in nature (see Chapter 8). Difficulties in providing basic needs and education are most frequently reported. Now, let us find out whether it is true that the economic pressure of bringing up children does not impinge solely on the biological parents. As discussed in Chapter 5 the extended family exists at societal level but the influence of functional and structural joint or extended family is less than one-fourth at any given point of time. Nevertheless, eighty-five percent of all newly married couples start living either in stem or joint type of families after marriage. Even after establishing a nuclear family the practice of exchange, borrowing and accounting is common among close kin including father and brothers. But, if a son refuses to repay borrowed money to his father, the father may decide to distribute his property less the worth of the borrowed sum. The exchange of labour between relatives is not only regarded as reciprocal but also is accounted although not converted into monetary terms. As Caldwell has pointed out, familial relationships and emotional ties have begun to nucleate and the family is in a process of disengagement from the network of extended family relationships (1976a : 346) even in rural south India. The concern and expenditure on one's children and management of the family economy is by and large self-supporting. Therefore, the responsibility of bringing up children rests primarily with the biological parents. Though in a joint family child care is shared, the quality of child care, allocation of food, continuation of children's education directly depends on the current economic status of the biological parents. Children of such parents who contribute incomes regularly to the joint budget are better cared for and clothed than those whose parents contribute less or irregularly. The economic status of different couples within the same joint establishment differs according to the amount of personal wealth owned and the extent of support they offer to the other family members both on a regular basis and in times of crisis. The distribution of income within the families is dependent upon the relative contribution of its adult members.

Economic pressures appear to discourage a large number of births. Apart from the direct costs of food, clothing, schooling and so on people feel that a pregnancy not only adds to the expenditure but also reduces the total income of the households due to the loss of wages incurred during pregnancy, child birth and child care till the child grows old enough at least to provide for itself. Another mechanism which affects having a large number of children is that given the static levels of income the parents have to defer or even forego present consumption to raise children. Some parents think that it is sensible to consume more by having small family than to have less per capita availability because of large family. The actual as well as opportunity costs of the couple, especially the wife, initiate a cognitive process which appears to motivate them to postpone or control future fertility. The costs, however, are primarily determined by evaluating the intensity of the sex preference of another child.

These concerns, along with the growing fear of ill health to the mother during pregnancies, mould the individual preferences regarding additional children. However, it should be emphasized that the birth of a minimum number of boys and girls is an absolute necessity to parents and the question of having additional children or recognizing the fact that they have too many children comes only after that minimum is reached. The desire to have a son is so great in this area that all couples who had only daughters were determined to have more births in an effort to get at least one son irrespective of economic and health considerations.

(*iii*) *Marriage and Residential Arrangements*

In understanding the nature of fertility decision-making, the pattern of marriage and residential arrangements immediately after marriage are important. The type of marriage has not only a profound effect on the husband-wife relationship (Ross,

1961 : 13) but also on that between the couple and the kin group. Marriages are still arranged, usually with no say at all from the girl while the boys have only a limited veto power. Caldwell *et al* (1982a) brings out clearly the relationship between the residential arrangements, family structure and family decision-making in his study area about two hundred kilometres away from the area examined in this thesis. They write :

> Despite the fact that half the population lives in nuclear families, only one couple in 11 failed lo begin marriage with the husband's parents, and only one in eight lived for less than the first five years with them. More importantly, two-thirds of all births and over half the sterilization decisions take place while the couple are still living with the husband's parents. In these circumstances, the significant family changes that bear on decision-making are not those of family structure but of changing relations between the generations. . . The younger couples do not seem to wrest decision-making powers from the old during overt conflict, but rather the old increasingly retire from various arenas of decision-making. (p 701).

Nevertheless, it is observed that the capacity of sons to decide in the matters of their own sexual as well as family life has increased. In the past the most preferred brides were from among relatives but there is a decline in the frequency of such marriages because such relatives whose sons are ready to marry are in search of *better* girls both in quality, for instance more educated girls, and ability to bring relatively more dowry and who promise expensive gifts and continuous support after marriage. Thus the girl who is going to become a daughter-in-law can most probably be a far-off or a non-relative. In the research area the proportions of marriages falling into these categories are 28.9 and 26.7 respectively. Nevertheless, the newly wedded daughter-in-law is also likely to be much older than her mother-in-law was when she married.

There is little change as yet in the practice of virilocal residence after marriage. On an average, a newly wedded couple stays with the husband's parents for six and a half years, a duration sufficient to produce two to three children.[3] This duration in the past is expected to be much longer which is decreasing at present. For instance, the newly wedded son of one of the Lingayat couples decided to split from his parents within three months of marriage in spite of the effort by the parents to establish a supplementary hotel within the family hotel business. He instead established a separate tea stall adjacent to the village bus stop, investing money which he received from his father-in-law. Such changes are occurring frequently not only among those families whose occupation provides access to a flow of daily cash such as the *hotel* business, the shop, and the petty trade of collecting grains and selling them to the local traders, but also among the agriculturists of Laxmipura. Nevertheless, because of uneconomic and smaller land holdings, more and more sons are taking to non-agricultural occupations which provide direct and regular access to liquid cash as well as providing an opportunity to account for the exact contributions to the family and, therefore, an early division of the joint family. This facilitate the understanding of relative contributions to family, and the larger is the differential in relative contributions the greater is the chance that a problem arise and the family splits.

(iv) *Early Period After Marriage*

The period most important for a decision-making analysis is the first five to eight years of married life. This duration is the prime period in which the wife produces most of the children desired and an understanding of family relationships during this period will provide clues to the pattern of fertility decision-making within a specific family. Only two decades ago the female age at marriage was very low,[4] marriages were frequently arranged between relatives, the level of female education was low and the practice of dowry was not prevalent. All these factors worked against the newly wedded wife in achieving a status within the family and developing her independent motivations. The status was low compared to men and the elder women. In fact she would have been brought into the family to support the mother-in-law in household duties and to contribute to family labour. There has been a change in this regard. Sons are considered more valuable now than in the past not only because they take up diverse occupations which are believed to be more rewarding and provide better support to parents but also because they bring in a substantial sum in the form of dowry, sometimes as much as a year's family income. Parents attempt to benefit from this, which is possible only by controlling such children. One can, therefore, suspect dowry as being one of the reason which is reducing the male age at marriage recently.[5] Parents intend to redeem this wealth as early as possible, and retain their say in the way it should be spent, for instance, repaying outstanding loans, arranging the marriage of younger daughters or even investing in property. In recent times, the daughter-in-law is relatively more likely to be a non-relative or an outsider, more educated and possibly from a better economic background. Such girls are regarded as experienced, worthy and bold, and the community increasingly approves of these qualities in a daughter-in-law. Thus there has been shift from a submissive and deferential to a relatively less deferential and more outgoing daughter-in-law even in the early period after marriage.

The demographic behaviour of such younger women is distinctly different from that of older women. A major change has occurred in the timing of the consummation of marriage and birth spacing. These changes are modifications of the old cultural practices. The marriages are consummated sooner than before and often immediately. Parents intend not only to avoid expenditure on the second ceremony, namely *sobana*, but also to minimize the chances of the groom leaving his wife even before consummation. This is true among all the Low Caste Hindus, especially the Scheduled Castes and most of the peasant families. Instances are increasing where the bride-groom has refused to undergo the *sobana* ceremony unless more money, jewellery and gifts are given, and there are young girls who call themselves married but stay with their parents because the husband has deserted them even before *sobana* ceremony. Secondly, there is an overall reduction in the duration of birth spacing among almost all the younger women in this area. The value associated with the traditional abstinence and prolonged breast feeding has declined at least among the High Castes and the Peasants. Attitudes to sexuality have also changed to encourage a frequent and intimate relationship between the husband and wife. The predominance of neolocal residence has contributed to this change.

(v) *Kins, Affines and the Dyadic Power Structure*

The ralative power between various decision-makers which helps to measure the extent of disagreement between them for a certain decision to be taken is identified as a function of legitimacy (support of norms), reference group support, own expertise and information. For instance, dyadic power structure is based partly on individual characteristics and partly on the extent of outside support. A variation to this is a view held by Blood and Wolfe (1960) in terms of 'Culture and Competence' where the balance of power between the husband and wife is derived from the culture as well as individual competence. In their analysis it was brought out clearly that culture is not a sufficient explantion of power and that competence provides the chief basis for it (pp 14-15). They are the proponents of 'resource theory', which is highlighted in the following quotations :

> The sources of power in so intimate a relationship as marriage must be sought in the comparative resources which the husband and wife bring to the marriage, rather than in brute force. A resource may be defined as anything that one partner may make available to the other, helping the latter satisfy his needs or attain his goals. The balance of power will be on the side of that partner who contributes the greater resources to the marriage. (p. 12)

> Control over future resources is especially crucial, since decision-making involves the allocation of resources within the family. The partner who may provide or withhold resources is in a strategic position for influencing their disposition. (p. 13)

They proceed further to predict that 'if wives gain increased resources, old patriarchal notions are not likely to remain unaffected for very long' (p. 14). Heer (1963 : 139) also held similar views and believed that relative power depended upon the resources obtained from outside the marriage.

This line of thinking fits in perfectly with the kinds of changes taking place in Indian rural society. The resource theory provides a basis for seeking explanations of the nature of shift in the household power structure and decision-making. In the following we will discuss the source of such power among the rural population of south India especially with reference to the women.

(1) Firstly, certain women in the study area appear to derive substantial power from their contribution of monetary incomes earned either as wage labourers or secured from their natal homes. Once a girl is married she becomes a member of the husband's family where she ordinarily lives and spends most of her time in household duties and, if required, works in the family farm or in the family occupation. Among most of the families in this area, especially those who have marginal land holdings, women contribute to the family income by working as labourers.

(2) Although the presence of a matured daughter is no more shameful in many families especially those belonging to Settys, Brahmins and a few Balagigas, every effort is made to arrange her marriage as soon as possible.[6] The require a suitable boy who is also more likely to demand substantial sums in dowry. The local practice or custom also ensures a substantial transfer of wealth in the form of gifts, support during child care and emergencies, and help in establishing the business which continues for a long time after the marriage from the girl's parents to the boy or his parents. The girl's parents are obliged to do so because of the fear that the son-in-law and his family may discard or divorce their daughter which not only increases their economic burden but also adversely affects their social prestige and status. This is one way by which the boy and his parents maximize the wealth flow from the girl and girl's parents. On the other hand the situa-

tions are felt to be such where the girl's parents are obliged to please the boy and his kin in accepting her as the bride. The nature of the boy's parents can appropriately be described as exploitative as they intend to maximize not only the social benefits of the new relationship but also the flow of wealth involved in their son's matrimony. The economic forces based on this exchange are strong enough to create an imbalance in the power structure between the kin and affine groups. This also elevates the social status of the boy especially in the affinal circle. Beals also observes from another area in south India, that in the process of building relationships through marriage, the boy is in direct competition with member of his own and fraternally related lineages (1962 : 32). A greater affection from the parents-in-law along with the flow of wealth and emergency support seems to influence boys to assume new responsibilities and become patriarchs themselves by splitting from the joint family with the support of affinal relatives. During the process of this change in the pattern of relative power, the wife (daughter-in-law) appear to draw a substantial power enabling her to participate in the household decision-making. Conklin (1981 : 20) has provided a convincing evidence to the fact that dowry in the northern parts of Karnataka has increased the wife's say in the external matters[7] of the family decision-making thus refuting Kolenda's (1967) speculation of an opposite effect. Another study of an urban sample of educated girls in Bangalore city has also provided support to this contention (Blumberg and Dwaraki, 1980).

(3) The role and status of patriarchy is declining due to the incapacity of the patriarch to provide substantial inheritance to his sons, while sons are seeking alternative off-farm jobs and depending less on the share of family land. Another most important source of power a woman gains over time in her husband's family is her ability to manage a sub-budget and acquire personal wealth. It is universal among the responsible women in the family to have a sub-budget and have individual savings over time. Among these rural families, apart from access to the husband's income to be spent on family requirements, a woman usually can sell small quantities of grains and

other family produce on the sly. Women also claim a portion of cash earned by selling the produce of animals which they maintain like milk, eggs and chickens. The money received from selling vegetables, oil seeds and wild nuts, which a woman and her children collect, is generally her own property. Over time, a woman tends to save a substantial amount which she uses to buy gold ornaments thereby enhancing her power and status. A similar situation has been noticed by Srinivas (1976 ; 155) and Epstein (1962 : 237) in other parts of the region.

(4) There appears to be a situation in which the families of origin are unequal both in social and economic status. This situation initially emerged in the upper and middle class urban populations where the educated boys were getting married to girls belonging to a higher economic class and frequently the girls' fathers were themselves highly educated, working as high bureaucrats and officials. This kind of hypogamous marriage is becoming familiar to the rural population in spite of only a slight increase in the level of education of boys in the last two decades. This phenomenon also has supported the emerging pattern of an increase in affinal influence on the newly married couples. All these factors in combination have enhanced the ability of affines to influence the husbands although they have not completely eroded the effect of kin influence. This change has enabled the wife to derive power and status in her husband's family.

In the contemporary nuclear family, the relationship between the husband and the wife appears to be relatively more cordial and affectionate than in the past and in the extended family. As noted in Chapter 5, the women in these families are relatively older and have more children, and they have considerable influence and authority in day-to-day family management. It is appropriate here to quote Fortes :

> During the first two or three years of wifehood, the majority of young wives continue to reside with their *husband or* own kin. Young and inexperienced, they cling to their mothers *and mothers-in-law*. As they advance in maturity, the pull of conjugal ties increases and reaches its maximum at the peak

> of the child-bearing years, in the thirties. By this time they have perhaps three children, for whom it is an advantage to be under their father's care. Finally, when their child bearing years are over and their children are grown, the desire to establish their own households becomes strong in many women, the more so if they are widowed or divorced (1949 : 78-79) [emphasis added].

Thus Fortes clearly brings out the process, motivations and capabilities to acquire a greater say in the family establishment and management among the Ashanti women. Similar process, motivations and capabilities are found to be present among the South Indian women with certain variations. The desire to establish a family clearly develops at an advanced age, but the widowed and separated women stay in complex families. Nevertheless, the power and authority maintained and developed by a wife appears to be always derived from her husband and own kin. In an extended family system these relationships become more complex because the joint family usually have an elaborate system of avoidance patterns which serve to keep the husband and wife form becoming emotionally close (Goode, 1963) and the older generation tries to continue its hold on the younger couple especially through the control of property and sexual behaviour.

An important area of intra-family relationship useful in decision-making analysis is the balance of power between the husband's and wife's kin both of whom try to maintain their influence on the newly wedded couple. The husband's kin, in their effort to maximize the wealth flows, may eventually yield to the power and influence of the wife's kin which is gained by offers of dowry and other tangible transfers. This area of change in the intra-family power and relationships has not sufficiently been emphasized in social research in India. Such a change from a unilineal system to a bilateral system of kin relationships appears to have been taking place for two to three decades associated with an increase in the pecuniary interest of the community.

These are the changes which have begun to occur since independence and the beginning of commercialization which has led to a situation where the extended family and kin influences are declining and affinal influences are assuming prominence leading toward a bilateral kinship system. Thus the wife draws power and demands status in the husband's family and may even have a say in important matters like sale, purchase and even borrowing. This process of change is one of the salient features of the modern society which have gathered momentum since the introduction of modern values through education and urbanization and the advent of dowry which occurred almost at the same time in the research area. Thus, there appears to be a shift toward an egalitarian relationship between the husband and the wife and there also appears to be a cession of power from the older generation even while the new couple are relatively young.

Another study which has presented similar results was undertaken in Hong Kong and the Philippines by Liu, *et al*, (1973). They concluded that :

> . . . bilateral system of kinship network allows a more egalitarian relationship than the unilineal kinship system. Such structural determinants of conjugal power relationships become more important if the family is open and society is closed. (p. 84)

The situation in South India is very near to the above explanation to the extent that nuclear dwellings are predominant but they are open to kin pressures and the village society itself has not shown signs of openness and retains its close structure and distinct identity as judged from the way of life of the majority of the families in this area. Nevertheless, unlike the older couples among whom husband and wife communication was not essential (Poffenberger, 1968) for fertility and family planning decisions, the change in social status of younger married women warrants an increase in intra-family (including women) and husband-wife communication and egalitarian relationships (see also Conklin. 1973).

(*vi*) *Differences in Husband and Wife Motivations and Intentions*

Although husband and wife are two independent persons,

their intentions and motives regarding most areas of life including fertility and family life differ only rarely at least in the initial period after marriage in this area. In the later period the wife may feel the requirement to have more sons because she is the one who is more likely to remain widowed while she requires support from sons (Cain, 1978 : 431-432 ; Poffenberger, 1973 : 143). The intention to control fertility ordinarily and naturally originates from the woman who bears children. Therefore, the motivation to limit fertility is found to be relatively greater among women who have given birth to the minimum number of children they desire. Townes, Beach, Campbell and Wood (1980) found that the women's expectations carried about one-and-one-half times the weight of the men's expectations in determining the decision (see also Koenig, 1981). The reason is that in the absence of the practice of husband-wife communication in the early childbearing period, the origin of an intent is suppressed either due to the fear that husbands may get offended or because women are too modest to speak on these issues. In this area the knowledge and awareness of family planning, especially tubectomy, is not different between the dyad, yet the women are in an advantageous position because of their interaction with the female health workers. Therefore, when such a motive is communicated to the husband by the wife and if the husband disagrees, it is only because of a lack of knowledge on his part. When the motives of the spouses differ considerably even after a fair amount of knowledge, then acceptance is unlikely and the decision is postponed till such time as the wife feels confident to raise this issue with the husband or ask someone to intervene and convince him. Such instances are few and are mostly found among the Muslims and the Low Caste. Our data support the contention that practically all those who decided to limit the number of children and accept sterilization did so either with the agreement of the husband or with his consent. On the whole, women who could not accept family planning even after having the desired number and sex combination of children, are those who together with their husbands did not succeed in resisting the normative pressures and kinship group influences. The few occasions when the husbands did not permit their wives to be sterilized were not because they had different motives but because neither could comprehend any easy means to solve the fear of eventualities like the wife's or child's death and difficulties in securing emergency support.

Nevertheless, the first two or three births occur to a couple without explicit decision process. These non-decisions are regarded by researchers as passive decisions (Hollerbach, 1980; Leibenstein, 1981). It is not uncommon for husbands to express ignorance of their wives' pregnancy. Some husbands even said that they only became aware of their wife's pregnancy when the woman showed signs of sickness relating to pregnancy or when wife's physical appearance changed. The older women were of the universal opinion that they had neither opportunity nor need to discuss with husbands their fertility or the number of children to be borne. The younger women, however, are beginning to discuss fertility and family planning issues with their husbands at least after a few years of marriage. One evidence for this is that among the acceptors the decisions were taken within in a short time, sometimes spontaneously, while only a small number said that reaching the decision to stop future births was prolonged over a period by which time they gave birth to another child. The mehanism involved in this is that over time matters of children and family planning are discussed with reference to others in the community thus indirectly communicating the views and ideals. When they themselves reached such a situation, the decisions were made faster and with relative ease. Such decisions have a long passive period and a short active period of decision-making. In the absence of this pattern, decision-making becomes most active and the actors involved in decision-making will also increase thus increasing the chances either of postponement or even rejection of a particular idea. Another evidence of the increase in awareness and ability to think about the children is found in the confirmation of an increase in induced termination of pregnancies over a decade or so.[8] The IUDs too gained popularity within a short span of time mainly because women themselves decided to use this method and the husband's involvement was only superficial. Thus the persent situation is that even unmarried girls have some knowledge about the existence of family planning which they understand to be used to avoid child birth. After marriage the intention to restrict fertility is normally verbally communicated only after a minimum number are born ; the reason is not only female modesty but also the fact that the women know that they cannot use any family planning method till they have a minimum number of sons and those as soon as possible. The general notion is that the married couple should have a son as soon as possible so that the age gap between father and son should be minimum. This has also increased the speed of child bearing with an intention to stop after they achieve that goal.

In spite of the fact that motivations and intentions regarding fertility exhibit only small differences between spouses, there can be differences as to how their intentions are put into practice, their timing and arrangements. For instance, husbands are less specific than the wives in deciding when she can go for a sterilization—before or after another birth, while she is with him or while she visits her natal place, and whom to seek for emergency help for the household activities while the wife goes for sterilization. In this regard women generally have a better idea and they are normally the decision-makers on these issues. The husband permits the woman to undergo sterilization while the woman organizes the situation. It is normally affinal kin who provide active support and miscellaneous services.

(vii) *Referent Group, Status Group, Local Leaders and Expert Advice*

It is optional that couples contact the referent group (status group) and others and seek expert advice. This happens when the couple has failed to reach consensus because of a lack of knowledge or because there is opposition from the kin group. The referent group could provide trustworthy information to help solve the issues. They may also reach local leaders which consists of village panchayat members, bureaucrats and even the land-owners who generally are the employers. The most often sought leaders are those with whom the husbands or other male adults have occupational contacts and they are more likely to be large landholders. These land-owners would also be the panchayat members and local leaders as well as the caste group elders. Expert advice is also sought from the medical and para-medical health personnel. The health personnel are, however, contacted to give the services once a decision is made. Expert advice is crucial for a decision especially in a society where the understanding of the complexities of modern contraceptives is relatively limited. This stage is the one where the apprehension about whether or not to act on a decision is the greatest. In fact, the decision-makers may again review the whole process to make sure if there are any factors which are left out. However, the process of decision-making terminates once a particular decision is put into action but the post-acceptance situation is crucial from two viewpoints. As a result of acceptance there could be what is called satisfaction but if any of the fears and anticipated side-effects occur, then the decision-maker is subjected to criticism and ridicule. This is the main reason why autocratic decisions are less frequent. A satisfied acceptor is the most authentic and effective member of the referent group especially so if the person is a relative.

Summarizing the above discussion, we arrive at the following :

1. The approach to the study of fertility and family planning decision-making should essentially be an anthropological and sociological one.
2. The unit of analysis is more appropriately the marital dyad in spite of the predominance of the extended family system in the area.
3. The fertility and family planning decisions are identified as following the same process and path and in fact the latter may precede on many occasions.
4. Although the social and economic environment provides general guidance for a behaviour its influence is weakening especially as the extended family influences and the individual and dyadic factors are gaining prominence.
5. The dyadic power and consequent decision-making behaviour are influenced by the changing nature of the kinship patterns from unilineal to bilateral one which helps the affinal influences to gain prominence.

6. Fertility and even family planning decision-making is essentially the women's concern. Nevertheless, the husband's consent is required to meet the programme's regulations.
7. Autocratic decisions are rare but the common pattern can be at best described as a syncratic one with less emphasis on the role of the husband in the decision-making.

In the following chapter we will describe the actual supports to the discussion initiated in this chapter and provide data and explanations from the case studies and observations from the four south Indian villages.

NOTES AND REFERENCES

1. The extended family for our purpose includes not only unilineal descent groups but also residential (local) and affinal relationships.
2. Data collected on desired family size or desired number of total children in the rural Indian context appear to be useless and meaningless.
3. This duration is calculated using data from all those families where at least one currently married couple lived at the time of the start of the field work.
4. Thirty per cent of all currently married women aged less than 30 years are married before they were 14 years of age and majority of them did so before puberty. This proportion for those who were above 30 years of age was 37 per cent in the research area.
5. The primary reason is that young men are becoming independent owing to their open access to the wider world through education, transportation, communication and possibility of securing outside jobs, while parents feel a danger of losing them and their income unless they are controlled by compelling them to marry a girl of their own choice (Caldwell *et al* 1982a). Among thirteen most recent marriages in the study area it was found that on average the age difference between the husband and the wife was only 5.3 years.
6. One hundred and six or 13 per cent of all women in age group 15-24 years were unmarried. All 22 unmarried girls aged above 25 years were in Shetty, Brahmin and some Balagiga families.
7. Conklin used the following three questions as examples of external

matters : (a) Going to visit a festival, (b) If wife should seek work outside the home, and (c) How much education the son should get (Conklin 1981 : 12).

8. We have discussed elsewhere the fact that the termination of pregnancies were resorted to eliminate unwanted pregnancies or those which were thought to be immoral. Nevertheless, for the last decade the termination of pregnancy has been used within marriage.

8

Acceptors and Non-Acceptors of Family Planning, and the Decision Making Process

In the preceding chapter we discussed the background and conceptual framework for an analysis of fertility and family-planning decision-making. Details of the source and pattern of the flow of power enabling a decision is also discussed. In Chapter 6 we learnt that the fertility and family planning decisions are almost synonymous and that tubectomy is the only method currently being practised. We also mentioned that there are kinship and neighbourhood cluster patterns of acceptance in the larger village, namely Ramagere. In this chapter we will substantiate the earlier findings from the data pertaining to acceptors and non-acceptors with whom we had prolonged informal conversations on the decision-making patterns. Nevertheless, some of the core data collected from them is also presented. An attempt is made to bring out differences between acceptors and non-acceptors as well as between the villages wherever possible. The analysis is based on the primary data from 88 acceptors and 61 non-acceptors and the substantive evidence is drawn from conversations with 82 acceptors and all 61 non-acceptors.

8.1 Acceptor and Non-Acceptor Characteristics

In the following section we present some essential socio-economic characteristics of the acceptors and non-acceptors of the area. This analysis is based on the 50 acceptors in Ramagere, 31 in Laxmipura and one from the remaining villages who were contacted over a long period of time and with whom a series of prolonged conversations were under-taken. The only acceptor from the last two villages is in-cluded in the figures on Laxmipura. Data on 42 non-acceptors from Ramagere and eleven from Laxmipura are also presented for comparisons. A quick comparison of the characteristics of acceptors and non-acceptors from Ramagere and Laxmipura suggest that the predominance of male over the female children which is evident from the high sex ratio is an important factor leading to acceptance in both villages; but this ratio is only slightly lower in Laxmipura (see Table 8.1). The sex ratio of the last living child is another decisive factor in fertility and family planning decision-making. Nevertheless, 80 per cent of the non-acceptors in Laxmipura are Low Caste who are least likely to be acceptors. The acceptor couples are found to be better educated in both the villages, but the level of education is much lower in Laxmipura. An-other feature to be noted is the fact that 90 per cent acceptors in Ramagere and all acceptors in Laxmipura are tubectomy users. The remaining 10 per cent in Ramagere have under-gone vasectomy. Twenty-four per cent of all the tubectomized women in Ramagere used IUDs ranging from three days to three-and-a-half years' duration. Some of these findings have already been revealed in the 'discriminant analysis' undertaken in Chapter 6.

Table 8.2 presents certain characteristics of acceptors in the area. All the current family planning acceptors found in the area are included in this table. It appears that couples currently residing in simple families are twice as likely to be

TABLE 8.1

Acceptor and Non-Acceptor Characteristics by Village

[All ages and durations are presented in years]	ACCEPTORS Rama-gere	Laxmi-pura	NON-ACCEPTORS [1] Rama-gere	Laxmi-pura
Total number of cases	50	32	43	11
Average current age of women	32.2	31.5	30.1	29.7
Women below 30 years (per cent)	34	41	42	55
Difference of age between husband and wife	9.9	7.0	8.0	10.9
Average age of women at acceptance	28.5	28.6	na	na
Average duration of acceptance	3.6	2.9	na	na
Per cent of women having three or less living children	48	40	na[2]	na[2]
Sex ratio of living children (M/F)	159	143	86	138
Sex ratio of last living child (M/F)	150	167	70	57
Average current age of the last living child	6.1	3.5	1.8	2.7
Type of women's occupation (per cent). Household work	26	19	16	0
Household work and work on own farm	54	49	69	50
Household work and agril. labour	18	30	13	42
Work on modern jobs	2	2	3	8
Average years of schooling				
Wives	3.8	1.3	1.4	0.4
Husbands	6.1	3.5	2.2	1.4
Type of the family of current residence (per cent)				
Nuclear	66	56	49	73
Stem	20	22	30	18
Joint	12	19	21	9
Tubectomy (percentage to total)	90	100	na	na
Past users of IUD (per cent)	24	0	na	na

1. Data on seven non-acceptors from the two smaller villages is not presented.
2. Note that the criteria used to select the non-acceptors is that they had to have at least three living children.

[na]=not applicable

TABLE 8.2

Distribution of Current Acceptors of Family Planning by Age and Socio-Economic Characteristics

	Percentage to all acceptors*	Percentage of all eligible women in the category
1. Current age of women		
less than 19 yrs	0	0
20—24 yrs	8	6
25—29 yrs	27	22
30—34 yrs	26	28
35—39 yrs	22	38
40 yrs and above	17	28
2. Caste category		
High Castes	13	28
Peasant Castes	65	26
Service Castes	11	19
Low Castes	8	7
Non-Castes (Muslims)	3	12
3. Literacy (women)		
Illiterates	52	15
1—6 standard	28	33
7 and above	18	29
4. Occupation (women)		
Household (HH) duties	24	24
HH+work own farm	55	22
HH+Labour	18	13
Outside work	3	20
5. Type of family of current residence		
Broad category		
Simple families	82	24
Complex families	18	12

* Total number of cases is 88.

the acceptors of family planning than those in complex (extended) family types. Nevertheless, a greater proportion of those who are now in simple families would have lived jointly with others in the earlier part of their married life. A life cycle analysis of living arrangements is discussed below which reflects the true picture. Secondly, couples belonging to the High Castes and Peasant Castes are found to be more progressive in accepting family planning whereas Low Caste women are least progressive. Thirdly, literates are more than twice as likely to be acceptors than the illiterates ; and lastly women who work on household duties and also work as labourers on paid work are the least to accept a family planning method.

8.2 Living Arrangements of Couples

(i) Living Arrangements of the Marital Dyad and Family Planning Acceptance

We have already discussed in detail the fact that the place of residence and the people with whom a couple live is an element important in the achievement of a certain level of fertility and also in the acceptance of family planning methods. It is customary in this region for a girl to join her husband immediately after marriage at her parents'-in-law home. Apart from the husband's parents, his brothers and their wives may also live together. Other unmarried brothers and sisters of the boy may also live with them. Traditionally, marriages were meant to establish relationships between two families rather than between the husband and the wife. The matrimonial relationships were sought within relative circle. In the study area we found that 35.6 per cent of the Hindu husbands and wives had a first degree relationship, such as cross cousins, maternal uncle and niece, and 8.9 per cent had a second degree relationship even before marriage. Another 28.9 per cent were the marriages where they were far-off (third degree relationship) relatives and remaining 26.7 per cent marriages were between the non-relatives. A relatively greater proportion of marriages between non-relatives was found among the Scheduled Castes followed by the Brahmins of these villages. The proportions were almost uniform for the other castes of the area. The practice of a boy bringing in his elder sister's daughter or mother's brother's daughter as a wife is still prevalent but on a lesser scale. In such marriages the brides just change from the home of their parents to another home which is known to them from childhood. The post-marriage residence after such marriages were inevitably with the joint or extended families in this area. Later on in the life-cycle, the couple normally decide to stay separately in nuclear families. The importance of living arrangements either in a nuclear or joint family type has to be understood in the context of the extended family system where even after separation the relatives live close to each other, often in the same building but having a separate budget and hearth.

Table 8.3 presents data on certain aspects of family types and family planning acceptance. As couples having three or more living children (of whom at least two are sons) are more to accept family planning, all such couples were singled out likely for this analysis. A total of 102 couples had three or more living children of whom at least two were living sons. This group includes both acceptors and non-acceptors of family planning. Fourteen of these couples started their married life and continued to live in the nuclear families (see Table 8.3). Only for two per cent of their total marital duration they were able to live in the extended families. Thirteen couples started living in stem families with their parents, while there were only two instances where the couples joined the wife's parents. They spent 58 per cent of their total marital time in a stem family and another 14 per cent in a joint family along with at least one other couple of the same generation. The remaining or 28 per cent of their marital time was spent separately. Another three-quarters of all couples started their marital life in joint families and spent 37 per cent of their marital duration in them. Thirteen per cent of the remaining time was spent in stem families and for the rest or 50 per cent of the period they lived separately with their unmarried children.

TABLE 8.3

Pattern of Residential Arrangement of the Newly Married and Proportion of Time Spent in Different Family Types for Selected Families

Family of residence after marriage	No. of couples	Mean marital duration	Per cent of time spent in Nuclear	Stem	Joint	No. of acceptors	Per cent acceptors
Nuclear	14	16.4	98.0	2.0	0.0	5	35.7
Stem	13	15.4	27.9	57.8	14.3	8	61.5
Joint	75	18.2	49.5	13.3	37.2	47	62.7
All	102	17.6	53.3	19.1	29.9	60	58.8

An essential qualification for these living arrangements is that couples who started their marital life in non-nuclear families continued to stay in them for an average of nine years immediately after marriage.[1] It is only in the latter part of their marital lives that they moved to nuclear type residence. Of all such couples who started their married life in extended family (stem or joint), only twelve per cent continued to stay in them, while the rest have established neolocal residences. Nine years is a sufficient time for a woman to bear three to four children by which time the family may feel the requirement for fertility regulation. However, it appears that the extended type of family does not discourage family planning acceptance. The results are drawn from a small number of case histories and the analysis is illustrative, yet it is sufficient to highlight the fact that the acceptance rate among those who started their life in joint families and lived there for an average duration of nine years is 63 per cent. The acceptance rate for those who started their lives in stem families and stayed in them for the same duration, as is the case with joint families, is 62 per cent and the rate is only 36 per cent for those who continuously stayed in nuclear families.

(ii) Reasons for the Division of the Family

A close understanding of the reasons for the breakdown of extended families will provide clues for the understanding of the decision-making process. Among these rural families the major reason for the breakdown of stem joint families is the shortage of land (details about the land ownership and related discussion has been done in Chapter 3 of this thesis). Sufficient land ownership has a demonstrable power for creating a binding relationship between siblings and keeping them together. The position of the eldest son is that he is culturally the inheritor of the headship and ancestral profession. Nevertheless, the transfer of authority from father to eldest son is only partial (Srinivas 1982 : 69). This is also one of the reasons why families split up sooner, after the father's death. This leads to a situation where the young have to diversify their interests and find alternative sources of income. The younger brothers may decide to go to urban areas in search of jobs. All those younger couples who moved away from the joint family residences did so even before the formal division of land took place and frequently they did so even before the death of the patriarch. A few of them, however, cultivate their share of land on an informal basis as a secondary occupation. The growth of individualism and the spread of westernization are believed to be the contributing factors for the family divisions. The following views of the respondents will substantiate these issues.

> In the past, as far as my knowledge goes, there used to be one earner, others used to work on family land, but for all practical purposes the head was the earner and a king-pin which helped in keeping a family together ; but now all adults (males) have to work and more often they work on different jobs or have separate sources of income. This is the root cause for the family splits. Urbanization and changing values have contributed to this phenomenon. For instance, the per-capita textile consumption has increased over time and everyone wants to spend on himself. [Ramagere, case 243]

> Modern developments in agriculture have changed the cultivation pattern, and now agriculture produce is exchanged for money. Hybrid seeds and chemical fertilizers have enabled to cultivate crops which are not eaten by the local population rather they are sold. The taste for money is the cause for changes in the living patterns of the society favouring division of joint families. [Laxmipura, case 22]

> A villager never used to enter a hotel (restaurant) or a theatre, nor did he travel by a bus, he used to stay back and work hard, listen to parents, but now individual tastes have developed and the head of the households themselves have become corrupt. They spend more time and money in towns to solve their land problems in the government offices. The young are much worse, they are lazy and have taken to fashion. [Ramagere, case 220]

Frequent debts incurred by individuals, especially the fathers or the elder brothers, offering land as security has created rifts and ill-feelings among family members. In the process of acquiring as much inheritance as one can, brothers fight with each other. Sometimes the problem arises because the property owned by the mother is not subject to inheritance laws. In the past, however, the division of property was a difficult affair involving cast and village leaders, but in the recent days it is an easy task because of the modern concepts in measurements and legal regulations.

> There used to be frequent quarrels involving parents and brothers before the division. The land was mortgaged long ago and we had no money to repay the loan. This split the joint family and now live separately. I have no hope of inheriting any land. [Ramagere, case 57]

> For eleven years I stayed with my parents and four other brothers ; now all of us are married. But the youngest brother started stealing grain which he used to sell ; this created confusion. There was also a loan of Rupees 1,650 incurred by father, and all the brothers had to contribute

to repay it and only after repayment it was, possible to divide the property. We were divided and now we have no problem and rifts, each one cares for his own family and children. This is a good arrangement. [Ramagere case 112]

Another important reason is the incompatibility among the women of the joint household, especially between the wife, and the husband's sisters or between wife and mother or between her and her husband's brother's wives. Men consider that such situations are generally solved easily by establishing separate living arrangements. After all, one has to get separated one day or another. This reason partially originates from the reasons discussed above and partially emerges due to competition between women and disagreements on the division of household work responsibilities. The following quotations highlight the situation very well.

This is a general feeling among us (adult males) that the daughter-in-law cannot stay together along with her sisters-in-law and mother-in-law for long. Therefore, the family splits sometimes even before the trouble starts and the change is towards family nucleation. [Ramagere, case 220]

One has to live separately one day or another and the sooner the better. The joint living is not an ideal any more. [Ramagere, case 29]

Nevertheless, the desire of a woman that she should live separately to enjoy life, to take care of her children and to acquire individual wealth slowly grows stronger over time which accentuates intra-family rifts resulting in division of families (see a quote by Fortes in Chapter 7).

8.2. Access to Outside Support and Balance of Power

(i) *Types of Outside Support*

The source and accessibility of outside support provides clues to describe the power structure of a family. Outside support for a couple after marriage[2] can be of three types : (a) customary gift exchange and support, (b) support during sickness and deliveries, and (c) support during economic crisis. The usual source of such supports are close relatives and the type of relationship determines the relative access to or responsibility to support.

Customary support comes from both husband's and wife's side in the form of kind, such as clothing and books given to school-going children, gifts given during ceremonies and festivals and small quantities of grain and other family produce on various other occasions ; and in cash such as, money given to a daughter to return to her husband's place, and gifts in cash given during marriages and naming ceremonies. This happens whenever a family member visits his relatives or when relatives visits them and during festivals and marriages. The system between siblings works as a reciprocal arrangement.

A family experiences crisis during the sickness of a family member and also during pregnancies. A woman is expected to to be at rest during deliveries and post-partum periods and similar rest periods are advocated for tubectomized women both by the doctors and the elders. The frequently reported rest periods for women after deliveries are from a minimum of three months to one year. The average is about sixteen weeks. The rest periods after tubectomy are longer which are advised by the doctors and strictly enforced by the family members. It is customary that a sick or pregnant woman goes to her natal home where she takes rest and receives various services. Since tubectomy became popular, women who wish to undergo tubectomy choose to receive the services in her natal home or in the presence of her close relatives. Psychic and emotional support is an integral part of this system which is believed to be essential on such occasions. It is said that this system costs a great deal for the person who extends such help in providing food, shelter, care, medical attention and travel. Therefore, the relative who is expected to provide such support tries to discourage too frequent requests for help.

The economic emergencies in this area are largely the result of crop failures which make it difficult for farmers to repay loans taken before the harvest. Economic support is also sought to arrange a marriage in the family. The support during distress is often in the form of large amounts of money, other forms are a grant of a piece of land, the provision of a a house for living and the temporary provision of care and education for young children.

(ii) Nature and Source of Outside Support

Now let us take a look at the nature and source of such support in the research area. Twenty-eight or 19 per cent of the 148 families belonging to all the villages from whom we collected data on this issue confirmed that they have neither relatives nor friends to rely upon for any kind of support. They either borrow from others on interest or suffer. These families have lost contacts with relatives because either they have migrated to this area from their birth place where other relatives live or all close relatives are dead. Secondly, over a period of time the filial bondage and contracts have decreased and along with this the access to support has become extinct. Another seven per cent or 11 families disclosed that they need not depend on outsiders for any support because they are either sufficiently rich or live in economically stable joint families. The remaining 109 families provided details of 193 recent events when they received different kinds of support from various relatives and non-relatives. Because a family received more than one kind of support from more than one source, this analysis is undertaken on the number of events reported (see Table 8.4). The source of support is split into three major categories based on the relationship with the marital dyad. They are (a) husband's side relatives, (b) wife's side relatives and (c) others.

Forty-three per cent of all the events referred to the economic support that couples had received followed by the customary support which constituted 34 per cent of the incidence of the support during sickness and pregnancy was 23 per cent. Regarding the source of support, 58 per cent of all the events involved support extended by the wife's relatives followed by 34 per cent from the husband's side and the remaining 8 per cent by other sources like employer, friends, co-operative banks and sons. The majority of these families have benefited from the farmers co-operative bank by receiving loans but only one family treated this source of

TABLE 8.4
Frequency of Source and Kind of Outside Support for a Selected Number of Families

Source of support Relationship to the couple	Type of Support: Economic support		Support during sickness and pregnancy		Customary gift givings and reciprocal exchange	
	N[1]	%	N	%	N	%
Relationship to the husband						
Parents	6	7.2	7	15.6	4	6.2
Brothers	19	22.9	1	2.2	15	23.1
Sisters	2	2.4	0	0.0	3	4.6
Others (paternal uncles)	6	7.2	1	2.2	2	3.1
SUB-TOTAL	33	39.7	9	20.0	24	37.0
Relationship to the wife						
Parents	19	22.9	19	42.2	19	29.2
Brothers	11	13.3	11	24.4	14	21.5
Sisters	4	4.8	5	11.1	8	12.3
Others (maternal uncles)	1	1.2	1	2.2	0	0.0
SUB-TOTAL	35	42.2	36	79.9	41	63.0
Others						
Employers	3	2.6	—	—	—	—
Friends/money lenders	9	10.8	—	—	—	—
Co-operative banks	1	1.2	—	—	—	—
Sons	2	2.4	—	—	—	—
SUB-TOTAL	15	18.0	—	—	—	—
TOTAL	83	100.0	45	100.0	65	100.0

[1] N=Number of events.

support as an emergency or economic support. Normally, the banks provide loans to buy fertilizers and agricultural equipments and has no policy to advance emergency support. For the first time in 1981, the farmers bank provided small loans of money ranging from fifty to six-hundred rupees for those families (including non-agricultural) who were involved in leaf-plate making. The loan was meant to be used to procure and store leaves so that the family members can work on leaf-plate making even after the leafing season is over. This scheme helped many of the Ramagere families and was as good as an economic support, but none gave this as an example of source of support.

Wife's relatives provide the bulk of support in all the three categories especially the support during sickness and pregnancy, and customary support. Economic support is provided almost equally by both side relatives. In this analysis the figures on customary support actually highlight the relative contacts and frequency of visits between relatives and the two other columns provide evidence for the incidence of the actual wealth flow. It is easy to comprehend the fact that the husband's side relatives will generally be closer to the couple and the gift giving and customary support is often limited to festivals and marriages. In contrast the wife's relatives are either frequently visited by the wife and her children or the relatives visit the daughter's or sister's family. The customary support is reciprocal between the siblings but it is largely one-sided in the case of the daughter's family from her parents in the early days after marriage which slowly declines in frequency and extent of support.

Support during sickness and pregnancies also originates from custom, and this involves a substantial transfer of wealth in terms of food, shelter, care, travel and medical expense. Factors like easy access to a health dispensary, or the presence of an old woman who will be useful at the time of delivery, will determine the choice of a relative and his family from where support can be sought. Nevertheless, a prolonged stay with the provider enables some kind of co-operative plans and arrangement for future. For example, a woman may be heavily influenced about the timing of her next pregnancy, or even a suggestion from elder brother for a tubectomy will be received positively by the pregnant visitor. This source of support is useful not only as a means of enhancing power but also helps in the development of trust, cordiality and feeling of indebtedness by the receiver which places the supporter in a position to influence the other.

Access to economic or emergency support is an extreme case of dependency as far as a rural family is concerned. In a patriarchal society it is normally expected to come from the husband's kin. Dependence on the affines is regarded shameful and is condemned. But our finding is to the contrary. We have discucssed in chapter 7 that the kins are often at competition for benefits from the same source and reciprocal economic support is relativaly less frequent than expected. The kins and affines are almost equally responsible in extending this kind of support in the research area. From the wife's side, her parents followed by her brothers are the major source while brothers are the best source of economic support from the husband's side. Because of a considerable age difference between the husband and the wife, wife's parents are expected to be younger and still productive whereas the husband's parents are more likely to be old or even dead.

The forms of economic or emergency support are varied. A frequent form is cash followed by agricultural produce. A third and important form is the provision of food, shelter and education to the school-going children. The last form of support is more frequently sought from the wife's parents followed by elder brothers. It appears that because of the system of cross-cousin marriages, this form of support is often provided with a vested interest of seeking matrimonial relationships in future. The fourth form is the effort of the wife's relatives in establishing the nuclear family either after marriage or after migration and help in finding a new job or occupation. There are two instances where the daughter and son-in-law were offered a home and some land for cultivation. The following quotations will give an idea about the issues involved in receiving support from the affines, the wife's relatives. Because, in the patrilineal families, women do not inherit immovable property in spite of the fact that they are now legally entitled to such an inheritance, they get compensated for by their possession of rights in both the households—natal as well as conjugal.

> Sisters complain that they are married to poor husbands. They also complain that the parents gave all the property only to sons and that they did not get any share of ancestral property. Therefore, all the time sisters agitate to get more in the form of gifts and loans which will never be repaid. [Ramagere, case 34]

> My father-in-law helped me in establishing the family, provided money to construct a home in which now we live, and he also takes care of my children and their education. He is the real decision-maker. Though we both are favourable to the acceptance of family planning, it is impossible to convince the old man. However, I have no reason to worry about this issue. [Ramagere, case 280]

> All my six daughters are married, the first daughter who is now separated lives with me in this house. After my husband's death I had to arrange four marriages, in the absence of a male earning member I had to sell the land. All daughters put together have delivered 21 children in this house. I sold more than half of the property (eight acres) to arrange marriages and the rest to meet the expenditure on daughters' deliveries. Now I am selling this house part by part. [Ramagere, case 300]

Although the fertility and family planning decisions do not appear to have a direct and tangible relationship with the residential arrangements and the access to extra-family support they are essential elements in the process of decision-making. Day-to-day interactions and influences of the relatives standardizes individual behaviour and decision patterns so that they appear as routine or passive decisions. The passive decision behaviour do not usually conflict with the interests if other family members and slight modifications are always tolerable. When active decisions are warranted, the experience gained during the passive period provides the basis for decision-making. It is during this situation of bargaining that the living arrangements and extra-family support assumes prominence in the decision-making process. The following quotes from the respondents highlights these issues.

> My husband was always against it, I experienced a complicated second delivery, and the doctors advised me to undergo tubectomy. I made up my mind to undergo tubectomy after the next child birth. But as I was with my husband's parents during delivery I got no opportunity. Thus I became pregnant for the fifth and the sixth times. But, during my sixth pregnancy, I had to decide in spite of the opposition from parents-in-law for an abortion (MTP) followed by a tubectomy. I was not prepared to tolerate deteriorating health and by this time the total responsibility of bringing up children was mine. [Ramagere, case 111]

> Because she (daughter-in-law) has undergone tubectomy, I have to work more. She often complains that she is sick and becomes tired soon. Though it is good to stop future births it is not good for the health of the woman. [Ramagere, case 263]

> It is disadvantageous for husbands if wives undergo sterilization. Now I have to do certain works which she (wife) used to do earlier, like drawing water, sometimes cooking and doing other tedious household duties. Now she can work only on simple jobs. [Ramagere, case 304]

> When my mother-in-law was alive she persuaded me to go to my elder brother's house for delivery and tubectomy services because of difficulties in receiving post-operative (follow up) services in this village. She was also frightened that I might die and was not prepared to take the responsibility. [Laxmipura, case 1]

(*iii*) *Outside Support Versus Dependence on Earnings from Young Children*

It is not always easy to receive support from other relatives because it depends not only on their capacity to help but also upon their willingness to approach for help and the willingness to extend support. For example 74 per cent of all the first births have occurred in the wife's natal place and this percentage declines thereafter with an increase in parity. The percentages are 47 for the second, 26 for the third, 17 for the fourth and 13 for the fifth child births. As one woman puts it :

> For how many deliveries can one expect the mothers (natal family) to provide help and support ; they are also 'sailing in the same boat as we are'. It is difficult for them to help us for more than one child birth especially when we are expected by the husband's parents to stay in the mother's place for six months to one year. [Ramagere, case 164]

It appears that access to the outside support slowly diminishes over time and the family has either to reach for outside support through borrowing, mortgage or sale of property or depend on children's earnings. Therefore, it regarded as essential that a couple should marry young and beget sons as soon as possible. But the views are equally divided as to whether children should start working at an young age or not. Those who support the view that children should start work from a young age argue that children discontinue schooling either due to lack of interest and repeated failures or that the parents cannot afford to keep children in school for various economic and personal reasons. For instance :

> Yes I have many sons and I could have continued to have more, but it is already difficult to educate the eldest and the second son was made to discontinue schooling in order to take care of the cattle. It is difficult to feed many mouths in these days of bad crops and the high cost of grain in the open market. [Ramagere, case 78]

The parents also believe that the younger the children start working the better capabilities and skills they acquire and that it is easier to control children while they are young. On the other hand the other view recognizes that education is essential for children at this age and good parenthood is to provide the minimum comforts to their children at young ages. Nevertheless, the wage earning opportunities for children have fast declined and their work contribution on family farm is not substantial. The exceptions are the children who have the Scheduled Castes parents, who work as bonded or permanent labourers (see Chapter 9). From Table 8.4 it is evident that sons as the source of emergency support was refered only by two families, this is because the age range of the parents of the selected families is younger and only a few had grown up sons.

8.4 Reasons for Fertility Regulations

In the following we will look into the specific reasons for the fertility and family planning decision making. The control of fertility directly depends on the number and sex combination of living children, health status of the woman, and the understanding of the concept of the good life suited to the local standard. The frequent reasons, however, cited by the respondents for the acceptance of family planning methods are economic in nature [see Table 8.5]. Almost a quarter of the responses relate directly to the economic problems. Another one-fifth are with the views that they had either too many or sufficient number of children. Economic issues are inherent in this reason as well. The cost of providing education and better health are recognized as the prime components in the economic reason. The anticipation of huge expenditures to arrange daughters' marriage are feared to cause economic disasters to the family.

> ... female children are the source of expenditure while the males are the source of future income. Nevertheless, the females are the ones who try to help their parents in old age ; the boys just ignore them. [Ramagere, case 152]

Only sixteen per cent of the responses emphasized the desire to improve the life style by controlling fertility. Westernization and associated attributes like individualism and the desire to meet selfish ends are the frequently cited reasons. One lesser professional who works in the city while his family lives in the larger village said that having few number of children will enable greater savings and he considers that this will also enable a better care for the children who are already born.

> We have the right number of children : two sons and one daughter, who are studying in schools. I work in Bangalore and travel to visit my family once a week. It is expensive to manage the family. If I were to have more children it would have been difficult to save for the future. [Ramagere, case 184]

TABLE 8.5

Frequency of the Reasons for Limiting the Family Size Acceptors of Family Planning

Reasons	Ramagere	Laxmipura	All	Percentage
Too many children	10	12	22	15.0
Right number of children	2	0	2	1.4
Planned life	11	12	23	15.7
Economic problems	19	14	33	22.5
Poor health of woman	19	5	24	16.3
No support during deliveries	7	1	8	5.4
Old age	5	1	6	4.1
Force	4	1	5	3.4
Has to work outside	1	0	1	0.7
Anticipated expenditure on daughter's marriages	5	8	13	8.8
Too many died	1	0	1	0.7
Sufficient Children from first wife	3	0	3	2.0
Superstition	1	0	1	0.7
Others did it	1	0	1	0.7
Small land holdings	0	4	4	2.7
All	89	58	147	100.0

(1) Number of cases=81.

> Too many children create complications in family relationships ; they fight and compete for a better share in property. With less number it is easier to maintain a minimum standard and also provide them with inheritance. [Ramagere, case 220]

Another sixteen per cent of the responses reflect health associated reasons. Women were the ones who were most concerned about this issue. The couples who had experience of complications like induced or Caesarian deliveries, or the women who suffered from illness before or after the delivery were more concerned. Thus, for them the experience of many pregnancies means danger to life. There, however, is a growing health consciousness among the younger women of the community. A few were also concerned that they are old and intended to have no more pregnancies ; therefore, they opted to undergo tubectomies. Nevertheless, repeated deliveries and associated complications were the only convincing reasons which were recognized by the elders in permitting the woman to undergo sterilization.

> I wanted to be sterilized after the fourth child, but my mother-in-law objected. She does not believe in hospitals because when one of her grand-children died after immunization, the death was attributed to immunization. This was the main reason why she did not allow me to get tubectomized. But when I had to rush up to a city hospital for an abnormal seventh delivery, the doctors advised me to undergo tubectomy and my parents-in-law had to change their views. [Ramagere, case 98]

Another prominent reason is the concern that the couples may beget more daughters who are expensive to maintain (the returns from daughters in the form of wages and other work is regarded relatively low to that of sons), and that they have to spend substantial sums to arrange daughters' marriages. This is the most direct effect of the dowry system which has interfered in the local marriage customs in the last two decades. The incidence of dowry payment is found among all the castes of the area including the Muslims. There is one couple in which the wife underwent tubectomy after having only three female children for the fear of begetting more daughters, incidentally this is a Muslim family. This feeling is relatively predominent among the Vokkaligas of Laxmipura followed by the Balagigas of Ramagere among whom dowry payment is clearly a measure of social status.

Lack of support during repeated pregnancies is felt relatively more by the Ramagere women. Substantial pressure is found to come from women's relatives especially elder brothers (who are the third major source of support to the families in the area) followed by elder sisters inducing the eligible women to accept family planning. A few women from Laxmipura who approached their brothers on their own to receive help to undergo sterilization did not get such help because their husbands were not involved. This emphasized the status and power of husbands in the fertility and family planning decision-making in this village. [case studies, 1, 2, 25, 162 not presented]. Only four land holding families, all from Laxmipura, were concerned about the small land holdings and felt that more children will create problems at the time of division of property, and also that children cannot inherit sufficient land if they are too many. This feeling among the Ramagere people has almost vanished because the land holdings are already small and people have managed to acquire new skills while reducing their dependence on land.

Other reasons which figure in this analysis are women's work outside the home ; too many children already dead and an unwillingness to bear any more agony of children's death, the influence of other acceptors and the superstition that if a daughter follows three sons she brings death and misery to the family.

8.5 Reasons for Postponement of a Fertility Regulating Decision

The analysis of the reasons for fertility decisions is only one side of the argument. Now let us examine the reasons for the postponement of the acceptance of a family planning method to a period after another birth. It has been found that all but seven acceptors had thought of acceptance even before the birth of the last child. The reasons given by the non-acceptors of family planning methods who had at least three surviving children are also discussed to have a comparative and contrasting feeling about the emphasis on certain reasons than the others which are different from the acceptors. The data for acceptors is presented by village and for non-acceptors the figures are for the study area as a whole. This analysis is also based on the number of responses rather than the number of cases.

The reasons fall into four broad categories : Sex preference, resistance and opposition to acceptance, imperfect knowledge and superstition, and fear of ill-health and death. All these reasons, however, are interrelated. Thirty-seven per cent of the responses emphasised the need to have more children of a particular sex of which two-thirds expressed the desire for one or more additional sons as the reason for the postponement of the acceptance. Preference for the second son and at least one daugther appears to be a strong factor which influenced the acceptors of sterilization.

> Before the birth of the last male child we had four daughters and only one son (fourth birth). Though it is true that not many children die, one must be assured of at the least one son who lives longer, because only sons can provide *bala* (meaning physical strength, signifies work) and *bembala* (meaning encouragement, signifies secure and confident future) in life. We, therefore, wanted to have the second son to make sure at least one survives. [Ramagere, case 137].

> There should be at least two sons and daughter in a family, for, even if one son dies, the other can continue the family tree. A daughter is not so essential in the family as she does not help in continuation of the family. [Ramagere, case 220].

> Two male and one female is the best combination of children any family can have, but if we were to have one son and two daughters even then we would have gone for sterilization because daughters can also help in the continuation of the family tree. [Ramagere, case 283 :—note the contradictory views about the value of daughters].

> Among the Brahmins, a female child is always respected. Even a woman with ten sons is considered sterile if she does not give birth to a daughter. A daughter is essential because only she can provide *punniya* (virtue) if she is given in *kanyadana* (this refers to the belief that arranging

daughter's marriage is like donating her to her husband). A son is required for *vamshaooruksha* (continuation of family tree). [Ramagere, case, 184].

The desire to have at least one daughter is found strong among the acceptors who already had two surviving sons and took a chance to get a female child in the third pregnancy. When they had a boy instead the parents did not take another chance of pregnancy rather decided for sterilization. Nevertheless, the responses which emphasised opposition from the spouse of other relatives, and a disapproval of family planning as reasons for postponement where found to be due to either sex preference or due to ignorance. Fifteen per cent of the reasons referred to poor knowledge and ignorance regarding family planning. A total disapproval of acceptance is not noticed among the acceptors. The contrast between the villages is that the families seems to have had a strong opposition from elder relatives in Ramagere whereas the discouragement from neighbours (non-relatives) affected the acceptance in Laxmipura.

TABLE 8.6

Frequency of the Reasons for Postponing Acceptance to after Another Birth : Acceptors of Family Planning

Reasons	Number of Responses Rama-gere	Laxmi-pura	All	%
Wanted a son	3	0	3	2.9
Wanted additional son	14	9	23	22.3
Wanted a daughter	8	4	12	11.7
Husband wife opposed	6	4	10	9.7
Elders opposed	3	0	3	2.9
Other discourage	0	4	4	3.9
Fear of death, ill health	8	6	14	13.6
Poor knowledge about FP	10	5	15	14.6
Poor health	2	1	3	2.9
Lack access to FP	3	0	3	2.9
Other method used	6	0	6	5.8
Not applicable	3	4	7	6.8
All	66	37	103	100.0

The fear that sterilization will bring permanent disability, or lasting ill-health or even death was expressed in seventeen per cent of the responses as a reason for discarding the idea of acceptance but later on such views were altered after obtaining additional knowledge and advice from either the health personnel (expert advice) or the reference group, a source of authenticity and confidence from the acceptors [see Table 8.7]. Only seven acceptors did not approach others to get advice and additional knowledge. Three acceptors said that they had to postpone acceptance because family planning services were not available when they wanted them and six others said that they initially used IUDs and underwent tubectomies only after expulsion of the IUDs. The lack of proper knowledge and the desire of people to pursue credible and additional knowledge is strong among all sections of study population.

TABLE 8.7

Frequency of the Source of Additional Knowledge

Source	Acceptors				Non-acceptors	
	Rama-gere	Laxmi-pura	All	%	All	%
Wife's relatives (acceptors)	23	15	38	35.2	10	13.9
Husband's relatives (acceptors)	13	2	15	13.9	4	5.6
Hospital doctor	9	5	14	13.0	10	13.9
FHW MHW	13	14	27	25.0	27	37.5
Neighbourers (acceptors)	6	1	7	6.5	15	20.8
Not applicable	6	1	7	6.5	6	8.3
All	70	38	108	100.0	72	100.0

Not all the couples who aspired for additional daughters could realize the desire, yet most of them were not prepared to take another chance of getting pregnant. On the other hand, most of the couples who reported that reason for postponement was the desire for a son continued to deliver till they obtained the desired number of sons. Some of these feelings can be understood in the quotations from case numbers 137 and 220 presented above.

8.6 Non-Acceptors and Reasons for Non-Acceptance

The reasons for non-acceptance are totally different than the reasons discussed above for postponement. Opposition and disapproval from relatives followed by fear of death and or illness, and sex preference are the major reasons obstructing acceptance. Although Tables 6 and 8 are strictly not comparable, it can be inferred that a relatively higher proportion of couples who are not yet acceptors, even after having three or more children, are those who have decision-making problems and have a poor knowledge of family planning. The desire to have sons is understnadable in this group because the sex ratio of the living children is relatively less favourable towards male children especially in Ramagere. The low educational levels among the non-acceptors appears to be the basis for imperfect knowledge. Nevertheless, as we have mentioned in chapter 6, the medical and para-medical staff have already neglected this group and are less likely to cover these families in future as they are considered less responsive to their motivation. It is useful to know at this stage that practically all non-acceptors belong either to Low Castes and Non-Caste groups and some are the poor Intermediary Caste people. The following views provide clues of the diversified reasons for non-acceptance.

> Let God forgive : We cannot afford to eat milk and butter, we are poor people who eat *ragi hittu* and *chatni.* I could never accept *operation.* [Ramagere, case 28].

> Both of us work as manual labourers, employers give us jobs because we work harder. They sometimes ask us to do difficult jobs like lifting and transporting loads. Therefore, there is a fear that if we accept tubectomy or vasectomy we may not get employment. I do not approve even of using the IUD because it is also dangerous. [Ramagere, case 19].

I do not care even if we get many children. I have an established business, sufficient land and substantial savings. There is nothing to worry about rearing children. I will not allow her to undergo tubectomy which she wanted to after the fifth child birth. It is against Islam. Both my parents are also against family planning. [Ramagere, case 35].

It (tubectomy) is not possible because she (the wife) is already weak ; there is no blood in her body after bearing nine children and she is pregnant again. If she undergoes sterilization she may develop more problems. I will find it difficult to handle the situation. [Ramagere, case 57].

The female health worker who used to stay next door encouraged me and my husband gave his consent to undergo tubectomy. I then wrote a letter to my husband's elder brother who is in a town far away about this decision. He sent his grown up son, a student in a college, who carried his father's message. The decision to accept family planning is a vital one and has to be informed to the elders. If they are not involved, in case of after-effects and complications after the acceptance they will not provide either moral or actual support which is essential to a family. My husband's nephew came and said that should any complication arise, none will care my children. Right now there is none to support them. He concluded that if I was determined to undergo tubectomy than I should poison all my children before I go to hospital. We both (the couple) have a regard and respect for the boy's words because he is a student and an educated man. [Ramagere, case 270].

Religion and disapproval of methods are other reasons which are emphasised. The belief that Islam does not permit the use of family planning methods is widespread, yet, three (all relatively young) the twenty-four Muslims are acceptors. One husband is vasectomized while two other wives are tubectomized. But they are treated as out-castes and their contacts with other relatives in the village are minimal. There is practically no support from any one and that they live amidst the Hindu neighbours instead of in the Muslim area. Family planning acceptance is partially responsible for such a tendency toward discrimination.

TABLE 8.8

Frequency of the Reasons for Non-acceptance of Family Planning Methods : Non-acceptors of Family Planning

Reasons	Responses All Villages N	%
Wanted more sons	11	14.7
Wanted daughter	1	1.3
Opposition from relatives	19	25.3
Fear of ill-health have to work hard	9	12.0
Fear of death	10	13.3
Poor knowledge about FP	4	5.3
Lack of help	4	5.3
Religious reasons	7	9.3
Disapproves methods	4	5.3
Others (too old, now pregnant, fear of expenditure, can take care many children)	6	8.0
All	79	100.0

Few other women consider that because they are currently pregnant they cannot undergo tubectomy and they cannot say what they would decide after child birth. A few others said that they were too old to get sterilized and not only will it be a health hazard but also the chance of future conception is minimal. It is, however, observed, that the reported sexual abstinence is substantially high among certain older non-acceptor couples and apparaently is being used to avoid future pregnancies.

8.7 Decision Makers and Decision-Making Process

In the following we will look into the process of decision-making and find out the prime decision-makers. We will divide the type of decisions into three categories : independent decisions, syncratic decisions and collective decisions. If one of the spouses is the sole decision-maker then it is an independent or autocratic decision, while if the decision is taken by both the husband and the wife it is a syncratic decision. If other people other than the marital dyad are instrumental then it is regarded as a collective decision. In Table 8.9 we identify the first two decision-makers and discuss how and when others come into the process of fertility decision making. The relationship is defined with respect to the husband ; for example, kins are husband's parents, brothers and other relatives while affines are wife's parents, brothers and other relatives.

The major concern for the family planning decision is not the choice of a method ; for instance the concern is not whether to accept vasectomy or tubectomy as a permanent method ? But the concern is whether the woman should get sterilized at all, and, if so, when and after how many children? Thus one of the major areas in the decision-making process, namely 'the problem of choice of a family planning method,' is almost absent in this area and the remaining issue is largely the worry of the women, thus her involvement in the process is decisive but not necessary essential. Nevertheless, in the study area wives are the most frequent prime dicision-makers for the tubectomy acceptance when compared with husbands. However, one in every eight prime decision-makers is either a member of kin or an affine. In two instances the decisions regarding the vasectomies have been made solely by the husbands on the advice of doctors and for health reasons and the remaining four vasectomies were done under the influence of force by the local leaders and health personnel.

One-quarter or 21 tubectomy decisions were autocratic, of which eleven were solely made by husbands and ten were independently decided by the wives. There were instances where the autocratic decisions were prolonged, where although the relatives especially the other spouses were involved, the final decision remained autocratic and the other partner had practically no say against the decision. For instance, of the ten wives, three informed their husbands only after they reached the hospital to undergo their tubectomies. In all the eleven instances where husbands took autocratic decisions, the wives just agreed even when they had their own independent feelings and fear of tubectomy. Such wives are applauded and are branded as 'good housewives', 'too ignorant to be able to understand the outside world', and so on. The following are a few views on this issue.

> My mother-in-law and husband suspected my intentions to undergo sterilization. She wanted me to bear as many children as I could possibly have and he was worried about the post-operative complications. But I was confident and had spoken to many people at the general hospital in Bangalore where I delivered two children. When I became adamant and stubborn, my mother-in-law kept a low profile and rationalized the situation that after all it was not her problem. When my mother-in-law became soft my husband did not interfere. Now that I am keeping good health after tubectomy, my mother-in-law could not object to the sterilization of two other daughters-in-law. On the other hand she encouraged them. After all someone has to take the lead. [Ramagere, case 97]

> After the third birth I was willing to accept the IUD. Many women in the neighbourhood were already using them. The female health worker also spoke to me, but my husband refused. I accepted the IUD without his knowledge and it worked well for three years after which time it was automatically expelled without my knowledge following which I conceived and delivered two more children. During this time I came to know about tubectomy from my co-sister and also from the female health worker. This time both my husband and father-in-law refused on the ground that I was the eldest daughter-in-law and a resposible person for the whole family, and lest something happened to me. I could not go against their wishes after the fifth delivery but by the time I was due to deliver for the sixth time I was determined and had spoken to my elder sister. This time both my husband and my father-in-law felt that I will be difficult to handle.

> Therefore, they did not interfere. In the meantime, my husband had also approached his friends and male health worker to get more knowledge and yet remained quiet. With the help of the female health worker, I underwent tubectomy immediately after the sixth delivery. [Ramagere, case 241]

There are a total of 36 instances of syncratic decisions taken by the couple, of which 21 are those where the wife was the main decision-maker and the husbands were either co-operative or passive but not against the decisions. Ordinarily it is difficult to differentiate between an autocratic and syncratic decision because the involvement of the wife in the tubectomy decision appears to be absolute and also due to the system of husbands giving written willingness that he is voluntarily willing for his wife's tubectomy make his involvement essential. Yet, it was possible for us to find out to what extent actually a person was involved in such decisions. In the case of the instances where husbands were the prime decision-makers, wives were either willing from the start or they agreed to the husbands wishes as a matter of deference and a feeling of sacrifice that they should be sterilized instead of their husbands.

The husband's kin are prominent participants with either the husband or the wife and they also prominent as the prime decision-makers in six instances compared with only three by the affines. The important factor, however, is that a relatively major role played by the wives as prime decision-makers and also a prominent role as secondary decision-makers is not because the decisions are about tubectomy and women automatically become involved in the process, but that they are generally influenced and supported by their kin inducing or allowing them increased participation. The role of a woman's kin in the direct decision-making process appears to be minimal because of the fact that they normally do not stay in the same village. Nevertheless, their involvement is the indirect encouragement to the eligible woman. Whenever a daughter has undergone tubectomy in her natal place, the relatives present around her before the sterilization have extensively participated in the process of decision-making.

TABLE 8.9

Prime Decision-Makers for Family Planning Acceptance in the Order of Importance

Decision-makers	Ramagere		Laxmipura		All	
	N	%	N	%	N	%
Husband alone	6		7		13	15.3
Husband and wife	8		7		15	17.6
Husband and his kin	0		5		5	5.9
Husband and his affine	0		0		0	
SUB-TOTAL	14	26.4	19	59.4	33	
Wife alone	6		4		10	11.8
Wife and husband	13		8		21	24.7
Wife and husband's kin	3		1		4	4.7
Wife and husband's affine	4		0		4	4.7
SUB-TOTAL	26	49.1	13	40.6	39	
Kin and husband	2		3		2	2.4
Kin and wife	4		3		4	4.7
Affine and husband	3		0		3	3.5
Affine and wife						
SUB-TOTAL	9	17.0	0		9	
Force	4	7.6	0		4	4.7
ALL	53		32		85	100.0

There are certain basic differences between villages in the pattern of decision-making. Ramagere, the larger village, is a multi-caste and relatively open in characteristics. In this village we find that women dominate in the fertility and family planning decision-making and also that the involvement of kins and affines in the process of decision-making is substantial. On the other hand, Laxmipura is relatively homogeneous and characteristic of a male dominant society yet, has a relatively low level of extra-couple influence in the process of decision-making. Nevertheless, patterns of village exogamy have a direct correlation with the nature of both affinal and consanguinal kin ties among these villages. The larger village is exogamous as well as multi-directional in its contacts while the other is partially exogamous and nearly uni-directional in contacts and relationships. A related trend is that the larger village has been subjected to frequent convulsions emitted from within the nature of multi-caste structure as well as due to its phenomenal growth in trade, commerce and government bureaucracy. On the contrary, the other village is largely unchanged in its traditional structure and settled agricultural life style, but the response to fertility and family planning acceptance has emerged due to a consistent and uniform improvements in standard of living and education. Yet, the social relationships within the village have hardly changed over time.

What can be the reason as to why elders are not prominent in fertility and family planning decision-making in Laxmipura which would ordinarily be expected? The answer emerges from the culture and tradition itself, that the force of male domination appears to outweigh generational domination and sons are becoming responsible for the family economy while they are still relatively young. This is the main reason for changes in agriculture and cropping pattern, and a subsequent increase in standard of living. The fact that the wives have figured in the decision-making structure is proof that husband and wife communication has improved and that there is a change toward egalitarian relationships emerging from within the apparently homogeneous structure of the society.

Nevertheless, the origins of fertility and family planning decisions are directly related to the source of primary knowledge of family planning. Since, the male health worker is more popular in Laxmipura than in Ramagere, males are the primary recipients of knowledge who were also more likely to reconsider the issue of fertility and family planning as a matter of sheer curiosity and later due to self-interest. This is another reason why the males dominate family planning decisions as they do in any other segment of the family and the family economy. The male health worker in Ramagere, on the other hand, is a native of the same village, belonging to an intermediary caste group. Both these attributes together worked against his popularity in the multi-caste community. The female health worker, in spite of living in the village, appears to be only partially successful in disseminating family planning information, because of the difficulty in dealing with a diverse community on the one hand and due to the frequent transfers on the other. As we have stressed elsewhere in Chapter 6, the flow of the family planning knowledge in Ramagere is multidimensional through diverse contacts with the outside world (frequent visits to towns, more institutional deliveries of the pregnant women and so on) as well as inter-village communication emerging from village exogamy and reference group influence.

The uniqueness of fertility and family planning decisions in Ramagere is the fact that a greater proportion of the decisions originated from women who wished to undergo tubectomies. They had greater access and exposure to knowledge about family planning through both voluntary and involuntary sources. These women have also received relatively more influence and support from their natal families and such decisions appear to have originated when they were in the natal home rather than while they were in the conjugal family. This activated the involvement of the husband's kin as a deterrent to the wife's wishes because of the suspicion that the daughter-in-law may take over even other areas of of the family decision making. If in Ramagere the husbands were to initiate such decisions, the involvement of kin and elders would be expected to be minimal though not totally absent.

A common practice, however, found among all the acceptors is that, but for a few earlier acceptors in Ramagere, practically all tubectomized women had at least one other relative who was an acceptor or had a neighbour who had undergone tubectomy. Thus, the non-acceptor sisters, and co-sisters of the sterilized women and the non-acceptor neighbours belonging to the same caste as that of the acceptor are the most likely potential acceptors in Ramagere. In the family system of the kind found in the area these relationships fall well into the ambit of the functional extended family. Once an younger woman or man is able to make headway either by convincing or by rejecting the influence from older generation, the process of decision-making becomes easy and fertility becomes the independent concern of the young especially women.

There is another pattern of the fertility and family planning decision-making which is based on the age and parity of the woman. The younger the woman is the greater is the expectation of the community that she will bear children. This expectation slowly decline over time, and much later in the life cycle, by which time a woman would have had many children, the desire for more children logically falls. But to certain extent it is noticed that the older the wife is (and, therefore less able to bear children) the higher she values fertility. Nevertheless, it has been gathered from the case histories that the younger the woman is the greater is the chance that she will desire to limit fertility and the less is the chance that the older generation will object to her undergoing tubectomy. On the contrary, the older the woman is, the relatively greater is the chance that the husband and other relatives will oppose her tubectomy and the decision-making process is most likely to be collective and prolonged. This pattern is consistent with the common belief that younger women are relatively healthy, and physically strong and will tolerate the pain and agony involved in the tubectomy operation (see Chapter 6). A woman who is relatively old is believed to be weak after having undergone repeated pregnancies and the danger from tubectomy is assumed to be relatively more likely to be fatal when compared to the danger from more pregnancies. Nevertheless, those women who have undergone tubectomies after their fifth or sixth deliveries are those who have experienced complications during earlier deliveries and have used this as a pretext to convince their husbands and elders to permit them to undergo tubectomy by challenging the belief just mentioned above. Thus, once a woman has the right number of children, at a relatively young age, say less than 25 years, and if the desire to control fertility is strong, then involvement of others and the duration of the decision-making process is shorter than for those who are above 25 years of age. This age is arbitrarily chosen because the concept of age in this area depends not only on what age a woman belongs to, but also what life-stage she is in. One of the main criteria to determine what life-stage a woman is in is the number of children she has already delivered.

Traditionally, fertility decisions were controlled by elders and males used to dominate, but now this has changed. Family planning decisions are now regarded as modern and the young especially the women are, becoming involved in the decision-making process. These changes are the result of a fundamental change in the social and intra-family relationships. The reasons are changes in primary relationships between young and old, between men and women and especially between the wife and husband and others as a result of the change in the subsistence economy, increase in education and increase in the flow of power and support from the wife's kin.

NOTES AND REFERENCES

1. The average duration of stay works out to be the same for both stem and joint type of families.
2. Discussion about the transfer of wealth in the form of dowry is excluded from this analysis. This aspect has been covered in Chapter 7.

9

Value of Children and Education

9.1 The Children and Their Contribution to Family

(i) *The Children and Their Importance in Rural Families*

Children are important in this society and they are regarded as the source of joy, amusement, help, future security and religious fulfilment to the parents and other members of the family in India. They are essential to a married couple to obtain social acceptance. A childless couple cannot claim many of the religious and social privileges like blessing a bride during a marriage ceremony for begetting children. Children are essential for future economic support to the family, sons to take care of the family farm and daughters to help the mother in the kitchen and other household work including child-minding and support during the mother's pregnancy. In addition, children are required to play with. They amuse grand parents and parents alike, and parents see in them future security. An Indian child grows up within the security of the extended kinship (Lannoy 1971 : 90). He is then moulded to suit the village and family's labour requirements. Generally, children contribute their time and labour doing simple works for the family. Their work is estimated to be a significant contribution to the volume of work done by the whole family (Mamdani 1972 : 808 ; Caldwell 1976a : 343 ; Nag, White and Peet 1978). Children work, and in doing so, slowly learn their occupation as well as becoming socialized into their culture. This is one of the ways of achieving upward social mobility in the family and social hierarchy (Kakar 1979).

It is most common that young children, especially girls aged 7 to 10 years of age, take care of younger siblings at home while parents devote their time to agriculture or earn wages and work on household duties. As this child grows he helps his mother and other members on common errands, such as carrying pieces of firewood from the backyard to the kitchen, scaring away chickens from the house and doing small shopping. As the child grows, the type of work he handles involves more time and demands increased energy and dexterity. The work contribution of children is substantial not only in terms of the labour input but also in terms of savings of the parents' time and allowing its alternative productive use. Children do important work like collecting firewood from the bush, collecting cowdung for the family's organic manure pit, washing clothes, drawing water, and cooking and caring for children younger than themselves. One can observe children spending a substantial time collecting firewood and looking after the family cattle. Because of the lack of forest and other nearby sources of firewood, children spent sometimes whole days in collecting bits and pieces of wood and dry bark of the trees for a day's family requirement. All these activities add to the value of the household economy. Since children's activity can be of considerable gain to the family, their time and way of life are closely regulated by the family members ; the claim of the family on the lives of its children is total. A similar observation has been made by Mamdani in north Indian villages, and he narrates that it is not uncommon to find a man without any small children carrying his own water from the pump or well and cursing his fate for not having bestowed enough children upon him (1972 : 130). In south India, a scene with similar implication is the grazing of animals, sometimes a lonely cow or buffalo, by an adult, which is both less prestigious and uneconomical because it is an under-utilization of adult labour. Thus, the contribution of children's work is of a type not usually preferred by adults (Caldwell 1976b). The nature of the rural families and their economy is such that it requires many children to help in sustaining the family economy. Furthermore, the above discussion has ignored the monetary contributions children make toward the family by working as paid workers either in the fields or in the house of a rich landlord or in the local grain shop. Such contributions enhance the utility of children and also signify an upward flow of monetary wealth.

Given an unchanged pre-modern social and economic order under a particular culture, the description ot the usefulness of having many suriving children was given by Caldwell (1976a : 343). To ensure that the desired number of children survive until adulthood or a workable age, a woman may have to bear twice as many children. In a sex-selective and son-preferring society like India, this number is far greater than in a society where children are regarded as of equal value. But the social and economic order does not remain unchanged. Modern technology has brought dramatic results in reducing mortality, thereby increasing the chance of survival of the children. Nevertheless, May and Heer (1968) have demonstrated for India, that there seems to be a curvilinear influence of the death rate upon the intrinsic rates of increase, which suggests that only a fast and high rate of death reduction can effect a decline in fertility, whereas intermediate levels of the death rate decline have little effect.

The cultivation pattern among the majority of the families in the study area is still largely of a subsistence type using traditional methods and the exchange or sale of produce is only partially done by modern means. Land is tilled using conventional tools such as the wooden plough and a pair of bullocks, while sowing, transplanting, weeding and harvesting is done by hand. Transporting the harvest requires considerable labour. Thus, agriculture is labour-intensive and time-consuming. The rural families require cattle for agricultural use and for dairying which is also labour intensive. Within the household, cooking, cleaning, washing and household maintenance are labour intensive and tedious. Each day, from dawn to dusk, there are innumerable tasks to be done : drawing water, cleaning the frontyard, going to fields on jobs like ploughing, watering the fields, weeding, reaping, collecting firewood and cow dung, picking spinach, plucking vegetables, doing shopping, cleaning the ragi, milling it, cooking and serving it, washing utensils cleaning the kitchen, washing cloths, and many more tasks apart from caring for the children. This list never seems to have an end. Females particularly have less time to rest and sleep in a rural household. Traditionally, however, these jobs are grouped and allocated to different members of the family as their prime duties based on sex and age. If there are more persons in the family, the amount and type of work done by an individual would be less. Household duties including child care, are the women's responsibility ; major agricultural activities are always the responsibility of men ; and other simple and small jobs are usually entrusted to children of different ages. During the peak agricultural season women and older children are drawn to the fields to work.

As the hiring of labour is uneconomical and expensive, a small farmer utilizes family labour. A decline in average size of land holding does not seem to decrease the family's labour input into cultivation, on the other hand, it increases the degree of participation of the family members in agricultural activities. This is partly explained by the fact that it is the smaller landholder who undertake labour intensive cultivation in an attempt to reap sufficient yields. Mechanization and agricultural modernization have not reached the small farmer.

The parents under such situations expect to have a large number of children, especially male, and the motivation to limit family size is almost certainly marginal for them. The need for children is universal among these families and parents may decide to bear successive children because of the apparent net benefits from them. However, in a situation where children are becoming more independent and less submissive at older ages, parents, are concerned and anticipate help at least from one of many children in future. A majority of the parents, however, intend to use the labour of the children while they are still young, at an age when it is easy to control them. In such a situation, probably they need more sons so that at least one can take care of old parents.

Although it is strictly not a part of the Hindu religion, it is often believed that a deliberate action to limit future birth amounts to obstructing an old soul from reappearing in a new body. Children are often named after their dead grand or great-grand parents. Such a custom seems to perpetuate the memories of the deceased and extends emotional support to the population. To ensure this emotional and religious benefit in a high mortality situation, parents wish to have as many children as they can.

(ii) *The Nature of Children's Work and Education*

In the above discussion, we have raised issues which are believed to be beneficial but they need not be so in actuality. In the following, we will, therefore, look into the aspects of value of children especially in terms of their labour contribution and monetary earnings. Education, which is a major factor in evaluating the value of children, is also discussed. Discussion of the psychic and religious values are used as supportive arguments.

Children in the research area work as wage earners in addition to contributing their labour services to family agriculture. Girls also work in certain home industries, namely *leaf-plate* making and the cleaning of tamarind, at least in the largest village. In the following tables (see Tables 9.1 and 9.2), we present the proportion of children working as wage earners and on the family farm as unpaid workers by age. It is evident from the data that children start earning wages and provide labour to the family from an early age and this proportion is higher for children who are above 12 years of age. Most of the children go to school but in many families they are drawn to fields during the peak agricultural periods. Such a practice is noticed mainly in the remote villages where the only primary school is not opened on certain days of the peak agricultural season for want of students. Nevertheless, the value of educating children is little in these villages and, therefore, this practice is nothing more than a convenient strategy for child socialization. Some boys from these remote villages, who were on continuing education studying in the larger village, were found to perform many other tasks apart from attending school, which otherwise would have required an exclusive visit by others. For instance, boys from these villages carried the daily produce of milk to be delivered to the milk producer's co-operative while at the same time attending school, and carried back the family requirement of groceries after purchasing them in the larger villages.

Nevertheless, the proportion of boys who worked on the family farm was substantially higher than the proportion of those who worked in wage-earning activities, which suggests fewer employment opportunities for children. However, if both the proportions are added together, we reach a situation where there appears to be a substantial contribution from children to the rural economy. The trend in girls' participation is slightly different from that of boys. Girls only rarely undertake regular wage employment (as their primary activity), but as secondary employment their contribution is substantial. This is because this labour is marginal and is drawn upon only during the pressing periods of high-labour demand and temporary shortage of labour. A similar trend is found for those girls who work on their own farm. Nevertheless, the proportion of female primary workers either as wage earners or working on the family's own farm is negligible for ages between 15 and 19 years suggesting that unmarried females are withdrawn from the active labour force upon attending puberty.

The practice of making young children work for wage labour still predominates among the Scheduled Castes of Ramagere and Laxmipura, the Bovis of Shivadurga, and certain poor families among Gollas and Kurubas of Ramagere. Nevertheless, there is differential demand for child labour between villages and the proportion of child labour is a function of seasonality and demand for labour. Some children are made to work as bonded labourers (see Chapter 3). Another kind of paid work boys do is as shop assistants in Ramagere, where they largely come from some poor Balagiga families and other Service Castes of the villages. Some girls work in tamarind cleaning and leaf-plate making activity by which they earn a

TABLE 9.1

Participation of Male Children in Rural Production Activities (all villages)

Age in years	Number of Males	Primary activity[1]		Secondary activity[2]	
		% earning wages	% working on own farm	% earning wages	% working on his farm
< 6	276	—	—	—	1.0
6	58	—	1.7	—	32.8
7	47	2.1	8.5	2,1	42.6
8	52	2.1	13.5	0.0	57.7
9	26	11.5	15.4	0.0	61.5
10	52	11.5	16.2	0.0	44.2
11	41	9.3	10.3	0.0	61.0
12	60	14.3	33.3	1.7	38.0
13	37	10.1	32.4	2.7	54.1
14	38	15.8	28.9	5.3	50.0
15	42	19.1	35.7	11.9	40.5
16	24	20.8	41.7	20.8	29.2
17	15	33.3	40.0	20.0	0.0
18	42	35.7	47.6	21.4	23.8
19	21	9.5	57.1	33.3	9.5
>19	768	22.7	54.0	21.4	26.4
All ages	1599	15.2	34.4	12.4	2.73

(1) Primary activity is defined to be an activity in which a person spends most of his time round the year. Full-time wage-earning activity is categorised as primary activity.

(2) Secondary activity is the one which a person does in his spare time after performing the primary activity. The activity has to be for a gainful purpose. Persons reporting a secondary activity will definitely have some other primary activity.

daily income. All female children who work on farms as labourers come from the Scheduled Castes. Female labour in times of demand is hired in groups and, therefore, a girl works on the same farm where her mother or some other female relative works. Average daily wages for child labour ranges from two-and-a-half rupees to three-and-a-half rupees depending upon the age and season of work. Once children are sixteen years old they become eligible for the adult wage rate which is less for women than men.

TABLE 9.2

Participation of Female Children in Rural Production Activities (All Villages)

Age in years	Number of females	Primary activity[1] % earning wages	Primary activity[1] % working on own farm	Secondary activity[2] % earning wages	Secondary activity[2] % working on own farm
< 6	243	—	—	—	1.0
6	53	—	3.8	—	28.3
7	48	2.0	18.8	—	31.3
8	59	0.6	20.3	—	45.8
9	47	2.0	25.5	—	51.1
10	50	6.0	28.0	2.0	46.0
11	37	0.0	18.9	0.0	56.8
12	50	8.0	14.0	10.0	46.0
13	34	9.9	11.8	17.7	50.0
14	32	11.6	3.1	9.3	65.6
15	41	3.4	0.0	36.0	34.2
16	39	2.6	2.6	30.8	38.5
17	13	0.0	0.0	15.4	76.9
18	28	3.6	0.0	32.1	39.3
19	29	3.4	3.5	27.6	37.9
>19	756	2.5	2.4	23.4	38.8
All ages	1559	2.5	5.7	15.3	34.8

(1) and (2) See Table 9.1.

While children are young, the parents control the best part of wages earned by them and parents decide where the child is going to work. The most frequently cited relative, as a response to a question on which relatives helped in securing the first outside job, were parents. In the case of permanent labour contracts involving boys, the parents receive money in advance and send the child to work for a specific period. When the child works as a daily wage labourer, parents receive the wages from the employer and only a small portion is given for the child's personal enjoyment. Because at young ages children work and parents enjoy substantial monetary benefits, parents from these castes prefer to put children to work at young ages. For some of the agriculturists and Muslims, the reasons for putting a child to work at a young age is not only the monetary returns but that the children acquire necessary skills and dexterity to fend for themselves. This group of people do not regard education (schooling) as essential although they know that there are benefits from educating children. The school enrolment of children for the Scheduled Castes and Bovis together is the lowest and by the age of eight or nine, children are withdrawn from schools. Only 22.3 per cent of boys and 7 per cent of girls from these castes were found to continue education and none were in fifth and higher standards.

TABLE 9.3

Proportion of Boys and Girls Aged Between 5 and 19 Years Continuing Schooling by Caste

Caste	Boys		Girls	
	N	% continuing education	N	% continuing education
b 1 ;				
Scheduled Castes and Bovi	121	22.3	128	7.0
Madivala, Bhajantri, Ganiga, Achari and Kumbaria	72	57.1	78	34.0
Golla and Kuruba	125	38.4	133	17.3
Vokkaliga, Ediga and Balagiga	260	63.4	268	36.7
Brahmin, Lingayat and Setty	60	80.0	51	66.7
Devanga and other Hindus	9	55.0	13	35.7
Non-caste (Muslim)	40	42.5	60	51.7
All Castes	687	51.0	731	31.0

Because the age at marriage for both boys and girls is low and the practice of joint living is also relatively higher among the Scheduled Castes, the benefits accruing from sons are high, increased by the fact that a son will bring into the household a daughter-in-law who comes in also to work for wages and to contribute towards the survival of the family. For this group of parents, high fertility is advantageous because children of either sex contribute incomes from a fairly young age. A major force which is beginning to discourage parents from having a large number of children is a steep decline in the demand for child labour in the area, in recent years this is counteracting the parents' calculations of monetary incomes.

The other major category of parents are those who make children work on their own farm. These are the families who at least have average size of cultivable land. The large farmers employ modern technology such as tractors, electric-driven water pumps and modern methods of marketing the produce, but an average farmer is incapable of doing this. Average farming is labour-intensive and the greater number of family labour a farmer employs the more he saves the wages which he otherwise would have spent on hired labour. In the research area, although the proportion of children working on the family's own farm is high, the actual worth of such work is far less than expected. It is not only the nature of work which children do that is less important but also that they do not work all through the year. Agriculture is dependent on the monsoon, and the local varieties of dry crops require very little labour. We know from Chapter 3 that the size of landholdings is small and, therefore, the prospects of a continuous demand for child labour either on the family's own farm or as paid labourers is small and only marginal in Ramagere. In Laxmipura and the grouped villages the relative contribution of children to family agriculture is higher because children undertake supportive agricultural activity of rearing and caring for cattle. However, the farmers in Laxmipura have easy access to the hired labour from the Scheduled Castes of this village, and thus the pressure on their own children to work on family farm is limited to peak demand periods. In effect, it appears that, although the proportion of children working on family farms, is high, the net contribution is low and affected by bad rains and seasonality. The crucial aspect, however, is that children are employed as marginal labourers, and in emergencies they readily substitute for some adult activities to relieve adults to perform more important functions.

The children belonging to Service Castes are increasingly loosing familiarity with their traditional occupations as more and more families are shifting from ancestral occupations due to a decline in demand for these services. Some youngsters are able to learn the modern version of the traditional occupations like managing a barber shop or a local version of a cloth washing and pressing enterprise. Due to a fast displacement of labour, the demand for child labour in the village servicing occupations is almost non-existent and, therefore, the proportion of children continuing education is higher than those of Scheduled Castes and the Gollas and Kurubas. Nevertheless, they are struggling to seek opportunities in non-traditional and agricultural sectors which is their priority.

The remaining categories of population groups are the High Castes, business men, agriculturists, bureaucrats and Muslims. These are the people who send their children to school regularly and the emphasis on sending children to earn wages and to work on family enterprise or agricuiture is less. A majority regard education as an investment but some consider that training children in traditional occupations from a young age is also important. But there are a wide range of views and preferences on how much of education children should get and which of the children should get it. The common pattern is preferential education for boys as long as they can continue to pass and do well in examinations while the girls can only continue until they attain puberty or the maximum of a Secondary School degree. Fifty one per cent of the boys and only 31 per cent of the girls are found to continue schooling in the age range 5 to 19 years, per cent for boys and only 31 per cent for girls. Because of an *Urdu* primary school in Ramagere, the proportion of Muslim girls going to school is higher than those of boys, but none were found to study beyond fourth standard because they have to travel 16 kilometers to attend higher standards. If the primary school were not in Ramagere, the proportion of Muslims girls in schools would have been negligible. The Muslim boys work on various non-agricultural occupations from a young age. Bureaucrats who are mostly the migrants are younger on average (many are bachelors) and have fewer and relatively younger children. Therefore, the eventual educational pattern of their children is not yet clear ; nevertheless, the expectations of high education and the high returns are strong among them. The Settys are business-oriented and expect sons to take up the family profession fairly early and only a few boys and girls go to higher education. The Brahmin and Lingayat families value education most and the highly educated adults and children belong to these castes in this area. Among the agriculturists of both Ramagere and Laxmipura there is an acceleration in the effort to educate sons, especially because of the views of the parents that, in these modern days of increasing government activities at village level, only educated children can maximize all benefits by coping with the system. The proportion of boys continuing education is almost twice as great as to the proportion of girls in this caste group. The following are some of the views regarding education :

> Expenditure on children's education is a waste ; the girls go away to their husbands and sons leave us after marriage to care for their wives and children, leaving us (their parents) helpless. [a Golla couple in Ramagere]

> Females have to be provided with education to the extent that they are capable of understanding the complexities of life, while the males should be educated as much as possible to secure a better job and higher income. [a Vokkaliga woman in Laxmipura]

> In the cities even girls can earn and, therefore, they study ; in villages we do not give importance to the education of daughters because their world is within the limits of four walls. But I like daughters to study as much as sons do, so that they can be equally good and at the same time they learn work from a young age. [a Kuruba woman in Ramagere]

All our four sons have left school, not only because we cannot afford the expense, but also because they refused to continue. We expected that at least one of them would be a wise boy but none managed to continue. Therefore, we put them on agriculture. [a Balagiga couple in Ramagere]

Apart from an active participation in income-earning functions, children undertake a wide range of household duties which are described above in this chapter. The most important duties which have demographic implications are the child-care functions and performance of household duties during the sickness or pregnancy of a woman. It is essential to re-emphasize the fact that many women choose to undergo tubectomy because of lack of support in performing household functions during repeated pregnancies and after child-birth. Thus the presence of a grown-up child, especially a girl, will help in this regard among the average families in the study area. But the contribution from a daughter to the parents when they are old is believed to be negative because she has to be given in marriage after which she stops to help the parental family. Parents also intend to avoid the births of female children at advanced ages because of the fear that it would be almost impossible to arrange their marriages. On the other hand, a son brings in a wife who cares for this family when parents are old.

It appears that economic forces are operating on the rural families in such a way as to reduce the economic value of childern across the cross-section of the population, although different groups have been affected differently. The main factor is economic stress due to an increasing reliance of the rural population on the market economy to procure essentials including grains and other basic food commodities while the wage rates have not changed over time. Secondly, because of a slight increase in the schooling of the children, although education is free, the expenditure on school-going children is substantial in terms of good clothing, books, stationery and extra care and the attention which such children demand is adding to the economic stress. Thus, there is a situation where for the majority of the population the economic transfer or the wealth flow is from the parents to children. Consequently a very essential support to induce high fertility has weakened.

A consistent increase in the acceptance of family planning in the two large villages partially confirms that villagers are beginning to evaluate the relative costs and benefits which will decrease family size in future. Such a thinking has not yet developed among the families of the two smaller villages. Nevertheless, the oral evidence of those couples who have accepted family planning suggests, that the 'unit value' (both economic, in terms of increased monetary expectations and support, and psychic) per child has enormously increased. This is because, in falling fertility conditions and relatively unchanged economic situation, parents in future expect to receive help from a lesser number of children than otherwise would have been the case under the high fertility and falling mortality conditions. It has been argued by many that a decline in the net value of children will reduce the family size ideals and people will resort to fertility regulations, but this does not appear to be an equilibrium situation because soon the counteracting forces operate, the unit value of children increase and may consequently increase the desire for more children. The parents by then are old or incapable of producing more children to maximize returns from additional children. But such views and expectation may create forces at the societal level which affect new parental desires and values. It also appears that the smaller the family size, the greater will be the unit value of children. It can also be speculated that a fast decline in fertility in the absence of the implementation of labour-saving agricultural innovations at a village or regional level may create pressures on children who may be forced to undertake more physical jobs and also bear a greater burden of the family affairs at young ages in the absence of other siblings to share responsibilities. In fact, this situation may also lead to a fall in the school enrolment and literacy levels in future. These tendencies along with two other factors, namely (a) almost stable and fairly high infant and child mortality, and (b) an increasing risk that sons may not provide support in old age, will enhance the desire for having more children as an insurance against such risks. As long as this counteractive relationship persists in the rural areas, the government's objective to bring down the net reproduction rate to *one* by AD 2001 in India remains short of being a viable proposition.

10

Conclusion and Overview of Findings

Demographic transition is of recent origin in India. Various geographic areas are experiencing different phases of the demographic transition. South India is believed to have entered the intermediate stage of demographic transition where both the birth and death rates have been consistently falling since the middle of this century. Social, cultural and institutional factors are regarded as having maintained a stable high fertiliry regime in the past. Since the second quarter of this century, there have been profound social and economic changes in this country. It is, however, not a coincidence that the demographic transition and social change have occurred almost at the same time. Therefore, there is an interest in investigating the causes and mechanisms of the fertility decline and its association with social change in a rural population. Because the fertility decline and the acceptance of family planning is of recent origin, it is also possible to investigate the causes of destabilization.

It has been argued after a review of literature regarding the relative importance of economic development and value orientations to the study of family that, in the process of social change these two aspects are inseparable. Attention was drawn to the fact that, while the social and economic transformation occured, the old values and stereotypical behaviour altered and a series of other changes took place. Of these the most important in explaining the decline in fertility are the changing relationships between old and young and between spouces. The pattern of family and fertility decision-making reflects these changing relationships. A society in transition appear to give new ways and opportunities to the young, facilitating relatively affective conjugal relationships and encouraging secular values to flourish while traditional patriarchy loses it authority along with a weakening of old social values. Such a transformation helps reproductive couples to choose modern fertility control methods if they are available to them. The acceptance of family planning methods itself is an indicator of change and a segment of the social change in general.

Social change is a cumulative effect of change in behaviour and response over time among a set of population, which has to be properly understood. Although surveys are a good source of data on large numbers across the cross-section of the population they lack the ability to provide qualitatve interpretations and an in-depth understanding of the nature of social change. It is argued that such a macro-perspective provides only superficial knowledge and fails to provide enough understanding to establish the interrelationships between social change and demographic transition. Therefore, the need of yet another approach, which cannot only help in an in-depth understanding of the society but also provide correlates for a macro-interpretation is emphasized. This methodology is a combination of both survey and anthropological tools and techniques and is identified as a micro-approach.

An essential feature of this approach is the emphasis on the requirement of acquiring first-hand knowledge and gathering facts from those who have been experiencing change. The micro-approach is different not only in its form but also in its structure and objectives. Because our broader objective is to investigate the cause of fertility decline in south India during the recent decades, it was necessary to know the nature of this change, how it occurred, what caused this change, and what are the responses to this change in the society. This demanded a detailed understanding of the society, which is less efficient by a quick administration of a set of questions on predetermined hypotheses and on a sample of population. With this intention, therefore, a cluster of four south Indian villages were chosen which were sufficiently away from the urban influence and a year-long period of field work was undertaken. Both anthropological and survey tools were used for data collection. The reason for choosing a rural area is obviously the predominance of rural population in India, and that the effects of social change are better understood in a place where the change is presumed to have a consistent pattern unlike the case in urban areas. The objectives and scheme of this research focuses on the institution of family, because a study of individuals in the Indian case does not approximate the reality. This necessitated a detailed description of the socioeconomic structure of the research area which is a precondition for understanding social change. This framework is latter appropriately modified to study the fertility differentials between the sub-groups, family patterns, responses to family planning, changing value of children, and fertility and family planning decision-making process.

The research area is a cluster of four villages found within a diameter of about nine kilometres and about twenty kilometers from an average sized town. Ramagere is the largest of the study villages with approximately 2000 population living in about 350 families. It is a developed village and a panchayat headquarters. Because of various government institutions, commercial and business activity, it caters to various needs of the people living in surrounding villages. Laxmipura is the second larger village with 150 families and the two other villages are remote and have about 50 families each. The caste system provided the basis for the understanding of the social structure which as yet is hierarchical in nature. In the absence of data on caste and social structure from other sources, it provided a unique opportunity to find out the effect of modernization and development on various castes which have distinct occupational identities. While predominant castes are

Intermediary-Peasants, the Scheduled Castes are found in sizable numbers. The High Castes are found mostly in Ramagere and there are some in Laxmipura. The Service Castes, who were traditionally known for their *jajmani* occupations and relationships, are found in Ramagere and Laxmipura and in one small village. Muslims constitute one-tenth of the population in Ramagere.

Agriculture is the prime source of income and 73 per cent of all the families have cultivable land over half-an-acre. The landless who are not bureaucrats and officials draw income from agricultural labour and other village occupations. Laxmipura is purely agricultural in its nature while in Ramagere, 14 per cent of the families receive salaried incomes. The other two villages depend on agriculture, wage labour and specialized occupations such as stone cutting and fire wood cutting and selling. Average annual income and per capita income is highest in Laxmipura followed by Ramagere (average level) and least in the two smaller villages. Ramagere is an educational centre for surrounding villages. The proportion of children continuing education to higher standards is higher in Ramagere, while the proportion is relatively low in Laxmipura and negligible in other two villages. Still the rate of growth of literates is highest in the remote villages because of the recent establishment of a primary school. Children who are not in school do work on various paid and unpaid tasks but the demand for their labour is restricted to certain periods of high demand. Nevertheless, the productive services of children in the smaller two villages appear to be essential to families than in Ramagere and in Laxmipura where there is easy accessibility to daily wage labourers.

There are wide disparities in the economic and social standards among villages and among different caste groups. High Castes are rich, more educated and progressive ; the Peasant Castes have acquired a strong motivation to follow the High Castes and some are successful in maximizing the benefits from the government-sponsored programmes such as agricultural loans, dairy development and marketing of produce. This was not possible for the Service Castes and Low Castes basically because the programmes are geared largely towards agriculture and they traditionally have been non-agricultural in their occupations. Thus the traditional affiliation to certain castes and certain specialized occupations have determined the present economic and social status of the population. The negative impact of modernization is highest for those families who were performing jajmani tasks in the past and their economic standard has declined due to lack of alternative employment and lack of occupational diversification. The landless labourers are increasingly feeling the pressure of inflation because they depend on the market system to procure essentials and food items while wage rates have remained same in real terms over years. The public distribution system of essential commodities which includes textiles has failed to reach the needy ; rather it has benefited the rural rich and the bureaucrats. The Muslims of Ramagere, who are also traditionally non-agricultural, have managed to keep their economic standards at an intermediary level because of their business, mechanical and other non-agricultural occupations. There has been a change in the pattern of daily wage employment in which there is no inhibition regarding working as wage labourers for the same caste employers. Thie has largely affected the wage earning opportunities of the Low Castes who were traditionally servants and labourers.

The population figures are available for these villages since 1941 decennial Census. There has been a 66 per cent increase in the total population in last forty years. The annual intrinsic growth rates are fairly consistent except between 1951 and 1961 in Ramagere and between 1971 and 1981 in Laxmipura. Ramagere has been experiencing a rapid growth in populations since the early 1960s because of relatively more in-migration. The change in population experienced by the other villages are mostly the result of natural increase. The age structure of the population has been relatively young yet it appears that there is a slight fall in fertility during last decade and this fall is substantial in Laxmipura. Nevertheless, the average birth rate for all the villages is 33 per thousand population for 1980-81 and there appears to be no statistically significant differential between villages. It is speculated that in future there will be significant differentials in the rate of growth between these villages because of the differential impact of socio-economic development and the acceptance of family planning.

Marriage is both a religious and a social institution and, therefore, universal. By the age of 30 practically all women are married ; the percentage of single women in age group 20-24 is only 10.6. Early and pre-puberty marriages are still found among the Low Castes and some of the Intermediary Castes. One-third of all ever married women in the area were married while they were under the age of 14 and in many marriages the bride was less than 10 years of age. Nevertheless, sexual intercourse is always sanctioned by a second post-marriage ceremony which is arranged only after the girl has attained puberty. Emphasis on early parenthood is strong throughout the community, but the motivation to bear children in older ages is fast declining except in the remote villages. This change first occurred in Laxmipura during the last ten years which is evident from low age specific rates for the older age groups and also that family planning acceptance is widespread in this village. Average age of women, who are either the tubectomy acceptors or the wives of the vasectomized men, is five years higher than those of non-acceptors. Nevertheless, when the age specific rates are compared with rates provided by Srinivasan *et.al* and Shariff *et.al* in the research area it presents a pattern of early childbearing immediately after marriage probably with short durations of birth spacing and then stopping the births by using family planning methods at more advanced ages.

An additional analysis on fertility was undertaken by constructing a cumulative index, namely the mean number of children ever born (MCEB) which is based on a large number of births. The MCEB for all currently married fecund women works out to be 5.7 while the mean number of living children is 4.7 indicating an average loss of one child per woman in her lifetime. In a preliminary analysis of differential fertility, both inter-village and intra-village differentials were noticed which are largely dependent on the differentials between various caste groups while for other categories the differentials was largely explained by age and marital duration. Therefore, multivariate analyses were undertaken to bring out the independent effects of various social, economic and demographic variables on fertility. A linear regression model established the statistically significant effect of variables, namely caste affiliation, infant mortality, mortality of children after one years' age, and marital duration, on the levels of fertility. Muslims followed by the Peasants (the dominant group) were the more fertile groups while the High and Low Castes were found to be less fertile. The total variance explained by all the fourteen variables used in the regression was 68 per cent which was statistically significant.

But it was found that the socio-economic variables had reasonably high predictive power in the absence of the demographic variable, namely marital duration. When demographic and non-demographic variables are used together in a regression, the socio-economic variables contributed only 12 per cent to the total explained variance. However, in the absence of any prescribed pattern of relationship between independent and dependent variables the multiple classification analysis is a useful device. The MCA results suggest that child mortality is a major determinant of fertility. Women who had experienced infant and child mortality had 1.6 children more than those who did not. Although the likelihood is that fertility is both the cause and the effect of infant and child mortality, the effect of child mortality on fertility may be strong and substantial. It was also discovered that the women currently residing in joint families had a lower fertility than those who lived in nuclear families. This analysis also presented a positive relationship of income with fertility. An interesting finding is that neither the regression nor the multiple classification analysis established a significant independent relationship of mother's formal education with the dependent variable. Thus, mother's education has no demonstrable effect on the levels of fertility at least in the research area, but it has been from a discriminant analysis that education is one of the main discriminating characteristic for family planning acceptance. With regard to the work status of women, and its relationship with fertility the MCA results suggest that only those women who work on modern jobs have low fertility, and those who are agricultural labourers have intermediate levels of fertility.

Women who worked both on household activities as well as on their own farm have higher fertility levels. Although there has been a decline in the levels of fertility in the research area, there are certain groups who are contributing relatively more to this decline.

The institutional nature of the extended family system is believed to keep fertility at a high level, and historically India is recognized to have a strong family system. Therefore, an attempt is made to find if it is true in our area. The family type categories are especially defined for our purpose. A distinction is made between extended-nuclear and residual-stem types of families which have a similar composition of relatives living in them. The distinction, however, is that in the extended-nuclear type the relative who is a widowed, separated or unmarried person moves in to join the other family members, whereas in the residual-stem type that relative continues to stay with the the family, and would have attained the above attributes because of the life-cycle events of death of spouse, separation or non-marriage. This distinction was essential becuause the relative power and status of the relative in the extended-nuclear type is extremely weak while their counterparts in the residual-stem type managed to retain a substantial power and sometimes enhanced it because of inheritance and control of property. Often the widowed persons in the residual-stem type were reported as head of the family while in extended nuclear they are the dependents.

Although the practice of joint living is universal in the initial period after marriage, the predominant family type found at a given point in time is the simple (nuclear) family. A newly married couple stays on average 6.5 years in an extended family type, a duration which is sufficient to produce two to three children. Nevertheless, families are appearing to split sooner than in the past and a moderate decline in mortality has activated the process of division of the family. In the research area the prevalence of joint living is found to be relatively high among the Scheduled Castes and least among the High Castes. The desire and opportunities to establish neolocal residence and separate agriculture has increased among the landed families of Laxmipura which is a prosperous agricultural village. These findings are contrary to the findings established by others, that joint living is characteristic of landed castes and the Scheduled Castes live in nuclear families. In our area the Scheduled Castes live together not only to maximize wage earnings by leaving behind only one person to attend to household duties but also that for them it is easy to provide evidence that they have a housing crisis while applying for a site and a grant for the construction of the house given by the government-sponsored public housing scheme. This scheme is highly successful in Ramagere and the tendency for joint living is, therefore, higher among the Scheduled Castes of this village. Emerging individual tastes and preferences and the declining strength of patriarchy are the reasons for the division of family while the conjugal bonds are in a process of strengthening the relationships although they are not yet egalitarian in nature.

With regard to family patterns and the nature of married women it has been found that women who live in complex families are 3.3 years younger than their sisters in simple families, and the proportion of married women in age group 15-19 years is almost two-and-a-quarter times higher in complex families. This suggests that newly married couples, along with their children, move out to live in simple families only after they have spent a substantial period with the original family. It has been found that the age-standardised CEB index is significantly lower for younger women living in complex families but the tempo of increase in fertility among these women is relatively greater in advanced ages, and women in either of the family types reach an uniform level of fertility. It has been explained that during the joint living period the opportunity and frequency of coitus is relatively low and that the sexual behaviour of the young is prescribed and controlled by the old. This is still the case because a substantial proportion marry very young and elders express authority, and also consider it their duty to control the sexual behaviour of the young couple. Post-natal sexual abstinence is followed relatively strictly in those families where there is an old woman residing in it. The instances of breaking this taboo are increasing more because the power and authority of the old is weakening and in simple families it is much easier to ignore such traditions.

An important fact which deserves attention is the role of education in combination with the type of family. It is found that illiterate women living in simple families have higher levels of fertility in all age groups when compared their literate sisters in simple families, and both literates and illiterates in complex families. Nevertheless, literate women less than 35 years of age, who live in complex families, demonstrate a higher fertility compared with those in simple families. It has been arguged that the literates in a complex family acquire a relatively higher status and they successfully repel the influences of the elders which results in higher fertility. The litrates who are in simple families are the most likely to use contraception after having a sufficient number of children. Education has been found to have an independant significant correlation with the acceptance of family planning methods whereas it is not significant correlated with fertility.

To understand the pattern of fertility control and associated social change it was felt necessary to know the perception of the family planning programme in the research area. The villagers are still governed by natural and traditional rules of the family formation which provides lesser opportunity for modern ideas to interfere. Family planning is visualised as an exogenous factor and the majority perceive contraception as unnecessary, unnatural, inconvenient, disruptive, dangerous and expensive. Family planning is also widely regarded as a part of allopathic health medicine. However, family planning is essentially a behavioural issue and certain families have understood its need and value. Although vasectomy was the first method to be introduced, the family planning programme has now turned to tubectomy and is a female oriented programme. This fits perfectly well into the cultural context of male dominance and female subordination and deference. Males as well as females perceive that pregnancy, child birth and child care is the woman's business in which males have little to do. It has also been noticed that rural wives cherish a sense of sacrifice by volunteering themselves for tubectomization, thus saving the husband from the danger of illhealth, impotency and shame. There were only two wives from among all the acceptor couples who refused to undergo tubectomy and the husbands had to accept vasectomy under the pressure of village leaders and health officials. Only a negligible proportion of current users are vasectomy users while all others are tubectomized women belonging to two larger villages. Family planning acceptance has a fairly long history in Ramagere whereas the people of Laxmipura have taken to tubectomy only in the last six to seven years. The programme has not reached the smaller villages not only because of the shortcomings of the programme but also because the information and communication channels are weak and highly restricted. The people living in these remote villages are still apprehensive to use a family planning method.

Decisions regarding acceptance of family planning and tubectomy are governed by various norms and principles : (a) Family planning is perceived as stopping future births and the concept of spacing is not yet recognized ; therefore, the emphasis is on tubectomy which solves the problem once for all. (b) Contraceptive intervention is discouraged for women who do not have at least two sons and one daughter. (c) Women below 25 years of age should not and those above 30 years of age need not resort to family planning because of the fear of sterility at early ages and death in latter ages. It is also believed that older women may not become pregnant again. Sexual abstinence is emphasized to be restored to in order to avoid births at older ages. Abstinence in this culture has religious significance at well. But it appears that the practice is much lower than is sometimes claimed. (d) For a woman it is convenient to undergo a tubectomy operation during the post-partum period so as to avoid problems involed in taking additional rest and seeking extra-family help a second time. (e) The IUD was repudicated by past users and new acceptors are discouraged in its use. Rumours against the IUD are widespread and the common complaints were spinal (back) ache and extra-menstrual bleeding. (f) The use of the condom is usually kept secret, and is condemned in public. Other problems frequently expressed with condom are that it is inconvenient, difficult and shameful to procure from commercial places and difficult to dispose of. (g) Men need not volunteer vasectomization, because they are the bread-winners and lest something should happen to them. (h) People desire easy contraceptives like oral pills, provided they need not be taken every day. There are instance where quacks sold medicine made of local herbs and chemicals which were dangerous to women's health. (i) The public acceptability of abortion is changing although not all those who want it go to a public dispensary. There are some instances when married women intending to abort a pregnancy approached a local Homeopathic practitioner, thus suggesting a voluntary demand for contraception.

In Ramagere the voluntary acceptance of family planning started from the Brahmins, Idigas and Balagigas. These caste people have wide contact especially with the urban areas. Settys too have these contacts but they have not yet picked up family planning. Since the castes earlier mentioned are contiguous in many ways the intra-caste information flow helped initially in the acceptance of the IUD during the sixties. The Kurubas, Gollas, Service Castes, Scheduled Castes and Muslims did not accept the IUDs, because of imperfect and poor knowledge. When the IUD users rejected it in favour of tubectomy acceptance, the flow of information remained the same in its pattern and direction in the initial periods. Nevertheless, the intensive dissemination of information during the mid 1970s and persuasion by a male health worker who is a Kuruba, helped some couples from Balagiga, Kuruba and Golla communities to accept tubectomies in Ramagere. The acceptance followed the principle of 'kin' and 'neighbourhood' clustering patterns and now any new acceptor has at least one relative who is an acceptor either from the kins or the affines staying either in same village or outside. Those women who have no such relatives are still the least likely women to accept tubectomies in Ramagere. It is argued that the normal pattern of diffusion of family planning has failed to communicate effectively to the target group ; therefore, it is suggested that various kinship and neighbourhood groups can be identified which normally have a central person who is effective and important in each group. If the programme concentrates their effort with such persons and provide sufficient and correct information to them besides the normal extension activities the diffusion of information will be faster and more effective.

The discussion of family planning is no longer regarded as shameful and embarrassing, and the sterilized women do not hesitate to disclose that they are sterilized ; rather they feel proud and distinctive as they have successfully undergone the operation while other non-acceptors fear it. Nevertheless, it has been argued that there still is resistance to the acceptance of family planning methods, especially among certain special groups such as the Muslims, Scheduled Castes, all living in the two remote villages. It has also been speculated that because the maternal and child health programme is integrated with family planning programme, the above mentioned groups of people will be disadvantaged because they do not accept MCH services from the same person who later will insist on family planning. The resistant group perceives MCH as a precursor to the imposition of tubectomies. There is, therefore, a need to rethink the aspects of the integration of various health and family planning programmes especially for the rural population. Nevertheless, a discriminant analysis on a selected sample of the non-acceptor and acceptor couples from all the villages suggest that the higher the education of women is higher is the caste affiliiation, and, if they have sufficient number of surviving sons, such women are most likely to accept the family planning methods with an intent to stop btrths in future. The length of marital duration and the type of family of current residence facilitate the acceptance. In this analysis almost 70 per cent of non-acceptors and 63 pet cent of acceptors are correctly classified.

The special interest of this research was to explore the pattern of supports and their influence on decision-making regarding fertility and family planning acceptance among the study population. Therefore, separate review of literature on the origins of fertility decision-making was done. It has been argued that the microeconomic model of fertility decision-making is inappropriate to meet the objectives of present analysis and a case is made for a sociopsychological approach instead. The nature of dimensions of decision-making are discussed, following which a framework for the present analysis is laid. A schematic model, which was presented by Backman (1978 : 6), has been appropriately modified and extended to suit the cultural and traditional context of the study population. Nevertheless, a case is made as to why even in the research area the primary unit of decision-making analysis has to be a marital dyad and that the extended kin and affine do play a direct as well as an indirect role. It is also argued that the fertility limitation ard family planning decision-making is almost synoymous in the absence of the acceptance of temporary family planning methods. Various supports to decision-making pattern within a family are discussed. The evidence is that the social and cultural norms are unintentionally creating anti-natal effects and the influence of economic forces are mostly felt by the biological parents as a result of changes in intra-family relationships, increased awareness of monetization and individualism. It is found that as yet there is no profound change in the residential arrangements of young couples immediately after marriage, although there is an increase in the participation of boys in marriage decision-making. The decline, nevertheless, is found in the duration of stay in the joint living conditions. There appears to be a change in the inter-family relationships, especially between the kins and affines and it is argued that there are signs of change from a unilineal extended system to a bilateral extended system working through the conjugal pair. It is only speculated that the relative power of kin is decreasing while at the same time the capabilities of affinal influences are sufficiently strong in changing the balance of power between kin, husband and wife. In the absence of post research on the relative influence of kin and affine influence on younger generation the above hypothesis is as yet arbitrary and requires further research.

In an illustrative analysis of the case histories of a selected group of families who had at least three living children of whom at least two were sons it has been found that the acceptance of family planning is higher among those women who had sufficient exposure to extended or joint llving conditions. It has been further argued that although the extended kin exert their interference in the family planning decision-making, there are the other couples of the same generation who are providing support for such decisions while the old, in most cases the mothers-in-law, either consider that family planning is the couple's business or that they co-operate with the decision-makers. This is perfectly compatible with the system because the women who are willing to undergo tubectomy are already old and have many living children. Nevertheless, the extra-couple influence is strong against acceptance of family planning when the target women are young.

It has also been found that for various reasons younger couples are establishing nuclear families which in itself reduces the pressures of the old to a large extent. It was possible to provide data on the frequency of source and nature of support for some of these rural families which highlight the fact that wife's relatives are as important a source of economic support as the husband's kin. There is also a substantial contribution from the wife's relatives in the form of support during sickness and pregnancy, and customary gifts and reciprocal exchange. This pattern of support is providing a base for the changing pattern of decision-making. This pattern is specifically found in Ramagere, the larger multi-caste and heterogeneous village. In Laxmipura the pattern is less clear and a major difference is that the sons among the Vokkaliga families of Laxmipura are assuming all major responsibilities earlier than before and their participation in the family planning decision making is relatively greater. Nevertheless, another reason for their greater involvement in decision-making is relatively low levels of knowledge and access to open ideas to the women of this village.

A major reason for the acceptance of tubectomy is found to be health of the woman, or the use of this reason by the woman as a convenient pretext to convince the elders that tubectomization is essential. Fears about health appears to be a major force for the women and their husbands to decide upon for tubectomization, and second only to economic reasons which are the most prominent, lack of support during repeated pregnancies, and fear of more female births are other important reasons. The most frequent reason (one-quarter of all responses) for the postponement of acceptance to after another birth was related to the want of a son or more sons. Another 14.6 per cent of the responses expressed lack of knowledge followed by 13.6 per cent reflecting fear of death and ill-health of the individual. On the other hand the major reason frequently cited for non-acceptance by non-acceptors is opposition from husband and his relatives followed by want of more sons and poor knowledge. Nevertheless, the prime decision-makers of the family planning method were wives in Ramagere while in Laxmipura they were husbands. Yet, even here, the proportion of decisions where the wives were prime decision makers was substantial, nearing 41 per cent in Laxmipura. The contrasting fact is that in Ramagere the kins and affines were moderately involved in direct and prime decision-making but they were not involved at all in Laxmipura. The reason is the dominance of the relatively young males in family management and decision-making. Nevertheless, 42 per cent of the decisions are syncratic and majority of them are wife dominated suggesting a greater role and participation of women in the fertility and family planning decision making.

A major change has occurred in the actual contribution of children to the family and the perceived value of children to parents. It is argued that in the research area children are employed as marginal labourers, and in emergencies it is readily substituted to relieve adults to perform more important functions. In effect it appears that although the proportion of children working on family farm is substantial the net contribution is low and is affected by bad rains and seasonality. The proportion of wage earners is not substantial either, excepting among the Scheduled Castes, because many adult males who were traditionally not wage earners are seeking wage earning opportunities due to a decline in demand for their traditional services. This has largely reduced the opportunities of children to work as wage labourers. The school enrolment and continuation of education was found to be closely related to child labour. Thus lack of work opportunities for children on the one hand and increased expenditure on their education on the other has discouraged parents to have a large number of children. Nevertheless, it is argued that a faster decline in family size will increase the unit value of children in future which many affect the fertllity ideals at the societal level. A fast decline in fertility in smaller areas may also create pressures on children who may be forced to undertake more physical jobs and also to bear a greater burden of the family affairs in young age, in the absence of other siblings to share responsibilites. Thus it is argued that the goals of fertility decline have to be moderate and they have to be achieved through a long term programme. Ambitious programme objective is not only difficult to achieve but may create imbalance within the society which may prove detrimental to the social well-being.

To conclude, social change has not only prompted a decline in fertility but it has also provided with venues for a further decline from where it is unlikely that fertility will increase in near future. There is an increase in the status of woman within the family as judged by her participation in the fertility and family decision-making. Yet this is not sufficient to conclusively establish her status because of various other factors which keep a woman relatively below the male in relative status. Some of these issues are : (a) The 'education trap' where a daughter is either discouraged or not encouraged to pursue higher education. Only a handful of villagers believed that there should not be preferential education to boys, aud majority consider investment in daughter's education as a waste of time and money. (b) The 'employment trap', while employment is contingent upon education, there is hardly any venue in a village setting for women to get employment. The scope is also limited for the occupational diversities for women. (c) 'The marriage trap' where even today there is no scope for a girl to interfere in the arranged marriage system which is an essential precondition for the emancipation of woman. And (d) the demographic dilemma namely the 'tubectomy trap' where the men and even women believe that her prime duty is procreation and child rearing and caring is of no concern of man. The bias that only females should undergo sterilization has created irresponsibility among men. One can only hope that in the near future the new forces of social change are more helpful for cause of women in India.

Further Readings

Bardhan, Pranab K and Ashok Rudra., (1980) "Types of labour attachment in agriculture", *Economic and Political Weekly*, 15 : 1477-84.

Bardhan, Pranab K., (1970) "On the minimum level of living and the rural poor", *Indian Economic Review* 5(1) : 129-136.

Beals, Alan R., (1955) "Interplay among factors of change in a Mysore village", in McKim Marriott (ed.), *Village India : Studies in the little community*, Chicago, University of Chicago Press, pp. 78-101.

——(1961) "Cleavage and internal conflict : An example from India", *The Journal of Conflict Resolution*, 5 : 27-34.

——(1962) *Gopalpur : A south Indian village*, New York, Holt, Rinehart and Winston.

——(1970) "Namahalli, (1953-1966) : Urban influence and change in southern Mysore", in K. Ishwaran (ed.), *Change and Continutty in India's Villages*, New York, Columbia University Press, pp 57-72.

Backman, Linda J., (1978) "Couples' decision-making process regarding fertility", in Karl E. Taeuber, Larry L. Bumpass and James A. Sweet, (eds.), *Social Demography*, New York, Academic Press, pp 57-81.

——(1983) "Communication, power, and the influence of social networks in couple decisions on fertility", in Rodolfo A. Bulatao and Ronald D. Lee (eds.), *Determinants of Fertility in Developing Countries*, Volume 2, New York, Academic Press, pp. 415-443.

Bebarta, Prafulla C., (1977) *Family Type and Fertility in India*, North Quincy, The Christopher Publishing House.

Becker, Gary S., (1960) "An economic analysis of fertility", in National Bureau of Economic Research, *Demographic and Economic Change in Developed Countries*, Princeton, Princeton University Press, pp. 209-231.

——(1976) *The Economic Approach to Human Behaviour*, Chicago University Press.

Blake, Judith., (1960) *Family Structure in Jamaica : The Social Context of Reproduction*, New York, Free Press of Glencoe.

——1965 "Demographic science and the redirection of population policy", in M.C. Sheps and J. Reley (eds.), *Public Health and Population Change*, Pittsburgh, University of Pittsburgh Press.

Blaikie, Piers M., (1975) *Family Planning in India : Diffusion and Policy*, London, Edward Arnold.

Blood, Robert O and Donald M. Wolfe., (1960) *Husbands and Wives : The Dynamics of Married Living*, New York, The Free Press.

Blumberg, Rhoda Lois and Leela Dwaraki., (1980) *India's Educated Women : Options and Constraints*, Delhi, Hindustan Publishing Corporation.

Burch, Thomas K (ed.)., (1980) *Demographic Behaviour : Interdisciplinary perspectives on decision-making*, Colorado, Westview Press.

Burch, Thomas K and Murray Gendell. (1970) 'Extended family structure and fertility : Some conceptual and methodological issues", *Journal of Marriage and the Family*, 32 : 227-236.

Burgess Ernest W and Harvey J. Locke., (1953) *The Family : From institution to companionship*, 2nd edition, New York, American Book Co.

Cain, Mead T., 1978 "The Household life cycle and economic mobility in rural Bangladesh", *Population and Development Review*, 4(3) : 421-438.

Caldwell, John C. (1975) "The containment of world population growth", *Studies in Family Planning*, 6(12) : 429-436.

——(1976a) "Towards a restatement of demographic transition theory", *Population and Development Review*, 2 (3-4) : 321-366.

——(1976b) "Fertility and the household economy in Nigeria", *Journal of Comparative Family Studies*, 7 (2) : 193-253.

——(1977) "The world population outlook", *Australian and New Zealand Journal of Sociology*, 13 (2).

——(1978) "A theory of fertility : From high plateau to destabilization", *Population and Development Review*, 4 (4) : 553-577.

——(1982) "The failure of the theories of social and economic change to explain demographic change : Puzzles of modernization or westernization", *Research in Population Economics*, 4 : 297-332.

——(1984) "Strengths and limitations of the survey approach for measuring and understanding fertility change", in J. Cleland and J. Hobcraft (eds.), *Demography of Developing Countries : Insights from the World Fertility Survey*, Oxford University Press.

Caldwell, John C and Pat Caldwell., (1981) "Causes and sequence in the reduction of postnatal abstinence in Ibadan city, Nigeria", in Hilary J. Page and Ron Lesthaeghe, (eds.), *Child-Spacing in Tropical Africa : Traditions and change*, London, Academic Press, pp 181-199.

Caldwell, John C ; P.H. Reddy and Pat Caldwell., (1982a) "The causes of demographic change in rural south India : A micro approach", *Population and Development Review*, 8 (4) : 689-727.

——(1982b) "The micro approach in demographic investigation: Towards a methodology", (in press).

Caldwell, John C ; G. Immerwahr and L.T. Ruzicka., (1982c) "Illustrative Analysis : Family structure and fertility", *Scientific Reports*, No. 39, International Statistical Institute, World Fertility Survey, London.

Caldwell, John C ; P.H. Reddy and Pat Caldwell., 1984 "The determinants of family structure in rural South India", *Journal of Marriage and the Family*, 46 (1) : Forthcoming.

Carr-Saunders, A.M., (1922) *The Population Problem : A Study in human evolution*, Oxford, Clarendon Press.

Cassen, Robert H., (1975) "Welfare and population: Notes on rural India since 1960", *Population and Development Review*, 1 (1) : 33-70.

——(1978) *India: Population, economy, society*, London, Macmillan Press,

Chandramouli, A.S. and M. Guruswamy., 1979 "Distance as a variable influencing the delivery of family planning and MCH services", *Journal of the Institute of Economic Research*, India, 14 (2).

Cicourel, A.V., (1967) "Fertility, family planning and the social organization of family life : Some methodological issues" *The Journal of Social Issues*, 23 (4) : 57-81.

Clifford, William B (II). (1971) "Modern and traditional value orientations and fertility behaviour : A social demographic study", *Demography*, 8 : 37-48.

Coal, Ansley J and Edward M. Hoover., (1958) *Population Growth and Economic Development in Low Income Countries*, Princeton, Princeton University Press.

Cohn, Bernard S., (1961) "Chamar family in a North Indian village : A structural contingent", *The Economic Weekly*, 13 : 1051-1055.

——(1971) *India : The Social Anthropology of a Civilization*, Princeton, Princeton University Press.

Conklin, George H., (1973) "Emerging conjugal role patterns in a joint family system : Correlates of social change in Dharwar, India", *Journal of Marriage and Family*, 35 : 742-748.

——(1981) "Cultural determinants of power for women within the family: A neglected aspect of family research", in George Kurian and Ratna Ghosh (eds.), *Women in the Family and the Economy*, London, Greenwood Press, pp 9-28.

Cutright, Phillips and William R Kelly., (1981) "The role of family planning programme in fertility decline in less developed countries 1958-1977", *International Family Planning Perspectives*, 7 (4).

Dandeker, V.M. and Nilakantha Rath., (1977) "Poverty in India", *Economic and Political Weekly*, 6 (1) : 25.

Das Gupta, Ajit ; Ranjan K. Som, Murari Majumdar and Subodh N. Mitra.

——(1956) *Couple Fertility*, Sankhya, 16 (3-4) : 230-434.

Davis, Kingsley., (1951) *Population of India and Pakistan*, Princeton, Princeton University Press.

——(1955) "Institutional pattern favouring high fertility in underdeveloped area", *Eugenics Quarterly*, 2 : 33-39.

——(1957) "Population Policy : Will current programmes succeed ?" *Science*, 158 (3802) : 730-739.

——(1963) "The theory of change and response in modern demographic theory", *Population Index*, 29 : 345-366.

——(1967) "Population Policy : Will current programmes succeed ?", *Science*, 158 (3802) : 730-739.

Davis, Kingsley and Judith Blake. (1956) "Social structure and fertility : An analytic framework", *Economic Development and Cultural Change*, 4 (3) : 211-235.

Demerath, Nicholas J., (1967) "Can India reduce its birth rates ? A question of modernization and governmental capacity", *Journal of Social Issues*, 23 (4) : 179-194.

Desai, P.B., (1975) *A Survey of Research in Demography*, Indian Council of Social Science Research, New Delhi, Popular Prakashan.

——(1980) "Family welfare planning in India", *Cyclostyled*, (paper prepared at the instance of the Department of Social Welfare in India).

Demeny, Paul., (1979) "On the end of the population explosion", *Population and Development Review*, 5 (1) : 141-162.

Demerath, Nicholas J., "Can India reduce its birth rates ? A question of modernization and governmental capacity", *Journal of Social Issues*, 23 (4).

Driver, Edwin D., (1963) *Differential Fertility in Central India*, Princeton, Princeton University Press.

Easterlin, Richard A., (1969) "Towards a socio-economic theory of fertility : A survey of recent research on economic factors in American fertility", in Behrman S.J. Leslie Corsa and Ronald Freedman, (eds.), *Fertility and Family Planning* : *A world view*, Ann Arbor, University Press, pp 127-156.

——(1973) "Relative economic status and the American fertility swing", in Eleanore B. Sheldon (ed.), *Family Economic Behaviour* : *Problems and Prospects*, Philadelphia, J.B. Lippincott Co., pp 170-223.

——(1975) "An economic framework for fertility analysis, *Studies in Family Planning*, 6 (3) : 54-63.

Epstein, T Scarlett., (1962) *Economic Development and Social Change in South India*, Manchester, Manchester University Press.

——(1973) *South India* : *Yesterday, today and tomorrow—Mysore villages revisited*, London, Macmillan Press.

——(1975) "The ideal marriage between the economists' macro-approach and social anthropologist's micro-approach to development studies", *Economic Development and Cultural Change*, 24 (1) : 29-45.

Epstein, T Scarlett and Darrell Jackson (eds)., (1977) *The Feasibility of Fertility Planning* : *Micro perspectives*, Oxford, Pergamon Press.

Eversley, D.E.C., (1963) 'Population in England in the eighteenth century: An appraisal of current research", *Proceedings of the International*

Population Conference, New York, 1961 ; Vol I, London, International Union for the Scientific Studies of Population, pp 573-81.

Fawcett, James T., (1970) "Psychology and population : Behaviour research issues in fertility and family planning, New York, The Population Council.

——(1973) *Psychological Perspectives on Population*, New York, Basic Books.

Fortes, Meyer., (1949) "Time and social structure : An Ashanti case study", in Meyer Fortes, (ed.). *Social Structure*, London, Oxford University Press, pp 54-84.

——(1958) "Introduction", in Jack Goody (ed.), *The Developmental Cycle in Domestic Groups*, Cambridge Papers in social Anthropology No. 1 Cambridge, Cambridge University Press.

Freedman, Ronald., (1961-62) "The sociology of human fertility : A trend report and bibliography", *Current Sociology*, 10/11 : 35-121.

——(1979) "Theories of fertility decline : a reappraisal", *Social Forces*, 58 (1) : 1-17.

French J.R.P and B. Raven., (1960) "The basis of social power", in C. Carwright and A. Zander (eds.), *Group Dynamics : Research and theory*, New York, Harper and Row.

Fried, Ellen Shapiro and Richard J. Udry., (1980) "Normative pressures on fertility planning", *Population and Environment*, 3 (3-4) : 199-209.

Frisch, R.E., (1975) "Demographic implications of the biological determinants of female fecundity", *Social Biology*, 22 (1) : 17-22.

Goode, William J., (1963) *World Revolution and Family Patterns*, London, The Free Press of Glencoe.

Goody, Jack., (1958) *The Developmental Cycle in Domestic Groups*, Cambridge Papers in Social Anthropology No. 1, Cambridge, Cambridge University Press.

Gould, Ketayun H., (1969) "Sex and contraception in Sherupur : Family planning in a North Indian village", *Economic and Political Weekly*, 4 (49) : 1887-1892.

Greenough, Paul R., (1982) *Prosperity and Misery in Modern Bengal : The famine of 1943-1944*, New York, Oxford University Press.

Gwatkin, Davidson G., (1979) "Political will and family planning : The implications of India's Emergency experience", *Population and Development Review*, 5 (1) : 29-60.

Hass, Paula H., (1974) "Wanted and unwanted pregnancies : A fertility decision-making model", *Journal of Social Issues*, 30 (4) : 125-165.

Heer, David M., (1963) "The measurement and bases of family power : An overview", *Marriage and Family Living*, 25 : 133-139.

Hermalin, Albert I., "Regression analysis of a real data", in C. Chandrasekaran and Albert I. Hermalin, (eds.), *Measuring the Effect of Family Planning Programmes on Fertility*, International Union for the Scientific Study of Population, Belgium. pp 245-299.

Hill, R ; J.M. Stycos and K.W. Back., (1959) *The Family and Population*

Control: *A Puerto Rican experiment in social change*, Chapel Hill, University of North Carolina Press.

Hobson, Sarah., (1978) *Family Web* : *A Story of India*, London, John Murray.

Hollerbach, Paula E., (1980) "Power in families, communication and fertility decision-making", Working paper No. 53, *Centre for Policy Studies*, New York, The Population Council.

——(1983) "Fertility decision-making process : A critical essay", in Rodolfo A. Bulatao and Ronald D. Lee (eds.), *Determinants of Fertility in Developing Countries*, Volume 2, New York, Academic Press, pp 340-380.

Howard, Alan., (1963) "Land, activity systems, and decision-making in Rotuma", *Ethnography*, 2 : 407-440.

Hull, Terence H., (1983) "Cultural influences on fertility decision styles", In Rodolfo A. Bulatao and Ronald D. Lee (eds.), *Determinants of Fertility In Developing Countries*, Volume 2, New York, Academic Press, pp 381-414.

Hull, Valerie J., (1982) "Breast-feeding and fertility", Paper presented at the WHO/NAS Workshop on *Breast-feeding and Fertility Regulation* : *Current knowledge and policy implications*, Geneva.

Ishwaran. K., (1970) "Mallur : Internal dynamics of change in a Mysore village", in K. Ishwaran (ed.) *Change and Continuity in India's Villages*, New York, Columbia University Press, pp 1-19.

Kammeyer, K.C.W., (1971) *An Introduction to Population*, San Francisco, Chandler.

Kakar, Sudhir. (1979) "Childhood in India: Traditional ideals and contemporary reality", *International Social Science Journal*, 31 (3): 444-456.

Kapadia K.M., (1959) "The family in transition", *Sociological Bulletin*, 8 : 74-79.

Karve, Iravathi., (1953) *Kinship Organization in India*, Poona, Deccan College.

Khatri, A.A., (1975) "The adaptive extended family in India today", *Journal of Marriage and Family*, 37 (3) : 633-42.

Knorr-Cetina K. and Aaron Victor Cicourel., (1981) *Advances in Social Theory and Methodology* : *Toward an integration of macro and micro sociologies*, London, Routledge and Kegan Paul.

Kocher, James E., (1976) *A Micro-economic Analysis of the Determinants of Fertility in Rural Northeastern Tanzania*, Ph. D. Dissertation, Michigan, University Microfiche International.

Koenig, Michael Alan., (1981) *Family Relations and Fertility Behavior in Rural North India*, Ph. D, Dissertation, Michigan, University Microfilms International.

Kolenda P.M., (1967) "Regional differences in Indian family structure", in Rober Crane (ed.) *Regions and Regionalism in South Asian Studies* : *An exploratory study*, Durham, N.C. Monograph Number 5 of the Duke University Program on Southern Asia.

——(1968) "Religion, caste, family structure : a comparative study of the Indian 'joint family' ", in Milton Singer and Bernard S. Cohn, (eds.), *Structure and Change in Indian Society*, Chicago, Aldine Publishing Co., pp 339-376.

Knodel, John E., (1977) "Breast-feeding and population growth", *Science*, 198 (4322) : 1111-15.

Krause, John T., (1963) "English population movements between 1700 and 1850", Proceedings of the International Population Conference, New York, Vol I, London, International Union for the Scientific Study of Population, pp 583-590.

Krishnamoorthy S., (1974) "Effects of sex preference and mortality on family size", *Demography India*, 3 (1) : 120-132.

Kulkarni, G.A., (1975) "An assessment of change in fertility", in R.S. Kurup (ed.), *Studies on Fertility in India*, Gandhigram, The Gandhigram Institute of Rural Health and Family Planning, pp 136-146.

Kuznets, Simon., (1964) "Notes on pattern of U.S. economic growth', in Edgar O. Edwards (ed.), *The Nation's Economic Objectives*, Chicago, University of Chicago Press.

Lannoy, Richard., (1971) *The Speaking Tree: A study of Indian Culture and Society*, London, Oxford University Press.

Leibenstein, Harvey., (1957) *Economic Backwardness and Economic Growth*. New York : John Wiley.

——(1974) "An interpretation of the economic theory of fertility: Promising path or blind alley ?", *Journal of Economic Literature* 12 : 457-479.

——(1977) "Beyond economic man : Economic, political and population problem", *Population and Development Review*, 3 (3) : 183-199.

——(1981) "Economic decision theory and human fertility behavior : A speculative essay", *Population and Development Review* 7 (3) : 381-400.

Liu, William T ; Ira W. Hutchison and Lawrence K. Hong., 1973 "Conjugal power and decision-making : A methodological note on cross-cultural study of the family", *American Journal of Sociology*, 79 (1).

Lorimer, Frank., (1954) *Culture and Human Fertility*, Paris, UNESCO.

Malthus, Thomas Robert., (1798) *An Essay on the Principle of Population as it Affects the Future Improvement of Society*, London, Johnson.

Mamdani, Mahmood., (1972) *The Myth of Population Control* New York, Monthly Review Press.

Mandelbaum, David G., (1970) *Society in India*, Change and Continuity, Vol 2, Berkeley, University of California Press.

Mauldin, W.P. and Bernard Berelson., (1978) "Conditions of fertility decline in developing countries, 1965-75", *Studies in Family Planning*, 9 (5) : 89.

Marshall, John F., (1971) "Topics and networks in intra-village communications", in Steven Polgar (ed.), *Culture and Population : A collection of current studies*, Carolina Population Center Monograph Series, No. 9.

——(1972) *Culture and Contraception : Response determinants to a family planning programme in a North Indian village*, Ph. D. dissertation, University of Hawaii.

May, David A and D.M. Heer., (1968) "Son survivorship motivation and family size in India : A computer simulation", *Population Studies*, 22 (2) : 199-210.

Meeker, Barbara F., (1980) "Rational decision-making models in interpersonal behavior", in Thomas K. Burch (ed.) *Demographic Behavior : Interdisciplinary perspectives on decision-making*, Colorado, Westview Press, pp 23-42.

Mencher, Joan P. (1971) "Family planning in Chingleput district Madras, India", in Steven Polgar (ed.), *Culture and Population*, Cambridge, Schenkman Publishing Company.

Miller, Barbara D., (1981) *The Endangered Sex: Neglect of famale children in rural North India*, Ithaca, Cornell University Press.

Mishra, G.P., (1981) *Dynamics of Rural Development in Village India*, New Delhi, Ashish Publishing House.

Misra, Bhasker D ; Ali Ashraf ; Ruth Simmons and George B. Simmons., 1982 *Organization for Change : A systems analysis of family planning in rural India*, Paper No. 21, Michigan Papers on South and Southeast Asia, Ann Arbor, Michigan.

Mosley, W. Henry., (1977) "The effects of nutrition on natural fertility", *Scientific Report 3*, Cholera Research Laboratory, Dacca.

Moore, W. E., (1965) *Social Change*, New Delhi, Prentice-Hall of India.

Mukherjee, Bishwa Nath., (1981) "Multivariate relationships between modernity value orientations and family planning indicators", *Population and Environment*, 4 (1) : 24-43.

Mukherjee, S. B., (1977) *The Age Distribution of the Indian Population*, Honolulu, East-West Population Institute, East-West Centre.

Myrdal, Gunnar., (1968) *Asian Drama : An inquiry into the poverty of nations*, Vol, III, New York, Pantheon.

——(1971) *Asian Drama : An inquiry into the poverty of nations*, An abridgement of the Twentieth Century Fund Study by Seth King, Penguin Books.

Nag, Moni., (1965) "Marriage and kinship in relation to human fertility", in Moni Nag (ed.), *Population and Social Organization*, The Hague, Mouton Publishers, pp 11-54.

——(1967) "Family type and fertility", *Proceedings of the Second World Population Conference, New York, 1965*, Vol. 2 : 160-163, New York, United Nations.

——(1972) "Sex, culture and human fertility in India and the United States", *Current Anthropology*, 13 (2) : 231-237.

——(1977) "Community studies for collecting fertility data", In Ashish Bose ; Devendra B. Gupta and Gaurisankar Raychaudhuri, (eds.), *Population Statistics in India*, New Delhi, Vikas Publishing House, pp 273-276.

——(1980) "How modernization can also increase fertility", *Current Anthropology*, 21 (5) : 571-587.

——(1982) "Modernization and its impact on fertility: The Indian scene", *Center for Policy Studies*, Working Paper, New York, The Population Council.

——(1983) "The equity-fertility hypothesis as an explanation of the fertility differential between Kerala and West Bengal", *Center for Policy Studies*, Working Paper, New York, The Population Council.

Nag, Moni ; N.F. Benjamin and Creighton R. Peet., (1978) "An anthropological approach to the study of the economic value of children in Java and Nepal", *Current Anthropology*, 19 (2) : 293-306,

Nag, Moni ; Richard Anker and M.E. Khan., (1982) "A guide to anthropological study of women's roles and demographic change in India", *Population and Labour Policies Programme Working Paper No. 115*, International Labour Office, Geneva.

Namboodiri N. Krishnan., (1980) "A look at fertility model-building from different perspective", in Thomas K. Burch (ed.), *Demographic Behavior : Interdisciplinary perspectives on decision-making*, Washington, D.C. Westview Press, pp 71-90.

——(1972) "Some observations on the economic framework for fertility analysis", *Population Studies*, 26 (2) : 185-206.

National Academy of Science., (1981) "Manuscript section on Indian vital rates", National Academy of Science, Washington D.C. Unpublished.

Notestein, Frank W., (1956) "The impact of anticipated trends and shifts in population upon American agriculture", Proceedings of *Agricultural Industries Conference*, Cornell University, pp 28-42.

Oechsli, F.W and D. Kirk., (1975) Modernization and the demographic transition in Latin America and the Caribbean", *Economic Development and Cultural Change*, 23 : 391.

Oppong, Christine., (1979) "Family structure and women's reproductive and productive roles : Some conceptual and methodological issues", *Population and Labour Policies Programme, Working Paper No. 79*, Geneva, International Labour Office.

Page, H.J., (1977) "Patterns underlying fertility schedules : A decomposition by both age and marriage duration", *Population Studies*, 31 (1) : 85-106.

Paige, Karen E and Jeffery M. Paige., 1981 *The Politics of Reproductive Ritual*, Berkeley, University of California Press.

Panandiker, V.A. Rai ; R.N. Bishnoi and O.P. Sharma. (1978) *Family Planning Under the Emergency : Policy implications of incentives and disincentives*, New Delhi, Radiant Publications.

Poffenberger, Thomas., (1964) "The effect of local beliefs on attitudes toward vasectomy in two Indian villages in Gujarat State", *Population Review*, 8 (2) : 37-44.

——(1978) "Motivational aspects of resistance to family planning in an Indian village", *Demography*, 5 : 757-766.

——(1969) *Husband-wife communication and motivational aspects of population control in an Indian village,* Central Family Planning Institute, New Delhi.

Poffenberger, Thomas and Shirley B. Poffenberger., (1971) *Reaction to World News Events and the Influence of Mass Media in an Indian Village,* Center for South and Southeast Asian Studies, The University of Michigan, Michigan.

——(1973) "The social psychology of fertility behavior in a village in India", in J.T. Fawcett (ed.), *Psychological Perspectives on Population* New York, Basic Books, pp 135-162.

Pope, H and N.K. Namboodiri., (1968) "Decisions regarding family size : Moral norms and utility model of social choice", *Research Previews,* 15 : 6-17.

Poston, Dudley L (Jr.) and Joachim Singelmann, (1975) "Socio-economic status, orientations, and fertility behaviour in India", *Demography,* 12 (3) ; 417-430.

Quinn, Naomi., (1975) "Decision models and social structure", *American Ethnologist,* 2 (1) : 19-45.

Rainwater, Lee., (1960) *And the Poor Get Children,* Chicago ; Quadrangle Books.

——(1965) *Family Design: Marital sexuality, family size, and contraception,* Chicago, Aldine.

Rao, Baskara N. P.M. Kulkarni and P. Hanumantha Rayappa., (1982) "Differentials in fertility in rural Karnataka", Cyclostyled, Population Research Centre of the Institute for Social and Economic Change, Bangalore, India.

Rao, Kamala Gopal., (1974) *Studies in Family Planning : India,* New Delhi, Abhinav Publications.

Rao, V.K.R.V., (1975) "On the Indian experiment in family planning: A review and suggestions for the future", in R.S. Kurup (ed.), *Studies of Fertility in India,* Gandhigram, Gandhigram Institute of Rural Health and Family Planning, pp 210-226.

Raulet, Harry, M., (1970) "Family planning and population control in developing countries", *Demography,* 7 (2) ; 211-234.

Raven, B.H; R. Centers and A. Rodrigues., (1975) "The bases of conjugal power", in R.E. Cromwell and D.H. Olson (eds.) *Power in Families,* New York, Sage Publications.

Reddy, P.H., 1978 "Family structure and fertility", *Social Change,* 8 (1) : 24-32.

Reinharz, Shulamit., 1979 "The ritual of survey empiricism", Chapter 2 in *On Becoming a Social Scientist,* San Francisco, Jossey-Bass.

Reynolds, Jack., (1972) "Evaluation of Family Planning Performance : A Critical Review", *Demography,* 9 (1) : 69-86.

Rindfuss, Roland and Philip Morgan., (1983) "Marriage, sex, and the first birth interval : The quiet revolution in Asia", *Population and Development Review,* 9 (2) : 259-278.

Rogers, Everett M., (1971) *Communication of Innovations*, New York, The Free Press.

Ross, Aileen D., (1961) *The Hindu Family in its Urban Setting*, University of Toronto Press.

Ryder, N.R., (1963) 'Notes on the concept of a population', *The American Journal of Sociology*, 69 (5) : 447-463.

Scanzoni, John and Maximiliane Szinovacz, (1981) *Family Decision-making A developmental sex role model*, Beverly Hills, London, Sage Publications.

Schneider, D. M., (1971) *India : The social anthropology of civilization*, Anthropology of Modern Societies Series, Prentice-Hall.

Schultz, T. Paul (ed.)., (1974) *Economics of Family : Marriage, children and human capital*, National Bureau of Economic Research, University of Chicago Press.

Sethuraman S. V. (1974) "Employment and labour productivity in India since 1950", *Economic Development and Cultural Change*, 22 (4): 673-90.

Shah, A. M., *The Household Dimension of the Family in India*, New Delhi, Orient Longman Limited.

Shankariah, C., (1969) *A study of differentiated communication patterns in a progressive and a non-progressive village*, Ph. D. Dissertation, New Delhi, Indian Agricultural Research Institute.

Shariff, Abusaleh ; M. Guruswamy and A.V. Diwakar., (1978) "Dual Record System : A preliminary Evaluation", *Newsletter*, 4 (4), Bangalore Population Centre, India.

——(1979) "Dual Record System : The vital rates estimation for the project districts—1977", *Newsletter*, 5 (4), Bangalore Population Centre, India.

Simmons, George B., (1971) *The Indian Investment in Family Planning* An occasional paper of The Population Council, New York, The Population Council.

Simon, H A., (1957) *Models of Man.* New York, John Wiley and Sons, pp. 196-200.

Slater, Gilbert., (1918) *Some South Indian Villages*, University of Madras Economic Series, Volume I, London, Oxford University Press.

Smelser, Neil J., (1965) "The social challenge to parental authority", in Seymour Farber, Picro Mustacchis and Roger H. Wilson, (eds.), *Man and Civilization*, New York, McGraw Hill, pp 67-72.

Solvic, Paul ; Baruch Fischoff and Sarah Lichtenstein., (1977) "Behavioural decision theory", *Aunual Review of Psychology* : 1-39.

Spengler, Joseph J. (1966) "Values and fertility analysis", *Demography*, 3(1) : 109-130.

Srikantan, K.S. (1977) *The Family Planning Program in the Socio-economic Context*, New York, The Population Council.

Srinivas M.N. (1942) *Marriage and Family in Mysore*, Bombay, New Book Co.

——(1959) "The Dominant Caste in Ramapura" *American Anthropologist*, 61 : 1-16.

——(1962) *Caste in Modern India and Other Essays*, Bombay Asia Publishing House.

——(1969) *Social Change in Modern India*, Berkeley, University of California Press.

——(1976) *The Remembered Village*, Berkeley, University of Calfornia Press.

——(1978) *The Changing Position of Indian Women*, Delhi, Oxford University Press.

——(1982) *India : Social structure*, Delhi, Hindustan Publishing Corporation.

Srinivas M.N. and E.V. Ramaswamy., (1977) *Culture and Human Fertility in India*, Delhi, Oxford University Press.

Srinivasan K., 1975 "Retrospective surveys", in C. Chandrasekaran, and Albert I. Hermalin, (eds.), *Measuring the Effect of Family Planning Programs on Fertility*, International Union for the Scientific Study of Population, Belgium, pp 301-350.

Srinivasan K ; P.H. Reddy and K.N.M. Raju., (1978) "From one generation to the next: Changes in fertility, family size preferences, and family planning in an Indian state between 1951 and 1975", *Studies in Family Planning*, 9(10/11) : 258-271.

Stycos, J.M. and K.W. Back., (1964) *Human Fertility in Latin America : Sociological perspectives* Ithaca, New York, Cornell University Press.

Teauber Irene B., (1958), *The Population of Japan*, Princeton, Princeton University Press.

Teitelbaum, Michael., (1975) "Relevence of the demographic transition theory for developing countries", *Science* 188 : 420-25.

Thimmaiah. G., (1983) *Inequality and Poverty*, Bombay Himalaya Publishing House.

Turchi, Boone A. (1975) "Micro-economic theory of fertility: A critique," *Social Forces*, 54(1) : 107-125.

Urdy, Richard J., (1983) "Do couples make fertility plans one birth at a time?", *Demography*, 20(2) : 117-128.

United Nations., 1961 *The Mysore Population Study*, Population Studies, No. 34, United Nations, New York.

——(1970), "India : UN mission evaluation of the family planning program", *Studies in Family Planning*, (46) : 4-18.

——(1977) *Levels and Trends of Fertility Throughout the World 1950-70* ST/ESA/SER.A/59.

——(1973) *The Determinants and Consequences of Population Trends : New summary of findings on interaction of demographic, economic and social factors*, Department of Economic and Social Affairs, Population Studies No. 50, New York, United Nations.

Vance, Rupert B., (1959) "The development of Status of American demography", in Philip M, Houser and O.D. Duncan, (eds.), *The Study of Population*, Chicago, Chicago Press.

Veatch, Robert M., (1977) "Governmental population incentives : Ethical issues at stake", *Studies in Family Planning*, 8(4) : 100-108.

Vicziany, Marika., (1982a) "Coercion in a soft state : The Family Planning programme of India", Part I, The Myth of Voluntarism, *Pacific Affairs*, 55(3) : 373-402.

——(1982b) "Coercion in a soft state: The family planning programme of India", Part II, The Sources of Coercion, *Pacific Affairs*, 55(4): 557-592.

Visaria, Pravin and Leela Visaria., 1981 "India's Population: Second and growing *Population Bulletin*, 36(4).

Weeks. J., (1977) *Population : An Introduction to concepts and issues,* Belmont, Wadsworth Press.

Weiner, Myron., (1983) "The political demography of Assam's anti-immigrant movement", *Population and Development Review*, 9(2) : 279-292.

Wolpert, Julian, (1964) "The decision process in spatial context", *Annals of the Association of American Geographers*, 54 : 537-558.

Woyn, John B and John E. Gordon., The Khanna Study : Population problems in the rural Punjab, Cambridge, Harvard University Press.

Yaukey, D.W. Griffiths and B.J. Roberts. (1967) "Couples concurrence and empathy on birth control motivation in Dacca, East Pakistan", *American Sociological Review* 32 : 716-726.

Appendix

DEMOGRAPHIC TRENDS AND HISTORY OF THE FAMILY PLANNING PROGRAMME

A-1 DEMOGRAPHIC TRENDS IN INDIA AND KARNATAKA

(*i*) *Introduction*

Human fertility is one of the subjects of demographic investigation, discussed frequently at length and expressed in varied measurements. There can be plurality in its expression as a result of diverse data bases of different size and quality, and arising from the numerous techniques used to estimate it. In India these figures have elicited the increasing concern of policy makers in the course of economic and social planning. Current policy objectives are to reduce the high levels of both fertility and mortality. The level of fertility and the consequent rate of growth of population is considered an impediment to development and national well-being. It has been argued that evidence for this is provided by the consistent increase in the Net National Product, while per-capita income remains almost constant.[1]

This has led to efforts by the Indian government to reduce fertility levels in the form of an ambitious government family planning programme which was the first of its kind in the world. This has occurred despite the fact that India is characterized as a country with a tradition-bound society where traditional values act as a bastion against change. However, it has also been described as a developing country with certain unique socio-cultural and economic aspects. Such characteristics as its predominantly rural and illiterate population, subsistence agriculture, and the family as the major socio-cultural unit, are believed to encourage large number of children per each married couple.

Nevertheless, it is important to describe the trends in fertility of the populations of India and Karnataka state which is the focus of this study. The discussion of trends in fertility has to start with a note of caution that the figures presented below are those which are generally accepted to be reasonably close to reality even though their validity is sometimes questionable for one reason or the other.

(ii) Demographic Trends for India

The earliest source for calculating fertility and mortality rates was provided by the decennial censuses. Though information on births, deaths and marriages was not collected, they gave an insight into population growth patterns for the whole country and its many subdivisions. The age distribution of the enumerated population provided a basis for estimating decennial birth and death rates by indirect estimation.[2] Davis (1951 : 85) calculated these rates for each decade from 1881-1891 to 1931-1941. The birth rate for 1881-1891 was estimated to be 48.9 which fell to 45.2 by 1931-41 [see Table 1.1]. This apparent decline in birth rate over six decades was neither uniform over that period nor considerable. Coale and Hoover (1958:31) stated that a high and nearly constant level of fertility was combined with a relatively high but fluctuating death rate between 1891 and 1921. Mortality declined by ten points from 41.3 to 31.2 during these years, although there was an eruption of high death rates associated with the influenza epidemic at the end of the period. Birth rates for subsequent decennial intercensal periods have been estimated by the Census Actuary as 39.9, 41.7 and 41.1 for 1941-51, 1951-61 and 1961-71 while the respective death rates were 27.4, 22.8 and 18.9. Coale and Hoover (1958 : 31 and 50) argue that the vital rates provided by the Census Actuary (Census of India, 1951) were lower due to different method of computation, and the understated infant mortality rate for India used in the official life tables. The most recent figures for the 1970s are provided by the sample Registration System as 33.3 for the birth rate and 14.2 for the death rate for India for the period 1971-78. The annual figures provided by the Sample Registration Scheme for recent years indicate that the death rate which decreased to a level of 15 per thousand in 1971 was still around the same level in 1977. Thus mortality appears to have stabilized whereas the birth rate, which was 37 in 1971 after a decline of four points from the 1961-71, level, dropped further to 33 in 1977.

TABLE 1.1

Birth and Death Rates for India from 1881 to 1978

Decades	Birth Rate Per '000 Population	Death Rate Per '000 Population
1881—1891	48.9	41.3
1891—1901	45.8	44.4
1901—1911	49.8	42.6
1911—1921	48.1	47.6
1921—1931	46.4	36.3
1931—1941	45.2	31.3
1941—1951	39.9	27.4
1951—1961	41.7	22.8
1961—1971	41.1	18.9
1971—1978	33.3	14.2

Source : Davis (1951)
Visaria and Visaria (1981)

Thus for India as a whole there has been a falling trend in both birth and death rates, the fall in the death rate being much the steepest (Coale and Hoover, 1958 ; Deasi, 1980). A report by the United Nations states that :

> ...the moderate level of estimated crude birth rates and gross reproduction rates for India and...suggest that, if any confidence can be placed in their quality, fertility is, or has been, declining. If these figures can be trusted, there has been a falling trend in birth rates since the fifties after a slight rise in forties, and a sharp fall in the seventies (1977 : 189).

Death rates, however, have been falling since the 1911-21 period and have now stabilized around 15 per thousand, although still exhibiting features like high infant, childhood and maternal mortality. Coale and Hoover in their classic work on the inter-relationships of economic development and fertility in the Indian context remarked about the falling fertility trend in India that :

> ...if the view that the declines in the birth rates until 1951 were minor is accepted provisionally, it appears that the course of the birth and death rates in India between 1918 and 1951 confirms closely to the course that the theory of demographic transition ascribes to a country in the incipient stages of economic development (1958 : 31).

Nevertheless, this remark is more relevant for the period between 1951 and 1971, because profound economic and social development of recognizable magnitude have occurred during this period, a fact which presumably partly explains the recent decline in the birth rates in India. There have also been certain definite changes in the cultural and social aspects of the population. Desai while explaining the most recent trends of of falling fertility and almost stabilized mortality rates concludes :

> This has raised a hope that the cherished trend in fertility decline has been set in, though it is in an incipient stage (1980 : 3).

The decade 1965-75 is considered a period during which there was substantial fertility decline in Asia, about 17 per cent, (Mauldin and Berelson, 1978 : 123) and India constituted the bulk of Asia's population. The small decline in birth rate that occurred during the 1930s has been mainly attributed to the extension of the average length of the birth interval due to a decrease in infant and child mortality (Caldwell, *et.al*, 1982a), there being no evidence for that period of deliberate attempts to control fertility other than induced abortions in case of socially unrecognized conceptions. The consistent decline in death rates is attributed mainly to the policy executed by the governments[3] to extend free sanitation, drinking water, health and medical facilities to the people, and its impressive achievement in preventive health measures and in controlling epidemics such as cholera, small pox and malaria.

The explanation for the decline in birth rates, especially since 1951, is still a matter for speculation and some controversy. Major socio-economic changes since 1951 among the population could be a general explanation but it is far from satisfactory. Certain developmentalists and demographers believe this and the slogan *development is the best contraceptive* captioned by the Bucharest Population Conference in 1974 summarises their thinking. This was a widespread belief during the sixties in India. However, a major question emerges in defining development and specifying the level of development at which fertility starts declining—a question which is addressed in the forthcoming section of this Appendix. Cassen while discussing the lower birth rates among island populations, states that, 'the general level of various indicators of social and economic development in these countries is well above the third world average' (1978 : 48). He implies that development causes a decline in fertility, although he later speculates on the extent of the decline that might be expected. Oechsli and Kirk (1975) United Nations (1967), Srikantan (1977) have tried to relate the fertility decline to the level of development but were not wholly successful ; due to what Caldwell (1976a : 333) termed the cultural dichotomy. Extending this dichotomy further Caldwell (1977 : 100) laid stress on the diffusion of westernization,[4] and its effect on fertility. He writes that : 'it is noticeable that fertility decline in the third world...have taken place most frequently in islands which have been largely westernized or christianized...'.

Another explanation given for the decline in the birth rate particularly after 1960, is the success of the family planning programme. It is substantiated by presenting the number of births averted due to the increasing acceptance of contraception, especially sterilization. Cassen estimates that : 'the family planning programme in India has reduced by about one million a year the number of births that might otherwise have occurred. That is something like 5 per cent of all births since 1968 or so or 2 points on the birth rate till 1972' (1975 : 58). However, this view has been widely attacked on the ground that the family planning programme has not been so successful that it could be credited with such a decline in birth rates. Srinivasan, *et. al.*, (1978) and Rao (1975) have analysed the data on family planning acceptance in India to substantiate this line of attack. Rao pointed to the decline in the birth rate in 1941-51 over 1931-41 being as much as 5.3 points (p 213) ; the credit for the fall of 4.5 points in crude birth rate between 1961 and 1971 cannot, therefore, go to the family planning programmes, which began in late 1950s. He further analysed the data on the proportion of protected couples which rose from 11 per cent in 1967 to 15 per cent in 1972 leading to the birth rate falling only by one point, from 36.7 to 36.6 according to the sample registration data. Srinivasan, *et. al.*, while comparing the fertility rates of the Mysore Population Study (United Nations, 1961) with the Bangalore Population Study (1975), expressed astonishment, at an apparently small decrease in the birth rate over twenty-four years. They state that this small decline raise the question about the effect of the family planning programme in India. However, at the theoretical level, few (Blake, 1965 ; Davis, 1968) have raised doubts about the ability of the family planning programmes to cause the decline in fertility.

The third explanation advanced suspects that the rates evidence under-enumeration because of poor quality data and inadequate estimation techniques. This group considers that the decline in vital rates is not substantial, especially the birth rates, and provides an alternative set of figures estimated with different assumptions; these rates often are considerably higher. Srikantan and Dyson and few other belong to this group.

Caldwell, *et. al*, (1982a) believe that the analysis of Indian data suggests crude birth rates of around 40 per thousand in the 1940s ; a moderate pre-transitional level, perhaps 2-3 points higher in the 1950s ; and probably close to 40 again in the 1960s. The birth rate for the 1970s of 33 per thousand provided by the Sample Registration scheme is however said to be debatable.

(iii) Demographic Trends for Karnataka

For Karnataka, the picture is not substantially different [see Table 1.2]. The birth rate, which was estimated to be 36.9 during 1951-61, increased to 41.6 during 1961-71 and declined to 29.1 during the 1970s. For Karnataka, a unique opportunity exists for the comparison of results from two fairly large-scale surveys almost a generation apart. A comparison of the first, the Mysore Population Study 1951 (MPS) (United Nations, 1961) with the other, the Bangalore Population Study (BPS) (Bangalore Population Centre, 1975), provided certain insights into the fertility and mortality changes during this twenty-four year period. A comparative analysis presented a weighted average birth rate of 39.3 per thousand in 1951 and 35.2 in 1975 for almost the same geographical populations. However, the birth rate for the rural plains[5] was 39.9 and 37.9 per thousand population. Thus, there are astonishingly small changes in the birth rates over 24 years. These modest differences have been explained by the authors of the latter study as due to (i) underenumeration in the earlier study and (ii) the effect of modernization which created a paradoxical situation by relaxing traditional restraints on conception and thus contributing to an increase in potential fertility (Srinivasan, *et. al.* 1978). The birth rates made available from other sources for 1977 also help to explain the trend. An experimental project, the Dual Record System, undertaken by the Bangalore Population Centre, gave a birth rate of 34 per thousand population 1976-77 for almost same geographical area in Karnataka State (Shariff, *et. al*, 1979 : 9). It is essential here to mention that the figures provided by the Sample Registration Scheme seem to be lower than the one presented by the Bangalore Population Study and the Dual Record System, which might be explained by the widespread agreement over the possible under-registration by the Sample Registration (National Academy of Sciences, 1981 : 12). In spite of the problem of choosing the best figures, the declining trend in the birth rates is traceable for Karnataka since the latter part of the 1950s. Caldwell, *et. al*, (1982a) presents for Karnataka a birth rate of no more than 30 per thousand in the early 1980s, close to 40 in the early 1970s and possibly as high as 45 per thousand in the early 1960s. However, while there is some disagreement about the magnitude of the fertility decline between 1950 and 1982, there is general agreement that among the southern states the fertility decline in 1950s and the 1960s was quite significant, most apparent in Kerala followed by Karnataka (Kulkarni : 1975).

TABLE 1.2

Birth and Death Rates for Karnataka since 1941

Years	Birth Rate per '000 Population		Death Rate per '000 Population	
1941—51	36.9		—	
1951		(39.3)*		(18.6)*
1951—61	41.6		—	
1961—71	39.9		—	
1970	33.0		13.1	
1971	31.7		12.1	
1972	31,5		12.8	
1973	28.9		12.4	
1974	28.0		10.8	
1975	27.2	(35.2)**	11.1	
1976	29.4		11.7	
1977	26.3	(34.0)***	11.1	(13.9)***
1978	29.2		12.1	

Sources :

Various Sample Registration Scheme bulletins.

* Mysore Population Study, United Nations (1961).

** Bangalore Population Study.

Srinivasan, *et al*, (1978).

*** Dual Records System, Shariff, *et al*, (1979).

A.2 FAMILY PLANNING : EVIDENCE FOR INDIA AND KARNATAKA

(i) *Introduction*

This section begins with a brief note on the concept of 'family planning'. Family planning is a relatively new concept, although at least some kind of planning was involved in family formation in the past. Family formation is a process involving the occurrence of events like births, marriage, migration and deaths. Births are a sequential occurrence which tend to happen as a natural biological course. They may take place without the conscious involvement of the actors, at least the husband and wife, involving a decision for the occurrence of a birth or its postponement. Family planning is also contingent upon the availability or acceptability of the means, as, for instance, abstinenee, abortion or contraception. Even primitive populations regulated fertility through the impositions of prescribed cultural actions (Car-Saunders, 1922 : 222-223).

Deliberate actions within the family by the reproductive couple, whether independently or under external influence, by the elders, local or national leaders and the media, to plan the birth of a child or its postponement is essentially the essence of family planning. The ordinary usage of the terminology, however. is different. It is frequently used to mean the means through which the couples may avoid conception and birth.[6] Thus, the terminology communicates a narrow meaning even in the academic literature. In the following account of the family planning programme in India and Karnataka these terms are used in this narrow meainng.

(ii) *History of Family Planning in India and Karnataka*

Though the propagation of birth control information and ideas were included in the first plan period (1950-51 to 1955-56) for the first time, the emphasis of the programme was at the ideological level and the rhythm method was advocated. The second plan period (1955-56 to 1960-61) laid the real foundations of the family planning programme and a family planning directorate was created within the Health Ministry of the federal government. The clinical approach to the promotion of family planning practice was adopted during the second and third five-year plan periods, while the services were provided through the hospitals and dispensaries. This soon led to dissatisfaction among the population for it was heavily based on the prototype of the western style service (Myrdal : 1968) which ignored the cultural bearings of Indian society. It was only after the census results of 1961[7] that efforts were initiated to establish a service based on an extension approach interpersonal communication to suit the illiterate society. The programme also emphasized the need for the community acceptance of small family norms. Sterilization as the major means of birth control was introduced ; and, after the initial success of vasectomy as a family planning method, the IUD services were also introduced in 1965. The IUD programme lasted only for a short duration and its dwindling popularity led to a different approach called the 'Cafeteria approach' enabling interested couples to choose from among a variety of contraceptives. Ultimately, the emphasis and demand was for permanent methods. During 1970-73 innovative mass camps were held which helped regain the popularity of vasectomies for a while only to come to a standstill in 1973-74. The acceptance of tubectomy has grown steadily since its inception in 1950 to fall only in the post-Emergency year (1977-78) with a return to a moderate level by 1980-81. In 1971 the Medical Termination of Pregnacy (MTP) Act enabled couples to choose induced abortions to avoid unwanted pregnancies. In 1976 the union government adopted a National Population Policy to serve as a guideline for a more systematic and rigorous implementation of the programme. However, after the change in the government in 1977, a new policy was drafted which retained many issues of the earlier policy statement. Though an explicit emphasis was laid on the voluntary nature of the extension of the programme [8] as well as on the implementation of a programme based on multipurpose health and family welfare workers on the lines of bare foot doctors in China.

The budgetary outlay on family planning in India grew steadily both in absolute amounts and as a percentage of the total plan outlays.[9] The allocation for the First plan period of one million Indian Rupees was 0.01 per cent of the total developmental outlay which increased to 10.1 billion Rupees or 1.04 per cent of the total outlay for 1980-85. However, the peak percentage of the total outlay was during the fourth plan period (1969-74) which was 1.98 per cent. The actual expenditure on family planning during and after the third plan period was in the vicinity of 85-90 per cent of the budgeted outlays. The per capita expenditure on the family planning programme during this period in India was the largest in the world (UN Mission, 1970 : 4).

A similar trend was found for the state of Karnataka ; where the outlay was about 0.73 million Rupees in the Second plan rising to 6.93 million in the third plan and 121.4 million in the Fourth Plan period. The draft Fifth Plan has allocated 482.5 million rupees to be spent on family planning activities. The percentage of this outlay to the total of Karnataka's development outlays increase respectively from 0.1 per cent to 0.3, 3.5 and 3.6 per cent.

The outlay on the family planning programme and actual expenditure suggests the commitment of the government to encourage birth control acceptance by the community through the intensification of the infrastructure in terms of hospitals, beds, trained doctors, midwives and other requirements. However, these provisions are still short of the total requirements of the population in accordance with the planned fertility objectives.

Government sponsored family planning clinics were opened in Bangalore and Mysore cities as early as 1930 by the then Princely State of Mysore ; this was this first time in the country and in the world that family planning was given recognition at the state or governmental level. Such services, including the ancillary facilities of training institutions, were extended to greater areas after Independence through the state plans. The UN Missions of 1969 remarked that the efforts to augment the family planning programmes effectiveness were characterised by a great deal of uncertainty and had been undertaken without the benefit of models and precedents from elsewhere (p. 5). The progress of the programme during these years in Karnataka was also the reflection of what was happening elsewhere in the country, because of the experimentative nature of the programme which however was hurriedly extended throughout the whole country. In doing this the initial emphasis on rhythm was shifted to vasectomy, then to the IUD, and then to the camp approach for vasectomies. The scheme for providing compensation to the adopters of family planning methods and to the service personnel like doctors and motivators was introduced during 1965-66 throughout the country and this continues even to day. Simultaneously, a few states, notably Maharashtra, enforced disincentives such as, any concessions, loans, subsidies, relief, grants or other benefits not being available to families who did not restrict their family size to three living children. The practice of assigning targets as a means of both planning and controlling field worker performance was adopted during 1966. This led to an increased incidence of harassing and administrative penalizing of subordinate workers in the family planning programme bureaucracy.

The programme works on a wide network of primary and secondary level institutions apart from the organizational units of State and District. At the block level there is at least one primary health centre[10] (the family welfare planning centre is a part of the PHC) in each taluka (few have two PHCs) placed with an Assistant Surgeon responsible for the implementation and extension of family planning programme (FPP).[11] Apart from this, there are bands of both male and female health workers, each of which constitutes a team, working for birth control propagation through interpersonal communication and periodic house visits. Each worker is stationed at a sub-centre established at a major village in the block responsible for covering the population living in the surrounding villages. A PHC usually has around thirty sub-centres. The female health workers are expected to specialize in maternal and child health (MCH) care beside propagating and disseminating information and the use of the family planning technology. This approach lays emphasis on motivation and persuasion through regular visits to the couples as well as to other persons in the family capable of influencing the decisions made by the couples.

As of June 1980 in Karnataka 269 PHCs and 3121 sub-centres were engaged in the provision of FP services. These centres, however, were far less than the number required to meet the minimum standards of health and family welfare delivery of a population of this size. To meet the requirement of establishing one sub-centre for every 5,000 rural population and one PHC for 50,000 rural population the government of Karnataka requires the investment of an additional 661 sub-centres and 174 PHCs. With regard to the positions vacant, almost ten per cent of the sanctioned posts of medical and para-medical staff were vacant as of June 1980. In 1976, there was a doctor for every 10,000 and a nurse for every 13,500 persons, as well as an ANM for every 7,000 population in Karnataka.[12] The intensification of both health and family planning would require a much lower population to be covered per doctor and each categories of para-medical personnel.

It terms of acceptance, for India sterilizations (vasectomy and tubectomy) which numbered 7,000 in 1965 rose to 887,000 in 1966-77, 1,840,000 in 1967-68, and 3,122,000 in 1972-73, but fell to 942,000 in 1973-74. The peak in sterilization acceptance was in 1976-77 at 8,216,000 which fell sharply to 949,000 in the following year but later rose consistently to 2,029,000 by 1980-81. The sex-wise breakdown of sterilization presents a consistent increase in tubectomy acceptance since its start in 1956, from 4,758 to about 1.6 million in 1980-81, with the exception of 1972-73 when it fell slightly from the previous year; and 1977-78 when the number fell steeply from 2.06 million to mere 742 thousand. Vasectomy acceptance had a wide and frequent variation in absolute numbers. It rose consistently from about 24 thousand in 1956 to 1.6 million during 1967-68 then fell till 1970-71 to rise again during the period of mass camps to 2.6 million only to fall again to a mere 434 thousand in 1979-81. However, a record vasectomy achievement was in 1976-77 when 6.2 million vasectomies were done throughout the country.

The cumulative sterilization rates up to March 1981 for India was 48.8 per thousand population compared with 46.9 per thousand for Karnataka for the same year. This rate is above 60 in many other states. For Maharastra it is 83.0, Gujarat 68.4, Tamil Nadu 68.0, Andhra Pradesh 65.0, Orissa 61.8 and Kerala 60.3. The IUD rate for Karnataka was 13.9 while for Haryana it was 46.1, Punjab 45.8, and Himachal

Pradesh 19.6. For India as a whole the IUD rate was 12.8 per thousand population as of March 1981. A short analysis of the couples currently and effectively protected by various methods gives a crude idea about the impact and efficiency of the FPP. The total estimated number of eligible couples in 1970-71 for the whole country was 93 million, of whom approximately 7.6 million were protected through sterilizations, 1.3 million used the IUD, and 0.98 million were effectively protected by the adoption of conventional contraceptives. The cumulative number of the couples effectively protected by all methods was 10.6 million in 1970-71 which rose consistently to 23.7 million in 1976-77 only to drop to 22.7 million in 1980-81. However, in 1980-81 the estimated number of eligible couples were 116.4 million in the country of whom 23.3 million or 20 per cent were sterilized ; 1.2 million or 1.1 per cent were effectively using IUDs and another 1.9 million or 1.7 per cent were protected through the use of conventional contraceptives. For Karnataka, in 1981 there were 6.08 million eligible couples, of whom 20.9 per cent (1,270,688) were sterilized, 1.5 per cent (88,106) were effectively protected by the IUD and another 0.9 per cent (54,420) were effectively protected by conventional contraceptives. This makes the total couples effectively protected 1,411,214 or 23.2 per cent.

A brief analysis of the age at acceptance yet confirms the fact that majority of the acceptors or wife of acceptor in case of vasectomy and condom, were of higher ages. During 1973-74 only 33.4 per cent of the vasectomy acceptors for whom the age data were available were less than 30 years of age (21.2 per cent were of age 25-29 years and 10.6 per cent were of age 20-24 years). The mean age of the wife for these vasectomy acceptors worked out to be 32.7 years. This age declined only to 31.9 years in 1979-80 ; however, the percentage of wives of ages less than thirty years of the vasectomized males rose to 38.3. If this decline of 0.8 years in mean age of acceptor's wives is coupled with almost the same duration in increase in age at marriage of women during these years, there is almost a net loss of 1.6 years of child bearing marital duration. This duration in case of tubectomy acceptors worked out to be 1.8 years from 1973-74 to 1979-80. In the case of tubectomised acceptors the mean age at acceptance during 1973-74 was 34.1 which consistently fell to 30.4 in 1979-80. During the same duration, the percentage of women less than 30 years of age accepting tubectomy increased from 37.7 to 50.1. The age distribution of the women who were effectively protected by sterilization however, indicates a peak percentage of around 30 for the age group 30-34. By this age generally women would have had a family size greater than the average family size of the community. As a result, the figures on total births averted seem to be not impressive. In terms of absolute numbers, the births averted during 1956-61 were 0.0335 million, followed by 0.0884 million in 1962, with a consistent rise to 6.7866 million in 1970-71 ; and for 1980-81 the estimated births averted were 44.1527 million. However, Simmons (1971) worked out the benefits accrued from the births averted which he puts far above the total investment in the family planning programme ; thus the results to him were impressive although not optimal.

With this background it may be useful to describe how the system works. As mentioned earlier the FPP was introduced as a government programme during the second Five Year Plan period. The programme was integrated with the department of health at the organizational level creating a separate administrative head for the implementation of the FPP within the Department of Health and Family Planning. Operationally, at the Primary Health Centre level, the FPP was integrated with the MCH programme. The rationale being that during the course of the extension of MCH care, the recipient woman (in this case the pregnant or lactating women would be vulnerable to the advice of the family planning message provided by the same person who gives the MCH care. This seems to be a rational approach at the implementation level. However, there is a dearth of any research in this area of the merits and demerits of the integration of MCH and FPP at policy as well at the administrative and implementation levels (Gopal Rao, 1974 : 13).

Though under the federal constitution health and FP are state-controlled matters, the allocation of funds and logistic supply is done by central funding. The state level FP Bureau administers the implementation in the respective states, through the district family planning bureau headed by a District Health and Family Planning Officer in each district of the state. Each district has a number of community development blocks, otherwise called taluka, having a PHC headed by a Medical officer of health and an Assistant Surgeon in charge of family planning. These two medical posts usually have overlapping responsibilities for preventive and curative health, family planning implementative responsibilities and also day-to-day administration. The last one, along with other legal responsibilities, absorbs the major efforts of these officers specialized in medicine and health care. They have to manage and organize around one hundred subordinate staff.

A PHC on average covers one hundred thousand population and measures about 15-20 square kilometres. The PHC is also the block level headquarters for many health and family planning sub-centres. There are two kinds of sub-centres mostly having overlapping areas of coverage. The Male sub-centre manned by the paramedical Male Health and Family Planning Worker (MHW : formally known as FPHA, BHW and Junior HI) whose duties are many, such as, preventive health activities, distribution of simple medicines, the propagation of the family planning message, school health, bleaching the source of drinking water, spraying DDT to the village streets and households etc. They usually cover a population between 10,000 and 15,000 population. The other kind of sub-centre, is the Female sub-centre often provided with a sub-centre building for both residential and clinical purposes, this is manned by a paramedical Female Health Worker (FHW : earlier ANM) whose primary duties are the delivering maternal and child health care (MCH) and the propagation of family planning along with the general duties of preventive health care. Detailed responsibilities include disseminating family planning knowledge among eligible couples, motivating them, referring them to the PHC for the provision of sterilization and IUD services, caring for them during sterilization operations and the follow-up services to be provided at the doorsteps of the acceptors after the sterilization operations. Ordinarily she is supposed to cover 10,000 population (non-intensive sub-centres), but certain sub-centres have been declared intensive areas, where the FHW covers intensively a population of around 5,000 spread out among a few villages. To co-ordinate and supervise these field or grassroots level workers there are supervisory staff at the PHC and Sub PHC level head-quarters. They are Male Health and Family Planning Supervisors (MHFPS : earlier BHE, SHI) and Female Health and Family Planning Supervisors (FHFPS : earlier LHV) who supervise and control sometimes as many as ten MHFPWs or FHFPWs.

MHFPWs and FHFPWs are the persons at the bottom of the official hierarchy who indeed are most important to the family planning programme. They are responsible for the most difficult task of communicating with the masses involving slow, expensive and strenuous methods of personal contact. They are also expected to meet the eligible couples repeatedly at regular intervals. They cover a fixed area or village each day of the week, and visit the women and children at their homes to provide services. Thus MCH and FP propagagation is extended to the people at their homes. This, in principle, is a welfare activity and in theory should work well. MCH services, are received well, the only constraints for this being the cultural inhibitions associated with caste differences, for instance, if the health worker is from a lower caste the high caste women of the community may not be willing to receive services from her ; or, if the health worker belongs to a caste relatively high in the social scale, she may not provide sufficient attention to low caste people.[13] Although the incidence of this discrimination is decreasing, it has now taken a different dimension based on class differences. This is due to certain direct and indirect personal gains which the health worker may receive and thus devote a major attention towards the households who are relatively better off.

Another aspect which may operate but not as frequently as the first one but which acts a constraint to the provision of the MCH care, is the emotional involvement of the elder women from among the kin who take pride in performing such a service to the younger pregnant women. It may also involve the small amount of money payment or gifts paid for such a a service which may induce the local-dai or a neighbour to influence the pregnant woman to refrain from taking the professional services of the health worker. The issue can also be other way round. A few persons, as yet, in the rural areas are unaware of the benefits of the FPP or are fearful of the after-effects of such an use. They may opt either to refuse or to refrain from demanding the MCH services from the health personnel, especially as it is also well known that she subsequently insist on the acceptance of temporary or permanent acceptance of some family planning methods. In this event family planning is viewed as something imposed through the advance incentives in the form of MCH services.[14]

However, the facts and figures presented above testify to the impact of family planning programme in India as well as in Karnataka including the study area. The conclusion of this part, however, has to deal with a brief discussion of the nature of family planning and its propagation in a society still retains a strong traditional value orientation in the presence of mass illiteracy. The argument concerns the contradictory pulls and pressures within the society. The fact is that there is general agreement among the populations recognizing the usefulness of contraception and there is no incidence of any public opinion against family planning,[15] yet people, especially rural residents, consider larger numbers are a great good. This arises from the presence of high mortality and the traditional methods of cultivation which are largely labour intensive. Another contradiction is between different segments of the same population. The segmentation due to class and caste associations result in economic segmentation. Thus the persons from the segments who are better-off economically would accept the usefulness of family planning but the disadvantaged segment would not endorse the programme for the obvious traditional reasons of the usefulness of many children, especially sons. Further, the desire to have at least one child educated or in an urban job may require services or contributions from many family members especially other sons. Because of such contradictions it is inevitable that the programme implementation in its present integrated form would suffer both in the provision of MCH care and in the family planning achievement. The recent figures suggest that about 23 per cent of the eligible couple currently practice some kind of family planning methods, a great majority practising either of the sterilization operations. As early as 1969 the UN Mission felt that : 'As regards the sterilization figures, it appears that the peak has been reached ; in any case, the Mission did not find the optimistic views to the contrary convincing' (p. 6). A close understanding of the characteristics of these acceptors suggests that most of the couples from the favourable and highly motivated group are already consuming the family planning services. Quite a percentage of these couple were illiterates and belonged to disadvantaged section of the population, who were brought into the programme by direct or indirect compulsion, and persuasion through incentives[16] (which is yet another indirect form of compulsion). Many of these acceptors are either not satisfied fully or are dissatisfied. It seems that the time has arrived when the strategy of the family planning programme as a programme imposed has to be reversed through a social work approach at the community and household level so as to in fact create demand from within the society. To ensure proper health and MCH care the disintegration of the service delivery system may have to be undertaken. While discussing the constraints inhibiting the expansion of the family planning programme in India, Simmons (1971) states that (i) the problem of appropriate technique does not seem to be a major limitation and (ii) that the programme stagnation argument does not seem to have its complete validity. He had, however, hypothesized the inadequacies of the Indian family planning programme of its unimpressive performanae and inadequate administrative apparatus.

It will be shown later that the village data clearly reveals the fact that the first two constraints are very much valid in 1980-81 and the last one continues in its original form. Simmon's suggestion of two alternative strategies, one aiming at change in tastes and price parents pay for children, through a fundamental alteration in the approach to birth control, and the other which helps to expand the programme without a fundamental change in approach. Yet a few suggestions about the incentives and disincentives are unacceptable as they directly affect the development and prosperity of the child.

With regard to the reorganization and expansion of the programme, it is again emphasized that the integration of health and family planning at the operational level is disadvantageous to the programme. Yet another reason for this is that the field personnel have enormous amount and varied duties which would allow no room for specialized effort either to implement MCH care or the family planning programme.

Another bottleneck in the programme is the over-emphasis on sterilization as a means of birth control, where less attention was given to other modern and traditional methods of contraceptions. IUD was popularised in 1965 but it did not take long to lose its credibility in many peoples' view. Since then there has been no effort for its revival. Other conventional contraceptives have proved unsuitable for the Indian conditions and no alternative is yet available to replace them. The remarkable success of the oral pills as a conventional contraceptive in Taiwan, South Korea, and Indonesia have put the Indian programme under suspicion and criticism. An innovative approach for the propagation and wide use of temporary methods as means of spacing and controlling unwanted pregnancies is required immediately. Medical Termination of Pregnancy act has legalized induced abortion, but this can hardly complement other contraceptives, both because of its nonrepeatability on health grounds and the moral criticism based on religious beliefs. Secondly, the provision of the MTP services in the present structure is far from sufficient both due to the lack of knowledge among the population about its legal availability and the long distance of abortion centres from the village.

India's FPP heavily depends for its evaluation on the proportion of the pre-fixed targets[17] having been achieved. The sense of target achievement among the personnel has drawn them very close to the excitement of adding to the annual cumulative figures on 'number of cases motivated and provided with service' which are not related to the level of the infrastructure at the worker's level. They have compulsory monthly targets to be met for each method, but the targets achieved for sterilization remove the importance of other methods to oblivion. As a result the average age of the women from among the couples who have accepted sterilization is much higher so as to be closer to the age at which normally they achieve the completed family size at least have few other children. This seem to be due to (a) the relative case in convincing the couples to accept FP methods after a substantial number of birth, (b) because by then older couples would have had sufficient children from their own point of view and (c) the relatively greater temptation of these couples toward incentives, as these couples by then would have been closer to being dependent upon the younger generation for a living.

NOTES AND REFERENCES

1. The Net National Product for India consistently increased from 342.35 thousand million Rupees in 1970-71 to 443.28 million thousand million Rupees during 1979-80 at 1970-71 prices or 901.73 thousand million Rupees at current prices, while the per-capita income rose only from Rs. 632.8 to Rs. 677.8 at 1970-71 prices or Rs. 632.8 to Rs. 1,378.8 at current prices (Ministry of Health and Family Welfare, 1982).
2. The Indian censuses prior to 1981 census collected and published data on parity ; information on current parity or births during the year prior to date of census, was for the first time collected during the 1981 census on a sample basis. Data on the marital status by age was made available at least after 1981 decennial census. A separate organization namely the Sample Registration Scheme provided data on the births and deaths on almost one per cent sample for states as well the country since 1968-69.
3. India being a federation, the State governments have certain areas under their discretion and control—health and education are two of them.
4. Westernization is a concept distinct from modernization and development. For more on this see Srinivas (1969). *Westernization* has been explained by Schneider (1971) to mean broad cultural changes like the changes in values, ideas and life style as opposed to *Modernization* which means structural changes in social relations, stratification and basic economic structure. More (1965) considers modernization as a total transformation of traditional or pre-modern society in two types of technology and associated social organizations that characterized the 'advanced', economically prosperous and relatively politically stable nations of the western world.
5. The scholar has selected four villages for intensive research from this area of rural plain or maidan, a comparatively dry belt.

6. Family planning programme refers to the national level programme designed to achieve the objective of extension of birth control practice to reduce the fertility and hence the rate of population growth.
7. The 1961 census gave the figures on population size and distribution which was considerably higher than anticipated.
8. There, however, was no indication of the use of compulsion in the policy plan of 1976. Family Planning implementation and administration in India is the State's responsibility ; and few states noticeably Maharashtra took to compulsion to meet the imposed targets.
9. The data and figures presented in the following section are taken from the *Year Book : Family Welfare Programme in India 1980-81*, Government of India ; unless otherwise specified.
10. Abbreviation 'PHC' is used henceforth to mean the Primary Health Centre.
11. Abbrivation 'FPP' is used henceforth to mean the Family Planning Programme.
12. Statistical Abstract of Karnataka 1976-77, Bureau of Economics and Statistics, Bangalore, India.
13. A few evaluatory studies of India have presented this finding about the selectivity of households where the ANM provides the services to certain communities while certain others do not receive any.
14. There is some evidence on this issue available from the in-depth interview from the villages studied. It is also found that while implementing a nutrition programme in a PHC area in Karnataka, the recipients, at some stage, refused nutrition supplement, because the ANMS involved in the nutrition programme were simultaneously working on the family planning programme. (Nutrition in IPP districts ; Bangalore Population Centre).
15. The only time when the public opinion was against family planning was because of compulsion during the days of the Emergency. For more detail see Gwatkin (1979).
16. Veatch (1977) places the role of incentives close to coercion (p 103), and suggests the preservation of freedom by avoiding incentives that are in effect, coercive (p 107).
17. 'Target' refers to the number of persons accepting specific birth control methods.

Index